THE JERUSALEM POST LAW REPORTS

THE JERUSALEM
POST
LAW REPORTS

Reported and Edited by

ASHER FELIX LANDAU

former President of the
District Court of Jerusalem

THE JERUSALEM POST
THE MAGNES PRESS, THE HEBREW UNIVERSITY, JERUSALEM

The Jerusalem Post
The Magnes Press
The Hebrew University of Jerusalem
The Faculty of Law
The Harry and Michael Sacher Institute for
Legislative Research and Comparative Law

Distributed by
The Magnes Press, P.O. Box 7695, Jerusalem, Israel 91076
and
The Jerusalem Post Book Department,
P.O. Box 81, Jerusalem, Israel 91000
or 211 E. 43rd St., Suite 601, New York, NY 10017, USA

ISBN 965-223-827-9

Printed in Israel
Layout: Judith Fattal

TABLE OF CONTENTS

CASES REPORTED IN CHRONOLOGICAL ORDER*

* As published in *The Jerusalem Post*.

FOREWORD

Awareness of the rule of law, its deeper meaning and meta-formal contents, and the understanding in all respects of its binding and educative force, are vital concomitants of any open and free society. The above-mentioned awareness is based on an acquaintance with the legal processes, the ways of judicial reasoning, the qualitative norms of the legal systems, and the components of material law.

The factual reporting of the events in the courts does not provide by itself the background sufficient for an intelligent appreciation of the data. On the other hand, perusal of the full text of judgments is out of reach and too cumbersome for laymen. The Law Reports of *The Jerusalem Post* serve, therefore, as an excellent compromise: they are a learned, comprehensive, but concise description of the contents of the judgments without an excess of technicalities. Moreover, they enable people not completely familiar with Hebrew to become acquainted with our law. In other words, the reports provide the public with an intelligent insight into the workings of Israeli law. This is law in action in an excellent presentation by an outstanding expert.

Judge (ret.) Asher Felix Landau, former President of the Jerusalem District Court, is most respected in the legal community. He is highly proficient, and possesses excellent qualifications to present our law. His preparation of the reports has been a great success. Laymen and professionals alike follow his reports avidly.

I congratulate *The Jerusalem Post*, the Magnes Press, and The Harry and Michael Sacher Institute for Legislative Research and Comparative Law, for the well-conceived idea of publishing a collection of these reports, in order to create a well-edited and lasting source of law. This collection will be of great importance for Israelis and people abroad, who are interested in Israel and its law.

Meir Shamgar
President of the Supreme Court of Israel

Jerusalem, January 1993

PREFACE

Law Reports were first published in *The Palestine Post*, the predecessor of *The Jerusalem Post*, in 1942. They were prepared by Advocate Henry Baker, later President of the District Court of Jerusalem, and appeared until 1945, when Advocate Baker was appointed legal draftsman in the British Mandatory Administration.

Publication of the reports was resumed in 1954. They were prepared by Advocate Doris Lankin, who was also appointed the paper's legal editor, and continued without interruption until 1981 when, for personal reasons, she resigned her post. The writer of these lines then continued the preparation of the reports, which appeared sporadically until 1988.

It was then decided, on the suggestion of the editor responsible, Joanna Yehiel, that the reports be published weekly, and thus provide a continuous and coherent picture of the work of the courts, particularly the Supreme Court. This policy has continued until now, some 300 summaries having been published from 1982 until the present time.

Some 80 summaries of those published until the end of 1981 were originally selected by faculty members of the Harry and Michael Sacher Institute for Legislative Research and Comparative Law at the Hebrew University of Jerusalem for publication in this volume. It was decided later, however, to exclude six important judgments which had already appeared in English in *Selected Judgments of the Supreme Court of Israel*, published by the Israel Bar Publishing House. Those excluded are the cases of *Barzilai* (H.C. 428/86, 40() P.D. 505), *Levi and Amit* (H.C. 153/83, 38(2) P.D. 393), *Sarid* (H.C. 652/81, 36(2) P.D. 197), *Neiman* (E.A. 2, 3/84, 39(2) P.D. 225), *Shakdiel* (H.C. 153/87, 42(2) P.D. 221), and *El-Affo* (H.C. 785/87, 42(2) P.D. 4). Also excluded is the summary of the judgment in the *Zerzevsky* case (H.C. 1635/90, 45(1) P.D. 749), which will appear in the forthcoming issue of the *Israel Law Review* dealing with political coalition agreements.

The summaries have been published in this volume chronologically. Appearing over so many years, they were revised before publication by many different editors of *The Jerusalem Post*. Moreover, during that period, *The Jerusalem Post* introduced American spelling. The *Post* has always honored its friendly commitment to alter the material as little as possible, but some differences of style and language have, of course, been inevitable. It was decided, therefore, not to strive in this volume for absolute consistency in the above regard but — subject, of course, to the correction of errors — to publish the material as it originally appeared.

I wish to express my sincere thanks, for their encouragement and assistance, to Nina Keren-David, director of the *Jerusalem Post* Archives, who initiated the publication in book form of a selected number of summaries, and to the deputy-director, Derek Fattal, for his continuous and devoted efforts in bringing the project to completion; to Professor Alfredo Mordechai Rabello, director of the Sacher Institute, and to Professor David Kretzmer of the institute, for their advice and support; to Professor Daniel Friedman, Dean of the Law School of the College of Management, Academic Studies, Tel Aviv; and to Advocate Anthony Casson, who initiated the interest of the college in this publication; to my colleague Judge Hadassah Ben-Itto, President of the International Association of Jewish Lawyers and Jurists; to Professor Reuven Yaron and to Advocate Yosef Hadani. I also thank Judith Fattal, who set up the material for printing, and last — but by no means least — Dan Benovici, director of the Magnes Press.

Asher Felix Landau

Jerusalem, January 1993

ABBREVIATIONS

C.A.	Civil Appeal
C.A.A.	Chamber of Advocates Appeal
C.C.	Civil Claim
Cr.A.	Criminal Appeal
E.A.	Election Appeal
F.H.	Further Hearing
H.C.	High Court (The Supreme Court sitting as a High Court of Justice)
IDF	Israel Defence Forces
M.A.	Miscellaneous Applications
M.K.	Member of Knesset
O.S.	Originating Summons
P.D.	Piskei-Din (Supreme Court Judgments-Original)
P.D.A.	Piskei-Din Avoda (National Labor Court Judgments-Original)
P.M.	Pesakim Mehosi'im (District Court Judgments-Original)
S.J.	Selected Supreme Court Judgments-English
S.T.	Special Tribunal

INDEX OF CASES REPORTED*

---

* The names of the parties are followed by a reference to the publication of the judgment in the Hebrew Reports.

INDEX OF SUBJECTS

INDEX OF STATUTES, REGULATIONS
AND OTHER SOURCES

PROPER PERMISSION FOR SABBATH WORK

ESHKAR LTD. v. MINISTER OF LABOUR

In the Supreme Court sitting as a High Court of Justice before the then President, Moshe Landau, Justice Menahem Elon and Justice Shoshana Netanyahu in the matter of *Eshkar Ltd.*, Petitioner, versus *Minister of Labour and Social Welfare and the Chief Labour Inspector*, Respondents (H.C. 171/78).

Labour Law—Refusal of Permit for Sabbath Work—Intervention by Supreme Court in Decision of Competent Authority—Hours of Work and Rest Law, 1951, section 12(a).

The Petitioner owns a chain of duty-free shops two of which are situated at Ben-Gurion airport. For many years the Petitioner received, as a matter of routine, an annual permit — under section 12 (a) of the Hours of Work and Rest Law, 1951 — to employ shop assistants at its airport shops on the Sabbath. However, in terms of a joint decision of the then Deputy Minister of Labour, Ben Zion Rubin, and Eli Paz, the Deputy Director-General of the Ministry, the permit was renewed in 1978 only until March 15 of that year. After that date, so the Petitioner was informed, no further sales on the Sabbath would be allowed.

The petition against the non-renewal of the permit was lodged on March 16, 1978, and the court issued an order nisi against the Respondents, ordering that the permit remain in force until the final decision of the court was given.

Section 12 (a) of the above Law provides that "the Minister of Labour may permit an employee to be employed during all or any of the hours of weekly rest, if he is satisfied that interruption of work for all or part of the weekly rest is likely to prejudice the defence of the state or the security of persons or property or seriously to prejudice the economy, or a process of work or the supply of services which, in the opinion of the Minister of Labour, are essential to the public or part thereof".

Section 12 (b) of the Law provides that "a general permit under subsection (a) shall be given only upon the decision of a committee of ministers consisting of the Prime Minister, the Minister of Religion and the Minister of Labour". Section 35 of the Law empowers the Minister of Labour to delegate his powers under section 12.

Justice Landau dealt first with the manner in which the renewal of the permit had been considered. He found on the facts before the court that at the time of the joint decision referred to, only the deputy minister had been authorised by the minister under section 35 of the Law to exercise his powers in the matter, while Eli Paz had been given no such authority.

Justice Landau accepted the principle, often laid down by the Supreme Court, that a competent authority, in exercising its powers under the Law, is entitled to consult experts and other persons, provided only that the final decision is its own. In the present case, however, the final decision had been made by two persons, one of whom was authorised and one of whom was not. The result was, Justice Landau continued, the joint decision referred to had been influenced conclusively by a policy decision of the committee of ministers constituted under section 12 (b) of the Law, taken on October 31, 1980, under which the duty-free shops and news-stands at Ben-Gurion airport would be closed on the Sabbath.

In his opinion, Justice Landau said, the reliance by the deputy minister and Mr. Paz on this policy decision was unlawful. That decision had been given by the committee under the previous government; the court was obliged to decide on the information before it, and no reference had been made to a decision of the present government supporting such a policy, which, if such were the case, proper administration would require.

Moreover, Justice Landau pointed out, the governmental authority responsible for the administration of the airport was the Airports Authority, which had extended its agreement with the Petitioner for three years from the date of its expiry, April 1, 1983.

Finally, Justice Landau found fault with the approach of the deputy minister and Mr. Paz requiring the Petitioner to satisfy them that the requirements of section 12 (a) of the Law had been fulfilled, namely, in the present case, that the refusal of the permit would seriously prejudice the economy, or the supply of services to the public or part thereof.

Justice Landau pointed out that the rule had been long and well established that the considerations applying to the renewal of a permit were different from those applying to its being granted initially, for once a citizen had received a permit under the law, he was entitled to assume that it would be renewed and arrange his affairs accordingly; it was for the competent authority to show good reasons for refusing the renewal. It was therefore wrong to place the onus on the Petitioner, and for this reason, too, the joint decision was unlawful.

Justice Landau therefore proposed that the order nisi be made final, and the permit requested be issued.

Justice Netanyahu agreed with the judgment of the former President.

In dissenting from his colleagues, Justice Elon disagreed with each and every conclusion they reached. After reviewing the facts, he held that both the deputy minister and Mr. Paz had been authorised by the minister to deal with the renewal of the Petitioner's permit, and there had therefore been no irregularity in their having given a joint decision.

On the contrary, as said in Ecclesiastes (Ch. 4 v. 9), *"Two are better than one; because they have a good reward for their labour"*. Even had he found, Justice Elon continued, that the minister had delegated his powers to the deputy minister alone, he would have found no fault with the joint decision, since it was clear that that decision was also the decision of the competent authority, whether the other party was authorised to decide the matter, or not.

Justice Elon also found no fault with the reliance placed on the decision of the committee of ministers. Firstly, it was clear from the affidavits filed, in Justice Elon's view, that the present government agreed with the policy laid down by its predecessor in regard to work on the Sabbath at Ben-Gurion airport, and there was no necessity for any further proof of this fact.

Moreover, there is, *prima facie*, continuity between governments in respect of their decisions or the decisions of their ministerial committees, and in any case the deputy minister and Mr. Paz were certainly entitled to assume that the present government would not take a more lenient view of work on the Sabbath than its predecessor.

Justice Elon was of opinion that the renewal of the Petitioner's contract by the Airports Authority was irrelevant, since it was the Minister of Labour who had the power to decide in regard to work on the Sabbath, and the Airports Authority was obliged to honour his decision.

It was clear, Justice Elon continued, that the policy of the government was only one factor which the competent authority had to consider, and that it was also obliged to weigh the application before it in the light of the criteria laid down in the Hours of Work and Rest Law.

Justice Elon then stressed that the principle enshrined in the Law, on the basis of national-religious values and social considerations, is that the Sabbath must be observed unless the competent authority is convinced that one of the exceptions justifying its non-observance, which must be accurately and strictly construed, has been proved.

He was therefore of opinion, Justice Elon said, that the general rule relating to the renewal of a permit, as stated by the former President, did not apply to the permit in question. Generally speaking, a citizen is entitled to conduct his business and therefore to assume that a permit once granted will be renewed. In regard to the Sabbath, however, the rule is that work on that day is forbidden, and he is obliged, therefore, to satisfy the competent authority that he is entitled to a renewal of the permit under one of the exceptions laid down by law.

In the present case, Justice Elon continued, the competent authority had asked the Petitioner, time and again, to give particulars of the loss it would suffer by closing its shops on the Sabbath, but the Petitioner, by all kinds of devious and doubtful means, had refused to supply this information.

The competent authority, Justice Elon said, must weigh the loss the Petitioner would suffer by closing its shops on the Sabbath against the ideological, social and economic conceptions of the government of the day regarding this complicated and delicate problem. The instant case furnished an exellent example of this approach. The responsible minister who had granted the permit to the Petitioner, was of the opinion, after weighing all these aspects, that preventing the sale of the Petitioner's goods at the airport on the Sabbath would seriously prejudice the economy of the state. The policy of the present government is to limit Sabbath work at the airport of the State of Israel, and the competent authority therefore decided that as far as selling cameras, watches and souvenirs is concerned, the religious, national and social considerations relating to the observance of the Sabbath, and the image of this airfield as an international airport, were to be preferred to the consideration of some possible financial loss to the Petitioner.

In Justice Elon's opinion, it was this change in government policy that was really at the heart of the petition, and it is against this that the Petitioner complains. It is clear that the Petitioner has no standing before the court in this regard.

Justice Elon therefore proposed that the petition be dismissed.

The order nisi was made absolute by majority decision, and the Respondents ordered to pay the Petitioner's costs, IS10,000.

Advocate Yehuda Karni appeared for the Petitioner, and Advocate Renato Yarak, Acting Director of the High Court Division, of the State Attorney's Office, for the Respondents.

The judgment of the court was given on July 27, 1982.

HEARING THE PLO

ZICHRONI v. THE BROADCASTING AUTHORITY

In the Supreme Court sitting as a High Court of Justice before Justice Dov Levin, Justice Yehuda Cohen and Justice Gavriel Bach in the matter between *Amnon Zichroni*, Petitioner, versus *The Board of Directors of the Broadcasting Authority*, Respondents (H.C. 243/82).

Administrative Law—Freedom of Expression—Broadcast of Interviews With Hostile Organisations—Broadcasting Authority Law, 1965.

On April 19, 1982, the Board of Directors of the Broadcasting Authority adopted the following resolution:

"1. The board is conscious of the duty of the Authority to provide listeners and viewers with adequate and reliable information of what occurs in the Land of Israel and the world. The radio and television will therefore continue to report events in Judea, Samaria and Gaza, subject to the professional considerations of the various departmental directors.

2. There will be no broadcast or television of interviews initiated by the Authority with elements which have declared their hostility to, or fight against, the State of Israel. The Palestine Liberation Organization is such an element. No interview, therefore, with public figures identified as regarding the PLO as the sole or legitimate representative of the Arabs in Judea, Samaria and Gaza, will be broadcast or televised".

On April 24, 1982, the court issued an order nisi calling upon the Respondent to show cause why the directive in paragraph 2 of the resolution relating to interviews with public figures should not be set aside.

On May 17, 1982, the board passed an amended resolution adding a statement at the beginning of paragraph 2 that the Broadcasting Authority is not obliged to provide a platform for enemy propaganda, and adding a paragraph authorizing medium directors to permit the publication, by reporters or announcers, of opinions expressed by the public figures referred to. The concluding portion of paragraph 2, however, was left intact.

The Petitioner argued, in the main, that his right as a citizen to receive full information of events included the right to see and hear the persons interviewed so as to be better able to judge their intentions, and the directive relating to "public figures" was far too wide.

In giving his judgment, Justice Dov Levin dealt first with the Petitioner's standing before the court. The Petitioner, he said, had described himself as an advocate who had paid his radio and television fees, and was particularly concerned with events and opinions related to the administered areas.

Not everyone, however, was entitled to petition the High Court of Justice for, as a general rule, a Petitioner had to show that some personal private right of his had been infringed.

Nevertheless, since the Petitioner had raised a question of great public importance relating to Israel's image as a democratic state and a serious infringement of the basic rights of every citizen, the court would entertain the petition; moreover, counsel for the Respondents had not attacked the Petitioner's standing before the court since, as she said, they too wished to receive the decision of the court.

It had been argued, Justice Levin continued, that only the Broadcasting Authority itself, consisting of 31 members, was empowered to make the decision referred to, and that the Board of Directors of seven members had exceeded its authority. However, after examining the relevant provisions of the Broadcasting Authority Law of 1965, Justice Levin rejected this contention.

Turning to the merits of the case, Justice Levin cited decisions of the Supreme Court in which the right of the citizen to disseminate and receive information of what transpires both in and outside the State, had been clearly affirmed. This right, however, was not entirely unfettered, for it would not be upheld where "damage would be caused to the vital interests of the State or an individual", or "where there was a near certainty" that the exercise of this right in a particular case would endanger public safety or the security of the State.

Justice Levin then quoted several sections of the "Palestinian National Covenant" of 1968. The State of Israel, he said, was in the throes of a relentless and unremitting military and political struggle against Palestinian terrorist organizations banded together under the PLO. It was clear and well known that the PLO endangers the security of the State, and even rejects its right to exist. For this very reason it was vital that information as to its nature, aims, methods of operation, actions and plan, also in Judea, Samaria and Gaza, should be published both in and outside Israel.

There are two questions, Justice Levin said, which must be considered in the light of the above principles. Is it proper for the Authority to preclude its reporters from initiating interviews with public figures identified with the PLO, and does a citizen have the right not only to be told the contents of the interview, but also to see and hear the person interviewed.

It was reasonable to hold, he said, that the broadcasting and televising of such interviews are liable to damage the vital interests of the State, and create a "near possibility" of real danger to its security and the safety of the community.

The Board of Directors was therefore entitled to decide as it did. It was reasonable to assume that anyone who accepts "the Palestinian National Covenant" would exploit the radio and television to incite his listeners to achieve the destruction of the State of Israel as an independent political entity, and the establishment on its ruins of a Palestinian state.

The Supreme Court had already held, in different contexts, that it is the elementary right of every state to defend its freedom and existence against enemies from without and from within; no regime can be expected to uphold basic rights blindly, and follow the flag of liberalism into destruction.

Counsel for the Petitioner had contended that the decision in question offended against the "fairness doctrine", which had been recognized by the Supreme Court on the basis of American precedent. It had been held by the courts that the "basic principle underlying the 'fairness doctrine' is the right of the public to be informed . . . To invoke the doctrine there must be a controversial issue of public importance, and the broadcaster must have presented only one side of the issue".

Moreover, the test as to whether the doctrine has been infringed is that of reasonableness. In his opinion, said Justice Levin, the decisions in question — the second one particularly — satisfied this test, for they enabled a full, fair and balanced presentation of facts, albeit that they precluded such presentation by certain persons.

Counsel for the Petitioner had also argued, Justice Levin said, that the decision in question was too wide, and that it was essential that every piece of information to be reported be considered separately on its merits. Counsel had stressed that not only interviews relating to security and political matters were banned, but also those concerning social and economic problems.

This argument may have been valid, Justice Levin held, were it not for the fact that the decision referred to interviews with people who were devoted to what they regarded as the "holy" objective of destroying the State of Israel, and who exploited every available forum, whether it related to health, sport or any other topic, to this end.

In so extreme a case the Respondents were not required to make fine distinctions, but were entitled to lay down a general policy, wide as it was. Moreover, counsel for the Respondents had pointed out that in most cases, the importance of the information depended on its early publication and the delay involved in considering every piece of information separately would render it useless for broadcasting or television.

In conclusion, Justice Levin said that had the decision related only to defined members of the PLO, it would have been completely valid from every point of view. The one difficulty, however, was that the decision does not define — and perhaps cannot define — who is to be regarded as "identified" with the PLO and who is a "public figure".

If every piece of information were examined separately — which the Respondents were not prepared to undertake — this difficulty would not arise, since it would be possible in each case to ascertain whether the person interviewed was a public figure identified with the PLO or not. It was true that counsel for the Petitioner had asked whether the compilation for this purpose of such a list would be permitted in a free democratic state, and who would compile it. In fact, however, there is no such list.

The result was, Justice Levin concluded, that although the decision in question was valid in principle, it could not be implemented unless the Respondents found a way to provide a clear and unambiguous definition of the expressions "public figure" and "identified with the PLO". For this reason alone, he proposed that the order nisi be made absolute, with no order as to costs.

Justice Gavriel Bach preferred to express no opinion as to the Petitioner's standing before the court, for since Respondents' counsel had not raised this point, there was, in his view, no need to deal with it. He agreed to the order nisi being made absolute, but not only on the narrow basis proposed by Justice Levin.

Justice Bach was of opinion that the wide and all-embracing language of the decision in question rendered it invalid, and not only the absence of clarity as to who were public figures identified with the PLO.

He agreed entirely with Justice Levin as to the nature of the PLO, and the limitations on the right of the citizen to receive information. These limitations, however, must be confined to those expressions which, in the words of Justice Holmes, constitute "a clear and present danger". It was a matter of proximity and degree.

The question was, Justice Bach continued, whether the element of danger was to be found in every utterance of a supporter of the PLO on every subject. He agreed that the supporters of the PLO exploit every platform, in and out of Israel, to damage the State, but he did not agree that this released the Respondents from the duty of examining each item to be reported, and entitled them to reject every item irrespective of its content.

It was important to remember that there was no obligation to make "live" transmissions of interviews initiated by the Respondents, nor was the court concerned in this case with "news-flashes", which become meaningless if not reported without delay, and the prior investigation of which is practically impossible. He saw no reason why recorded or photographed interviews should not be examined by authorized persons in accordance with fixed criteria to determine whether they endanger state security, public safety, or some other vital national interest.

He was not convinced that prior examination, although perhaps difficult, could not be carried out. In any case, the alternative proposed in the decision in question was unacceptable, since it unjustifiably infringed the principle of free speech and the right of the community to receive reliable information.

It was possible, Justice Bach continued, that the mayor of a town who supported the PLO would be criticized in a televised interview by a political opponent in a municipal matter relating to sanitation, transport, education or economic development, while an interview with the mayor defending his policies would be precluded. Since it was true that propaganda and incitement could be introduced into interviews on seemingly innocuous matters, he would not suggest that the broadcast of all interviews should be permitted.

The question, however, was not whether general permission for such interviews should be given, but whether it was legitimate to impose on them a complete and absolute ban. It sometimes happens that mayors and other holders of high office are attacked personally in radio and television interviews, and accused of serious lapses, and even of corruption. Is it conceivable that such a person should be prevented from answering such charges in a personal appearance, when there is no connection whatsoever between the subject discussed and his political views?

Counsel for the Respondents had said that the decision was not directed against "innocent" interviews of this kind. The strength of a chain, however, must be tested by its weakest link, and if the decision in its present form could lead to unjust and unreasonable results, it cannot be allowed to stand.

Respondents' counsel had argued, Justice Bach said, that the principle of "clear and present danger" was to prevent the publication of information, but the contrary did not apply; the court would prohibit the publication of dangerous information, but would not compel the Respondents to publish information which was not dangerous. While this may be true in an isolated case, Justice Bach continued, it did not justify a wide and absolute prohibition such as that now considered.

In this respect, he accepted the opinion of the American judge, Justice Brennan, that ". . . in the light of the current dominance of the electronic media, the most effective means of reaching the public, any policy that absolutely denies citizens access to the airways necessarily renders even the concept of 'full and free discussion' practically meaningless . . .".

Justice Bach then gave examples of some of the strange consequences of the decision in question. If a supporter of the PLO wished to influence that body to adopt a more moderate attitude, an interview with him could not be broadcast. Again, the decision referred to interviews initiated by the reporters of the Respondents, but there seemed to be no objection to the broadcast of a press conference called by a supporter of the PLO. There seemed to be no logic in this distinction.

Justice Bach then pointed out that the "fairness doctrine" was intended primarily to ensure the right of the public to receive full and balanced information, as distinct from news that was presented in a prejudiced, arbitrary and partisan manner. In this respect he saw a great difference between "live" interviews and those merely reported.

The result of the decision was that one opinion would be expressed by persons whom the public could see and hear, while the contrary opinion could only be reported indirectly by a third party. This certainly did not ensure a fair and balanced presentation of a problem, and was against the public interest. In his view, therefore, the decision offended against the "fairness doctrine".

For the above reasons, Justice Bach proposed that the order nisi be made absolute on all the grounds mentioned, and not only because of some vagueness, as held by Justice Levin. He also proposed that the Respondents be ordered to pay the Petitioner's costs.

Justice Yehuda Cohen concurred in the judgment of Justice Levin. The limits of the freedom of speech and the right to receive information, he said, are measured not only by the contents of what is said, but also by the personality who says it.

He agreed with Justice Levin that the ban on personal interviews with members of and sympathizers with the PLO was not unreasonable, and did not damage the right of the public to receive full and fair information of what transpires in the administered territories. For example, the expression of an opinion against the settlements in Judea and Samaria was legitimate when voiced by a person concerned with the interests of the State. The same opinion, however, when expressed by a public figure identified by the inhabitants of these territories with the PLO, would encourage incitement and treachery, and strengthen their hostility to the State.

Justice Cohen was also of opinion that the absence of a clear definition of "public figures identified with the PLO" was not a matter for this court. This vagueness could create difficulties for the Respondents, and could lead to litigation in specific instances, but it did not affect the reasonableness of the decision.

For these reasons, Justice Cohen concluded, he would have dismissed the petition unreservedly, but in consideration of the opinions of his colleagues, he agreed to the order proposed by Justice Levin.

By majority decision, the order nisi was made absolute, as held by Justice Levin.

Advocate Avigdor Feldman appeared for the Petitioner, and Advocate Michal Shaked, Senior Assistant State Attorney, for the Respondents.

Judgment given on March 24, 1983.

IN THE INTERESTS OF THE CHILDREN

YEHIEL NAGAR v. ORA NAGAR

In the Special Tribunal, before the President Justice Meir Shamgar, Justice Menahem Elon, and Rabbi Yosef Kapah, in the matter of *Yehiel Nagar*, Plaintiff, versus *Ora Nagar*, Defendant. (S.T. 1/81).

Personal Status—Guardianship of Children—Jewish Law—Jurisdiction of Civil and Rabbinical Courts—Palestine Order-in-Council, 1922, Articles 51, 53, 55—Courts Ordinance, 1940, section 9—Rabbinical Courts Jurisdiction (Marriage and Divorce) Law, 1953, sections 1, 9—Womens Equal Rights Law, 1951—Capacity and Guardianship Law, 1962.

Under the terms of a divorce agreement between the parties, their two sons, aged 13 and 11, were to remain with their mother, who undertook to be responsible for their maintenance and education until they are 18. The agreement also provided that all disputes between the parties relating to their children after the divorce would be dealt with by the Rabbinical Court, whose judgment would be binding on them both.

At the time of the divorce both parents were non-Orthodox, and the children were placed in a secular school. Later, however, the father became Orthodox, and in January 1980 he applied to the District Rabbinical Court for custody of the children. In July 1980 he also applied for an order directing their mother to register them in the meantime in an Orthodox school.

On August 31, 1980, the court granted the order on the basis that since, according to Jewish law, the duty of educating the children was that of the father, he was entitled to decide what form that education should take. The mother then appealed to the Rabbinical Court of Appeals arguing, *inter alia*, that the Rabbinical Court had no jurisdiction. The Court of Appeals dismissed this argument of February 5, 1981, and directed the appeal to be heard on its merits at a later date.

On February 12, 1981, the mother applied to the District Court for custody of the children and an order that they be placed in a secular school, and on February 15, 1981, in the father's absence, the court granted the order sought. Thereafter it confirmed its order after a full hearing before both parties. Since the mother had secured the relief which she sought from the District Court, she applied to the Rabbinical Court on February 22, to withdraw her appeal. On April 13, 1981, that court decided that the District Court had no jurisdiction, and since the wife had withdrawn her appeal it confirmed the judgment of the District Rabbinical Court. Since at one stage, as a result of the litigation between the parents, the children did not attend school at all, the Attorney-General intervened. Later, however, the children returned to the secular school they had attended previously, and were still at that school.

Under Articles 51 and 53 of the Palestine Order-in-Council of 1922, the Rabbinical Courts have exclusive jurisdiction in matters of the marriage and divorce of Jews and "in any matter of personal status of such persons, where all the parties to the action consent to the Jurisdiction".

Under Article 55 of the Order and section 9 of the Courts Ordinance of 1940, whenever a question arises as to whether or not a case is one of personal status within the exclusive jurisdiction of a religious court, it must be referred to a Special Tribunal consisting of two judges of the Supreme Court and the President of the highest court of the community concerned, or his nominee.

Since the District Court had based its decision partly on the ground that the education of children is not "a matter of personal status" within the meaning of Article 51, the Rabbinical Court of Appeals referred the matter to the Special Tribunal which, by order of the President of the Supreme Court, was then convened to hear the matter.

The first judgment of the Tribunal was given by Justice Menahem Elon. Counsel for the mother had argued, *inter alia*, he said, that the term "exclusive jurisdiction" in Article 55 referred only to cases where the law imposed such jurisdiction on the religious courts, as under section 1 of the Rabbinical Courts Jurisdiction (Marriage and Divorce) Law of 1953, and not to a case such as the present one, in which the religious courts had concurrent jurisdiction with the District Courts, and the religious courts had exclusive jurisdiction only if the wife (under section 4 of that Law) or both parties (under section 9) so desired.

This argument was untenable, for it had been held consistently by the Supreme Court that once a party had chosen or agreed to litigate in a religious court, he was precluded from doing so in the District Court as well. He was not entitled to test his case in one court and, if the judgment did not suit him, sue in the other court for the same relief. The result was that once the jurisdiction of the religious court had been exercised by the consent of the parties, it became "exclusive jurisdiction" for the purposes of Article 51 of the Order-in-Council.

Justice Elon added that he had never come across a case in which a party had run from one court to another so blatantly as in the present matter.

The mother had agreed to the jurisdiction of the Rabbinical Court, specifically, in the divorce agreement, and impliedly by participating in litigation in that court, and even lodging an appeal to the Rabbinical Appeals Court. Nevertheless, the District Court had held that it was entitled to ignore the judgment of the Rabbinical Court on the grounds, firstly, that if it had jurisdiction such jurisdiction had been exceeded and, secondly, that in fact the conditions for its jurisdiction had not been fulfilled.

The District Court had based its first ground on the fact that the Rabbinical Court had failed to consider the views of the mother who, with the father, was the joint guardian of the children, and also on the interests of the children themselves. The duty to consider both these elements was imposed upon it by the Women's Equal Rights Law of 1951 and the Capacity and Guardianship Law of 1962, and in overlooking these Laws of the State, the Rabbinical Court must be regarded as having exceeded its jurisdiction.

It was true, Justice Elon said, that in some precedents such a failure on the part of the Rabbinical Court had been so regarded, though he preferred to describe it as a mistake in the application of the law. In either case, however, it was clear that substantive jurisdiction to deal with the matter had been conferred upon the Rabbinical Court by the consent of the parties, and it was therefore only the Rabbinical Court of Appeals and the Supreme Court sitting as a High Court of Justice which were entitled to set its judgment aside.

It had been held, Justice Elon said, that where a judgment had been given by a religious court without jurisdiction, it was subject to "indirect attack", in the sense that a litigant could oppose its being acted upon. This, however, was a very different thing from a District Court ignoring a judgment of a Rabbinical Court which had acted within its jurisdiction, and then itself dealing with the matter although the litigants had clearly and unequivocally agreed to the jurisdiction of the Rabbinical Court.

The position would be otherwise if the Rabbinical Court had acted without any jurisdiction whatever — for example, had judged a man for a criminal offence — or if a District Court had decreed a divorce. Any such assumption of jurisdiction would, of course, be completely void.

The District Court had based its second ground on the finding that the education of children was not "a matter of personal status" within the meaning of Article 51, and therefore not within the exclusive jurisdiction of the Rabbinical Court. According to the District Court, the Rabbinical Court had not dealt at all with the guardianship of the children as defined in the Capacity and Guardianship Law, but only with the right of the father to determine the education of his sons. Moreover, the District Court had held that guardianship, according to the Halacha, applied only to property and not to orphans, and was quite different from the conception of guardianship in the above Law.

Justice Elon then entered upon a detailed review of precedents of the Supreme Court, and the development of the Halacha in the matters at issue. He held that the conception of guardianship in the Halacha was fully in accord with that enshrined in the Capacity, and Guardianship Law. Moreover, he rejected the view that only the father was entitled to determine the education of his children. The guardianship over the children was the obligation of both parents.

In reaching this conclusion, Justice Elon demonstrated the capacity of the Halacha to adjust to developments in society, and keep abreast of modern conceptions in matters such as those which arose in this case. He emphasized that the interests of the children must always be the paramount consideration of any court in dealing with questions affecting their welfare. The result was that the question of the education of the children was "a matter of personal status", and that jurisdiction resided in the Rabbinical Court, and not in the District Court.

Justice Elon went on to consider what constitutes "the best interests of the children". Conceptions in this respect differ, he said. It was only natural that Jewish law embraced values and norms and ways of life, and it was to be expected that secular courts would differ in their approach to this problem. This feature, however, of the law following the judge, was not new, for there were different conceptions among the judges in the same court, secular or religious.

The legislature had created the two types of jurisdiction, and had therefore approved the existence of differing conceptions in regard to the matters now considered. The Rabbinical Court in the present case would have to consider all the circumstances, and, provided the principle of the best interests of the children were observed, and there was no extreme or unreasonable flaw in considering the facts, the Supreme Court would not interfere.

He proposed that the case be returned to the District Rabbinical Court to be reconsidered in the light of all the facts, including additional evidence and opinions of experts which the parties might bring before it. In the meantime, until a final decision was given, the children were to remain in the school which they attend at present.

The President agreed with Justice Elon. The religious and the secular courts, he said, exercised concurrent jurisdiction in regard to the education of children unless one of them acquired exclusive jurisdiction; and that had been acquired by the Rabbinical Court in the present case. Justice Shamgar also expressed some views regarding the "indirect attack" on the judgment of another court, but found it unnecessary to express a final opinion on this aspect. He also stressed that the children were to remain in their present school until some other order is made by the court

Rabbi Kapah also concurred in the judgment of Justice Elon. The District Court seemed to have thought, he said, that the legislature had intended to compel the Rabbinical Courts to rule against their religion and beliefs. However, this could only apply to matters of property, and it must be assumed that there was no such intention in respect of any other matter.

Much had been said, Rabbi Kapah concluded, about the best interests of the child as against the interests of the parents. As Justice Elon had pointed out, however, the court must consider all the circumstances. True, it must always weigh the physical and emotional interests of the child, but not at the expense of damaging the natural feelings of its parents.

Advocates Ido Divon appeared for the plaintiff, Noam Launer for the Defendant, and Renato Yarak, Director of the High Court Division of the State Attorney's Office, for the Attorney-General.

Judgment was given on February 24, 1984.

AN ADOPTION CASE: CONSENT AND REGRET

THE ATTORNEY GENERAL v. A.B.

In the Supreme Court sitting as a Court of Civil Appeals before the President, Justice Meir Shamgar, Justice Aharon Barak and Justice Eliezer Goldberg, in the matter of *The Attorney General*, Appellant, versus *A.B.*, Respondent (C.A. 577/83).

Personal Status—Adoption—Parent's Withdrawal of Consent—Adoption of Children Law, 1981, sections 1(b), 10, 13—Youth (Care and Supervision) Law, 1960—Legal Capacity and Guardianship Law, 1962—Penal Law, 1977, section 58—Transport Ordinance (New Version), 1961, section 63—Civil Procedure Rules, 1963, Rule 415.

In January, 1983, the Respondent, A.B., bore a son, and four days later signed a consent for his adoption. Since there was no such consent by his father, he was declared adoptable by the court and handed over to an adoptive family with whom he has since remained. A short while later the Respondent told the welfare authorities she had made a mistake, and in June 1983, she moved the District Court for leave to withdraw the consent. The leave was granted, and the Attorney-General appealed to the Supreme Court.

In giving the first judgement of the Supreme Court, Justice Aharon Barak stressed the difficulties in deciding adoption cases in which the maintaining or severing of the relationship between a child and its parents was decided irrevocably, and the test applied, "the best interests of the child" was complicated, embracing many more elements that are unknown rather than known.

The Respondent, an unmarried student of 23, became pregnant after relations with a married man of 43, the father of six. She had resolved while pregnant to give the child for adoption, for she wished to terminate her relationship with her lover, a member of an ultra-Orthodox sect (Haredim), who demanded that the child receive a haredi education. Moreover, her parents, members of the same sect, pressed her to take this step, and she realized the objective difficulties of a young woman in her position, without the support of a husband or other person in bringing up a child.

Thus she left the hospital without her child the day after he was born, leaving a farewell letter for him in which she explained the difficulties with which she was faced, and that it was for his own good that she had decided as she did. The child was then handed over to an adoptive family, who were bringing him up as an only child with devotion and love.

The Respondent thereafter changed her mind, as the District Court found, genuinely and honestly. This change was induced partly by a change in the feeling of her parents, who were now prepared to assist her in raising the child. She was about to complete her studies, had secured part-time employment, and had leased a two-room apartment in which she wished to live with her son.

She was now able to make her own way with her own resources. The identity of the child's father was not known to the court, and there was little fear of any interference on his part. A further fact to be considered, which had only been disclosed after the District Court had given judgment, but which the parties had agreed to bring before the court, was that the child was deaf. The Respondent had contracted measles in her second month of pregnancy, which she had not mentioned to anyone, resulting in the child's deafness, and the possibility of heart disease and mental retardation in the future. This fact, however, had not weakened the Respondent's desire to regain her child, nor the wish and readiness of the adoptive family to retain him.

The present case, Justice Barak continued, was governed by section 10 of the Adoption of Children Law, of 1981, which provides that "On the application of a parent, the court may invalidate his consent (to adoption) given before the birth of the adoptee or obtained by improper means, and it may, for special reasons which shall be recorded, permit a parent to withdraw his consent so long as the (final) adoption order has not been made".

This section gives no indication of what the "special reasons" are, but section I (b) of the Adoption of Children Law provides that "An adoption order and any other decision under this Law, shall be made if the court is satisfied that they are in the best interest of the adoptee". But the question is what are the "best interests of the adoptee"? And there is also the question of the relationship between the interests of the child and those of its natural parents.

The starting point must be that the natural family is the basic unit of society. Parents also have rights, and not only obligations. The parents have the right to fulfil their obligations towards their children. Their emotional bond with their children is one of their most treasured possessions, and it is fully recognized by law.

The state is not entitled to take children away from their parents only because "the best interests of the children" so demand. Even "bad" parents are entitled to rear their children, and the tendency must be to preserve the unity of the family. In order to justify disrupting the autonomy and privacy of the family unit and removing a child from its natural parents, some special and exceptional ground must be shown. The welfare of the child alone is not sufficient. It is for this reason that many child victims of the Holocaust were reunited with their parents who refused to give them for adoption. Where, however, some other legal ground for so doing does exist, the welfare of the child becomes the central element in deciding where the child should be placed.

The legal grounds for removing a child from its parents are found in many Laws such as the Youth (Care and Supervision) Law of 1960, the Legal Capacity and Guardianship Law of 1962, and also the Adoption of Children Law. Under section 13 of that Law the court may declare a child adoptable on the application of the Attorney-General on various grounds such as, for example, that the parents have abandoned the child. A special ground for intervention by the authorities is where parents have consented to the adoption.

Such consent in itself does not abolish the right of the natural parents toward their child, which terminate only with the making of the final order of adoption. However, such consent affects the order of priorities of the various elements involved, for once it is given, the principal factor to be considered by the court is the welfare of the child, the rights of the parents now taking second place.

In considering, therefore, whether to permit a parent to withdraw his or her consent, the court must consider, firstly, the interests of the child, and then the interests of the natural parents. It must also weigh the interests of the adoptive parents, though the rights of the natural parents will be preferred, provided there is no difference as far as the welfare of the child is concerned.

"The best interests of the child" should be weighed on the basis of the facts of each particular case, Justice Barak said, and not on the basis of generalities. The court must judge what will be best for the child — its return to its parents if leave is given to withdraw the consent to adoption, or its remaining with the adoptive family. The choice is hard, based as it is on predictions as to future events about which little can be known at the time. Thus, the authority Moonkin has said that: "The determination of what is 'best' or 'least' detrimental for a particular child is usually indeterminate and speculative. In most custody cases, existing psychological theories simply do not yield confident prediction of the effects of alternative custody dispositions. Moreover, even if accurate predictions were possible in most cases, our society today lacks any clear-cut consensus about the values to be used in determining what is 'best' or 'least detrimental'".

How can one gauge the damage to the child if he is to be removed from his adoptive parents, and what will be the damage in severing his links with his mother, and his growing up as an adoptee? There are those who hold that these are not really legal questions to be decided by judges, but until guidelines are laid down by the legislature itself, the court has no option but to weigh the alternatives by what it regards as the most appropriate considerations under the Adoption Law. Some authorities believe that, "In the long run, the child's chances will be better if the law is less pretentious and ambitious in its aim, that is if it confines itself to the avoidance of harm and acts in accordance with a few, even if modest, generally applicable short-term predictions".

Justice Barak did not accept this opinion, for an adoption order affects the child for the rest of his or her life, although the weight to be attached to short-term predictions is naturally greater than that relating to the remote future. The welfare of the child embraces not only his material but also his emotional well-being, and the situation must be judged taking into account both these elements jointly.

It must be presumed that a child is better off with his natural parents than with strangers, Justice Barak continued. On the other hand, an important factor in a child's life is continuity, and it has been said that "Empirical research by child development specialists indicates that revocation of consent after a child has been placed with adoptive parents is rarely in the child's best interests. If an infant or young child is uprooted from adoptive parents with whom he or she has formed a parental attachment and is returned to a biological parent whom the child now regards as a stranger, permanent psychological damage may result".

Moreover, the longer the child is with his adoptive parents, the greater the damage if he is taken from them. What is a short period of time for an adult may seem to a young child like eternity.

Another point to be considered is that it is preferable to act on the basis of certainty than on assumption. Thus if the removal of the child from his adoptive parents will certainly cause him damage, while the benefit he will derive from being returned to his natural parents is only speculative, he should remain where he is. Justice Barak then reviewed several precedents of the Supreme Court illustrating the application of these principles.

Justice Barak then considered the scope of the "special reasons" required by section 10 of the Adoption Law for the withdrawal of the consent to adoption. The court must strike a balance between two demands of judicial policy. On the one hand there was the basic right of a child's natural parents and the necessity for upholding this right. On the other hand, there was the importance of encouraging adoptions and strengthening the willingness of adoptive parents to undertake the responsibilities involved. This willingness would be seriously impaired if the natural parents would be permitted to withdraw their consent whenever they pleased.

It was true that adoptive parents have no legal rights until a final adoption order is made, but account must be taken of the enormous emotional damage they would suffer if the child is taken from them. The desire of parents to withdraw their consent is in itself certainly not a "special reason". What is required is a change of circumstances, such as the marriage of the parents if the mother was unmarried, or a change in their economic situation, or in the attitude of their parents. It must be a serious and meaningful change, relating to the facts of each particular case.

Justice Barak then analysed the facts of the present case as before the District Court, and concluded that the best interests of the child demanded that he remain with his adoptive parents. The damage he would suffer if removed from them was serious, clear and immediate, and would also last into the future.

As against this, the advantages he would gain from being returned to his mother were dubious, for there was serious doubt whether, because of her own lack of maturity and the problems she would face, she would be able to bring him up adequately.

His conclusion was strengthened by the subsequent revelation of the child's deafness. This feature would impose upon those concerned an additional continuous and heavy burden. According to the experts, the Respondent did not fully appreciate the difficulties she would face, and they were of the opinion that removing the child now from his adoptive parents would cause serious damage to his physical and emotional development.

For the above reasons, Judge Barak proposed that the appeal be allowed. He realized, he said, that this decision would be a serious blow to the Respondent. She should, however, find comfort in the knowledge that her consent to the adoption was a brave act in the best interests of her child, and that it was for this very reason that the court now decided as it did.

Justice Eliezer Goldberg agreed with Justice Barak. He would have hesitated, he said, to have interfered with the decision of the District Court, given after the child had been with its adoptive parents for only six months, were it not for the fact of the child's deafness, which had subsequently emerged. Although the whole case had to be judged on the basis of imponderables, it was not difficult to imagine the problems the Respondent would face in bringing up a deaf child alone.

This task would impose upon her an almost unbearable emotional strain, and for the child her failure would be a tragedy. She had been described as weak and immature, and there was therefore a real fear that she would not be able to bear that burden. It was therefore in the child's interests that he should remain with his adoptive parents.

The President concurred with his colleagues. It was not enough, he said, for the purposes of section 10 of the Adoption Law, that a parent should change her mind. There had to be special reasons which, in the opinion of the court, were sufficient. The legislature, however, had not indicated what changed an "ordinary reason" into a "special reason" for this purpose. In some instances, such as in section 58 of the Penal Law of 1977 or section 63 of the Transport Ordinance (New Version), the normally unfettered discretion of the court was limited by the requirement that it record "the reasons" for its decision.

In other cases, such as in section 10, or in Rule 415 of the Civil Procedure Rules of 1963, the discretion was made even narrower by the requirement of "special reasons" for the decision, which have to be recorded. Since the Law says no more than this, the only inference is that "reasonable grounds" acceptable in ordinary circumstances, are not sufficient. There must be particularly weighty considerations that clearly justify the withdrawal of the consent. This means, he said, that there must be a meaningful change of circumstances such as that the child has not yet been fully integrated into the adoptive family, or that the mother has married and her husband is willing to share her responsibility.

Justice Shamgar agreed with Justice Barak in regard to the close and loving relationship between the child and its adoptive family. Nevertheless, he said, he would have hesitated to take the cruel and harsh decision of separating a mother from her son. After anxious consideration, however, he had agreed to do so mainly for the reason relied upon by Justice Goldberg, namely, the present state of health of the child, and the special treatment and conditions which he now requires.

There was grave doubt whether a single young woman, who would sooner or later have to support herself and overcome her own problems alone, would be able to cope with such a burden. She was undoubtedly willing to do so, but the difficulties she will encounter, in addition to the attachment formed by the child to his adoptive family, the emotional crisis he will face, and his physical limitations, all weigh the scale in favour of his remaining with his adoptive family, while what remains on the other side cannot create "special reasons" that would justify a special decision.

For the above reasons, the appeal was allowed.

Dr. Yosef Ben-Or, Senior Assistant State Attorney, appeared for the Attorney-General, and Advocate Bert Arwas for the Respondent.

The judgment was given on March 6, 1984.

DIFFERING CONCEPTIONS

WATTAD v. MINISTER OF FINANCE

In the Supreme Court sitting as a High Court of Justice before the Deputy-President, Justice Miriam Ben-Porat, Justice Eliezer Goldberg, and Judge Yaacov Tirkel, in the matter between *Mohammed Wattad and Hamed Heleita*, Petitioners, and *The Minister of Finance*, Respondent (H.C. 208/83).

Administrative Law—Grants to Assist "Yeshiva" Students—No Unlawful Discrimination—Connecting Such Grants with Those Given to Discharged Soldiers Insupportable—Discharged Soldiers (Reinstatement in Employment), Law, 1949.

The Discharged Soldiers (Reinstatement in Employment) Law, of 1949, empowers the Minister of Labour and Social Welfare, in consultation with the Minister of Finance and with the confirmation of the Finance Committee of the Knesset, to make regulations for the payment of grants to discharged soldiers and their families.

According to the Petitioners, members of the Knesset, and fathers of large families, a representative of the treasury had informed the Finance Committee, during a discussion on a proposed increase in the grants to soldiers for their children, that it was proposed to pay the same increase to students in yeshivot (schools for Jewish religious studies) for whom "study was their profession".

The Petitioners did not question the principle of compensating fathers of large families for their three years of army service, but they argued that there was no reason why they should not receive the same grants as those paid to others who had not done army service. They argued that making grants to persons other than soldiers on the model of the above Law was against the intention of the legislature, and they also voiced the impression that the government had decided, behind the scenes, to deny the grants in question to Arabs.

The Petitioners asked for an order restraining the Respondent from making any grants, on the basis of those paid under the above Law, other than to soldiers, and from seeking the confirmation of the Finance Committee for such grants.

After the petition was lodged, and on the instructions of the Attorney-General, the proposal complained of was withdrawn. However, the Ministerial Committee for the Interior, Services and Quality of Life laid down new criteria under which grants were to be paid to ensure an income for students in a yeshiva, or institution of higher learning for religious studies of other religions, for whom their studies were their profession and sole occupation.

The Petitioners, however, persisted in their application on the basis that there were no such higher institutions of learning in Israel for Moslems, Christians or Druse, with the result that the only recipients of the grants would be yeshiva students, while non-Jews would be the victims of unjust discrimination.

The first judgment of the court was given by Judge Yaacov Tirkel. The principles of equality and non-discrimination, he said, were already laid down in the Bible, and after the suffering of the Jewish people during thousands of years of exile and unjust discrimination, had been restated at the very opening of the Declaration of Independence of the State of Israel.

The Jewish people, therefore, more than any other, was bound to ensure that no unjust discrimination existed in its midst, or appeared to exist. It was usual to assert that unjust discrimination meant different attitudes towards equals, while different attitudes towards non-equals was not so defined. This latter assertion, however, was too facile, for it was necessary to examine whether the non-equality was real and genuine, and relevant to the different attitudes adopted.

For example, the application of different tax standards to rich and poor, or to those with small or large families, was not unjust discrimination. Where, however, the differences between the two groups related to religion, nationality, race or sex, the distinction was not easy to define, for it depended on the different conceptions of the communities concerned, their accepted values and their desire to protect and strengthen them, and these differed from place to place, and from time to time.

The Supreme Court had dealt with a similar problem in the case of an Arab who had been refused an apartment in the Jewish quarter of the Old City of Jerusalem since he was not "a citizen and resident of Israel who had served in the army or was released from service, or a new immigrant" — as the conditions required. It was held that he was not the victim of unjust discrimination.

The repopulation of the Jewish Quarter by Jews alone was the result of their having been driven out and their property despoiled. There was no unjust discrimination in preserving the unique character of the Jewish Quarter as that of the Moslem, Christian and Armenian Quarters of the city.

The Petitioners had alleged that there were no non-Jewish institutions in Israel similar to yeshivot. It was possible, however, that there would be such institutions in the future, and in that event there was no provision in the new criteria to deprive non-Jewish students of the grants. The question still remained, however, whether the grants to yeshiva students did not constitute unjust discrimination for so long as they alone enjoyed this privilege, and this in turn raised the question of the special place occupied among the Jewish people by religious studies and yeshivot throughout the centuries.

Judge Tirkel then cited talmudic and other sources from which he concluded that the granting of special support to yeshiva students was justified, even if there were no similar institutions of other religious groups. This was not unjust discrimination, but a just balance of values. He therefore proposed that the application be dismissed.

Justice Miriam Ben-Porat agreed with her colleague. In her opinion, the petition to the court — according to the conceptions of the Petitioners — was absolutely reasonable and understandable. They accepted the distinction between those who served in the army and those not liable for service, and there was, in their view, no reason why all those who did not serve should not be treated equally in respect to grants paid to their families. It was not surprising that they did not understand the significance of the expression "yeshiva student". This was not an Israeli invention, but a conception deeply rooted in the history of the Jewish people throughout the years of its exile, fostered as a means of ensuring its continued existence and identity.

The "yeshiva student", who engaged in religious study, was received by the community as an honoured guest, and invited to Jewish homes for meals to relieve him of the burden of supporting himself, and enable him to devote himself entirely to his studies. This time-honoured tradition was observed also in the State of Israel, and it was no wonder that the authorities changed the form of support for these young men, and enabled them to receive financial assistance from the state, as if they had served in the army, instead of having to go from door to door to assuage their needs. Since their sole occupation was study instead of some lucrative calling, they were regarded as worthy of such support.

Nevertheless, the Deputy-President continued, the Attorney-General had acted correctly in ruling that connecting the grants to yeshiva students with those paid to discharged soldiers was legally insupportable. This ruling, however, was given after the petition was lodged, and the Petitioners, therefore, could not be criticized for approaching the court.

In conclusion, Justice Ben-Porat also agreed that the fact that there was at present no institution similar to a yeshiva in the non-Jewish communities made no difference. Whatever one's personal opinion may be, the new criteria were reasonable, and they were also non-discriminatory since they entitled all students, irrespective of their religious affiliation, to enjoy the benefits in question.

Justice Eliezer Goldberg concurred. There could be no doubt, he said, that the government was entitled to assist students in religious institutions who do not support themselves, and for whom "study is their profession", provided there was no personal unjust discrimination. The argument that there were no such students in non-Jewish communities in Israel — and perhaps will be no such students in the future — proved in itself that the court was not concerned here with unjust discrimination between equals, but with a legitimate and objective distinction between non-equals.

For the above reasons the application was dismissed, and the Respondent ordered to pay the costs of the Petitioners in the sum of IS50,000.

Advocate Bezalel Reshef appeared for the Petitioners, and Advocate Renato Yarak, Director of the High Court Division of the State Attorney's Office, for the Respondent.

The judgment was given on July 25, 1984.

FORBIDDEN MARRIAGE

TAMAR FORER v. MARIO FORER

In the Supreme Court sitting as a Court of Civil Appeals before Justice Gavriel Bach, Justice Shoshana Netanyahu, and Justice Eliezer Goldberg in the matter between *Tamar Forer*, Appellant, and *Mario Forer*, Respondent (C.A. 592/83).

Personal Status—Jewish Law—Wife in Forbidden Marriage Not Entitled to Maintenance—Family Law Amendment (Maintenance) Law, 1959, sections 2(a), 17—Rabbinical Courts Jurisdiction (Marriage and Divorce) Law, 1953, sections 1, 2.

The parties, nationals and residents of Israel, were married in a synagogue in Florence, Italy, and the marriage was registered in the municipal marriage register. The wife was a divorcee, and the husband a cohen (a member of the priestly sect).

Subsequently the wife sued her husband in the Rabbinical Court for a restoration of family relations, while the husband sued for a divorce. Thereafter, on January 8, 1981, the wife claimed maintenance from her husband in the District Court, and that court granted a temporary maintenance order in her favour.

On September 16, 1981, the Rabbinical Court ruled that since the marriage was between a cohen and a divorcee, which is forbidden by Jewish law, the parties must be divorced. The wife's claim, therefore, was dismissed. The court also made no order for the wife's maintenance since the marriage itself was forbidden, and it rejected her argument that the fact that she had financial claims against her husband entitled her to maintenance from him. It decided further that it would deal later with any financial claims between the parties if an action for such claims were filed. The wife's appeal to the Rabbinical Court of Appeals was dismissed.

On December 31, 1981, the District Court cancelled the order for temporary maintenance in view of the decisions of the Rabbinical Court, and on September 2, 1983, it dismissed the wife's claim altogether. The wife then appealed to the Supreme Court.

The judgment of the Supreme Court was given by Justice Shoshana Netanyahu. There was a conflict between the parties, she said, as to whether the marriage was recognized in Italy both as a religious and civil marriage and, if so, whether such civil marriage was recognized in Israel.

She inclined to the view, and would assume, that it was recognized in Italy as a civil marriage as well, and she would also assume — without deciding the point — that it would also be so recognized in Israel. These assumptions, however, would be of no assistance to the wife.

It was not disputed that according to Jewish law the marriage was forbidden, but was recognized retrospectively. The parties were obliged to divorce. Some authorities held that the wife was not entitled to maintenance from the beginning, but it was agreed that whatever right she had came to an end when the court ordered the parties to be divorced, even if the divorce itself was not accepted by the wife. The husband would only be liable for maintenance thereafter if he delayed giving the divorce to his wife. In the present case the position was reversed — the husband was only too eager to give the divorce, but the wife refused to accept it. Therefore, it was clear that in Jewish law she had no right to maintenance.

The law to be applied was laid down in section 2 (a) of the Family Law Amendment (Maintenance) Law of 1959, which provided that "A person is liable for the maintenance of his spouse in accordance with the provisions of the personal law applying to him . . .". That law, in the present case, was Jewish law. It was true that Private International Law was introduced into the statute by section 17, which provided that the duty of maintenance between spouses shall be governed by the law of their place of residence, or that of the spouse liable, but since the parties in the present case were residents of Israel, section 2 (a) contained the relevant law.

It was noteworthy that the above statute provided otherwise in respect of children and certain other relatives, who were entitled to maintenance even if their personal law did not give them this right. In regard to spouses, however, their personal law applied.

Counsel for the wife, Justice Netanyahu continued, had tried to draw a distinction between the effects of the religious marriage of the parties, and of their civil marriage. Even if the former gave the wife no right to maintenance, he argued, the latter, recognized by the State, did give her this right. Counsel relied in this regard on precedents of the Supreme Court that had held that a civil marriage outside Israel, though not recognized by the Rabbinical Courts, was recognized by the civil courts. Those cases, however, dealt with spouses who were neither nationals nor residents of Israel, and to them section 2 (a) did not apply. Not only did the distinction suggested by counsel have no legal basis, but it would create conflict and uncertainty as to the rights of spouses which could never be resolved.

Justice Netanyahu also referred in this context to sections 1 and 2 of the Rabbinical Courts Jurisdiction (Marriage and Divorce) Law of 1953, under which "Matters of marriage and divorce of Jews in Israel, being nationals or residents of the State, shall be within the exclusive jurisdiction of Rabbinical Courts" and "Marriages and divorces of Jews shall be performed in Israel in accordance with Jewish religious law". The result was that whether the marriage was religious or civil, or both, the only competent court which could deal with the divorce was the Rabbinical Court, which applied Jewish religious law. According to that law, the wife's claim to maintenance did not exist.

A further argument of counsel was that Jewish law imposed certain financial obligations in favour of the wife on a cohen who had knowingly married a divorcee, and for so long as he failed to carry out these obligations she was not obliged to accept a divorce. She was, therefore, entitled to maintenance until the divorce was effected. This contention was based on analogy — since such a husband who refused to give a divorce was liable to pay maintenance, a wife who justifiably refused to accept a divorce was entitled to maintenance.

Counsel also based his contention on the law of contract, arguing that the husband's financial obligations and the wife's obligation to accept a divorce, were reciprocal. The answer to this argument was that the Rabbinical Court had exclusive jurisdiction to deal with this subject. The husband had lodged his claim for divorce in the Rabbinical Court before the wife had lodged her claim for maintenance in the District Court, and he had already linked the question of maintenance to his claim by asking for a ruling relieving him of the obligation.

Moreover, the wife had accepted the jurisdiction of the Rabbinical Court. It was clear from that court's decision of September 16, 1981, that not only had the wife not challenged its jurisdiction on the question of maintenance, but had actually asked for an order of maintenance and submitted her arguments. Her claim, however, was rejected.

Justice Netanyahu then pointed out that in subsequent proceedings in the Rabbinical Court the husband was ordered, with his consent, to pay the wife IS200,000 linked to the index, on her receiving the divorce, but that should she persist in her refusal to do so, he would be granted a licence to remarry, and would be obliged to pay the wife only what was owing to her in the Ketuba (marriage contract). Thereafter the Rabbinical Court of Appeals had stayed the issue of the marriage licence, but had not yet given judgment in the appeal on its merits.

Justice Netanyahu concluded, therefore, that there was no alternative but to dismiss the appeal. The result was that although the husband had married his wife knowing that he was forbidden to do so, she was obliged to accept a divorce without any right to maintenance, and with meagre compensation, which had been awarded to her not by right but only as a favour. For a person of secular opinions this result was intolerable. It was, however, unavoidable under Jewish law which, by legislative command, was to be applied to claims for maintenance by a spouse.

For the above reasons, the appeal was dismissed but, in the circumstances, with no order as to costs.

Advocate Matityahu Kaniel appeared for the Appellant, and Advocate Shoshana Broide for the Respondent.

The judgment was given on September 19, 1984.

NO BASIS FOR PUNITIVE CLAIM

MIRA SALOMON v. MOSHE SALOMON

In the Supreme Court sitting as a Court of Civil Appeals before Justice
Moshe Bejski, Justice Dov Levin and Judge Yehuda Weiss, in the
matter of *Mira Salomon*, Appellant, versus *Moshe Salomon*, Respondent
(C.A. 664/82).

*Personal Status—Jewish Law—No "Punitive Maintenance"—Rabbinical Courts
Jurisdiction (Marriage and Divorce) Law, 1953.*

The parties, a married couple with three children, have been engaged
in litigation in both the civil and rabbinical courts for the last 10 years. The
wife sued in the Rabbinical Court for a divorce, and in the District Court
for maintenance. The husband resisted these claims, and sued his wife in
the Rabbinical Court for a reconciliation.

On June 12, 1980, the Rabbinical Court ruled that the husband should
give his wife a divorce as a religious obligation, a ruling which obliges the
husband to give the divorce as a mitzva — a religious act alone, not
amounting to an actual order of court. Both parties appealed against this
ruling.

The husband did not give the divorce, and the wife sued in the District
Court for an increase in the amount of her maintenance in order to induce
him to do so. Her claim, however, was dismissed on the ground that there
was no legal basis for awarding "punitive maintenance" in order to coerce
a husband to divorce his wife.

On July 5, 1982, the Rabbinical Court of Appeals gave its judgment. The
husband's appeal was dismissed. The wife's appeal, however, was allowed, and the court made an order obliging the husband to give the
divorce, an order imposing a stronger obligation than performing a mere
religious act. The court added that if the husband persisted in his refusal
to give a divorce, the wife would be entitled to apply again to the Rabbinical
Court for relief. The wife then made a further claim in the Rabbinical Court
for an order compelling her husband to give the divorce, this being the
strongest order a Rabbinical Court could make. Her claim, however, was
dismissed.

On July 26, 1982, the wife again sued in the District Court for an increase
in maintenance, relying on the order made against her husband by the
Rabbinical Court of Appeals.

Her claim, however, was again dismissed on the ground that there was no legal basis for an order of punitive maintenance. The wife then appealed to the Supreme Court.

The judgment of the Supreme Court was given by Judge Yehuda Weiss, who referred at the outset to the leading precedent of that court on this subject, the case of *Rosenzweig* (H.C. 54/55). It was held in that case by the late Justice Silberg that even where the Rabbinical Court had made an order compelling the husband to give a divorce, there was no legal basis for punitive maintenance.

This ruling was based on section 6 of the Rabbinical Courts Jurisdiction (Marriage and Divorce) Law, of 1953, under which "Where a Rabbinical Court, by final judgment, has ordered that a husband be compelled to grant his wife a letter of divorce or that a wife be compelled to accept a letter of divorce from her husband, a District Court may, upon expiration of six months from the day of the making of the order, on the application of the Attorney-General, compel compliance with the order by imprisonment".

The court there held that it followed from the enactment of this provision that even if, under Halacha (Jewish law), the court could impose the payment of punitive maintenance, once an order compelling the husband to give the divorce had been made, the procedure laid down in section 6 was now the only sanction which could be applied to urge the husband to comply with that order.

Justice Silberg also warned that a possible consequence of a punitive maintenance order, namely, imposing the payment of maintenance in a amount exceeding the wife's reasonable needs, would be that the divorce would be regarded as artificial and invalid, having been given under coercion.

Judge Weiss pointed out that the decision in the *Rosenzweig* case had been criticized by some legal scholars. There would, however, be no purpose in examining the matter further since the only possible basis for awarding punitive maintenance, namely, an order compelling the husband to give the divorce, did not exist in the present case.

Under Halacha, Judge Weiss continued, a husband was entitled to deduct his wife's earnings from the amount of her maintenance. Where, however, he had refused to comply with an order of a Rabbinical Court to give her a divorce, he was denied the right to make this deduction. The Supreme Court had recognized this rule, and counsel for the wife had argued that this recognition amounted to an acceptance of the principle of "punitive maintenance", and an implied rejection of the rule in the *Rosenzweig* case.

Judge Weiss then examined the relevant decisions of the Supreme Court and the Rabbinical Courts on this point, and held that although the rule relied upon resembled a fine imposed on the husband to induce him to release his wife, it was nevertheless a rule relating strictly to the assessment of the amount of maintenance, as distinct from the question of punitive maintenance. In every case cited, the court was called upon to assess the amount of maintenance as such, without allowing the husband to set off his wife's earning against that amount. Not in one case had the power of the court to grant punitive maintenance, namely, maintenance without any reference to the wife's real needs, been considered. He was unable, therefore, to accept this argument of counsel.

The result was that the dismissal of the wife's claim by the District Court was correct. The appeal would therefore be dismissed, with no order as to costs.

Advocate Menashe Bar-Shilton appeared for the Appellant, and Advocate Mordechai Patbag-Bilker for the Respondent.

The judgment was given on December 12, 1984.

RIGHTS OF A ONE-MAN FACTION

THE KACH FACTION v. KNESSET SPEAKER

In the Supreme Court sitting as a High Court of Justice before the President, Justice Meir Shamgar, Justice Aharon Barak and Justice Eliezer Goldberg, in the matter of *The Kach Faction in the Knesset*, Applicant, versus *Shlomo Hillel, The Speaker of the Knesset*, Respondent (H.C. 73/85)

Constitutional Law—Right of One-Man Faction in Knesset to Move Vote of No-Confidence—Knesset Constitution, Rule 36(a)—Political Parties Financing Law, 1973.

On February 4, 1985, the Petitioner, a one-member faction in the Knesset, presented a motion of no-confidence in the government. It requested that the motion be dealt with on February 5, 1985, together with a similar motion of the Tehiya faction.

The Respondent rejected the request on the ground that a one-member faction could not present such a motion. The Petitioner then moved the High Court of Justice for an order nisi setting aside the Respondent's decision, at the same time requesting an interim order postponing the debate on other motions of no-confidence fixed for the same date. The court granted the order nisi, but refused the interim order sought. The motion of Tehiya, therefore, was debated, and rejected, but the Petitioner's motion was not dealt with at all.

The judgment of the court was given by Justice Aharon Barak. Respondent's counsel had mentioned at the outset, he said, that as a general rule the court would not entertain a petition where any order given would be ineffective.

Since Tehiya's motion had been defeated, counsel pointed out, Kach's motion had no prospect of success, and the court would not deal as a rule with a purely academic question. Nevertheless, with the Respondent's concurrence, counsel had submitted his arguments on the merits of the case since the point in issue was likely to arise again.

This attitude was correct, Justice Barak continued. The present case formed an exception to the general rule, for the Respondent's decision raised a matter of principle on an important constitutional issue which was likely to recur. Unless, therefore, it was absolutely clear that the matter was non-justiciable, this was a case with which the court should deal.

The Petitioner's motion, Justice Barak continued, was presented under section 36 (a) of the Constitution of the Knesset, which entitles every faction to present a motion of no-confidence. The section also provided that such a motion must be dealt with at the next session of the Knesset, and take precedence over all other business. There was, however, no definition of a "faction", nor was there such a definition in the numerous constitutional Laws dealing with the Knesset and the government save in the Parties Financing Law of 1983. That definition, however, was framed to meet the specific requirements of that Law and had no general application.

A "faction" could have different meanings in different contexts, but it did possess a basic constitutional "kernel", and included a list of candidates which participated in elections to the Knesset, and was represented in the Knesset without a change in membership.

This was not an exhaustive definition, but what it did include consti-tuted a "faction", obviously including one-man factions. Firstly, there was nothing in any Law or regulations to indicate otherwise. Secondly, a num-ber of parliamentary procedures laid down by law, which Justice Barak cited, could not be implemented unless a one-man faction was recognized. Lastly, the wide language of rule 36 (a) of the Constitution, and the absence of any contrary constitutional purpose, did not permit restricting the meaning of the rule as it reads.

The Respondent had cited a decision of the Knesset House Committee of March 20, 1967, under which a single member of the House was not entitled to propose a motion of no-confidence. The grounds for the decision were that it was unreasonable that a single member, even if he were a faction, representing less than one per cent of the members, and whose prospects of succeeding in such a motion were negligible, should be able to block a discussion of other topics, and paralyze the Knesset's work.

There was, however, nothing to show, said Justice Barak, that these grounds were considered by the Knesset when it enacted rule 36 (a); if so considered, they would surely have found expression in the rule itself.

The result was that a one-man faction could propose a motion of no-confidence. It must be stressed, said Justice Barak, that this result was based entirely on the interpretation of rule 36. The Knesset could change this situation if it so wished.

The decision of the House Committee of March 20, 1967, was repeated, in a different context, on July 30, 1979. The committee, in its discussions, left open the question whether a faction could consist of only one member, but again decided that a single member could not propose a motion of no-confidence.

Counsel had argued, said Justice Barak, that the Respondent, in giving effect to decisions of the House Committee, was acting in accordance with established and accepted parliamentary custom. These decisions, he contended, were binding not only on all the organs of the Knesset, but also on the court itself. He was prepared to assume, said Justice Barak, that the committee's decisions in regard to the interpretation of rule 36 were binding on the organs of the Knesset, but he rejected utterly the argument that they were binding on the court.

As was held in the U.S. by Chief Justice Marshall, in a democratic regime based upon the separation of powers, "it is emphatically the province and duty of the judicial department to say what the law is". Similarly, in dealing with the argument that the communications of the U.S. President enjoyed absolute privilege, Chief Justice Burger had said: "In the performance of assigned constitutional duties each branch of the government must initially interpret the Constitution, and the interpretation of its powers by any branch is entitled to great respect from the others. The President's counsel reads the Constitution as providing an absolute privilege of confidentiality for all presidential communications.

Many decisions of this court, however, have unequivocally reaffirmed the holding that it is emphatically the province and duty of the judicial department to say what the law is . . . Any other conclusion would be contrary to the basic concept of separation of powers and the checks and balances that flow from the scheme of a tripartite government.

We therefore reaffirm that it is the province and duty of this court 'to say what the law is' with respect to the claim of privilege presented in this case".

Indeed, Chief Justice Agranat had once pointed out that where the Supreme Court had interpreted a statutory provision, that interpretation became in fact part of the statute itself. Of course, the legislature was entitled to alter the court's interpretation by amending the Law, and it could also specifically confer the power of final interpretation of a Law upon some body other than the courts. It had not done so, however, in regard to rule 36 (a) of the Knesset Constitution.

In regard to the general powers of the House Committee relating to Knesset procedures, it was sufficient to point out that rule 147 of the Constitution empowered the committee to lay down rules "in matters not covered by the Constitution". Since the present matter was covered by rule 36 (a), which was to be interpreted as now laid down, it followed that the committee had no power to decide as it did.

Justice Barak then dealt with the Respondent's last and most important argument, that the matter in dispute was non-justiciable since the court would not interfere in questions relating to the internal proceedings of the Knesset. These, so it was said, must be solved within the framework of such proceedings in the Knesset itself.

The court, counsel contended, must exercise a self-restraint which would avoid conflict between the legislature and the judiciary. Counsel was aware of the decisions of this court in H.C. 652/81 and H.C. 325/85 (*The Jerusalem Post*, May 16, 1982 and September 9, 1985); he tried, however, to persuade the court to depart from those decisions and follow the British rule which completely excluded parliamentary proceedings from judicial review or, at most, to hold that the court would interfere only where a parliamentary body had exceed it functional jurisdiction.

Justice Barak was not prepared to accept this argument and adhered to his opinion that the court was fully empowered to interfere in Knesset proceedings, the only question being one of discretion — when to exercise that power and when not to do so. Counsel was correct, he said, in contending that the test laid down by the court for the exercise of its discretion was difficult and uncertain, but no more accurate test could be devised. The test had to be wide and flexible.

The court did not accept the principle of absolute judicial restraint nor, in the same measure, did it believe in full judicial activism. The court's power, however, to interfere where it saw fit to do so, was beyond doubt. Justice Barak then examined a number of Israeli and American authorities and repeated the court's opinion that closing its doors on every petition dealing with internal parliamentary proceedings would infringe the rule of law, the legality of government, and the very basis of our democratic regime.

The question remained, said Justice Barak, whether the court should interfere in this particular case. It would examine, as it did in previous cases, the extent of the damage caused by the Respondent's wrong decision to the fabric of parliamentary procedures, and the influence of that decision on the foundations of the structure of our constitutional regime. Although given in good faith, the Respondent's decision caused grave damage.

One of the Knesset's principal functions, along with its legislative powers, was the control of the executive arm of government. The most extreme expression of this control was a motion of no-confidence, and the denial of this expression deprived an opposition faction of its sharpest parliamentary weapon, and damaged the legislature's control of the executive. This was no mean matter; a faction unable to propose a vote of no-confidence suffered a deep and lasting parliamentary disability.

It was true, as counsel argued, that the prospects of a one-man faction, unsupported by other factions, in a motion of no-confidence, were minimal.

When asked, however, what would happen if there were a number of one-man factions, counsel replied that the court was not concerned with hypothetical questions. That was true, but where a concrete constitutional question demanding solution did arise, as in the present case, the court was obliged to consider the whole constitutional spectrum including, in this case, the possibility that the whole opposition would consist of one-man factions.

The reply to counsel's suggestion that in such a case the Knesset would surely amend its constitution, was that it could not be assumed that organs of government would always find legal and suitable solutions to their problems.

For the above reasons the court confirmed the order nisi, and declared that the Respondent was not empowered to reject a motion of no-confidence proposed by a one-man faction in the Knesset.

Advocate Meir Shechter appeared for the Applicant, and Advocate Renato Yarak, Director of the High Court Division of the State Attorney's Office, for the Respondent.

The judgment was given on August 1, 1985.

THE SHOSHANA MILLER CASE
UNITY OF THE JEWISH PEOPLE IS PARAMOUNT

SHOSHANA MILLER v. MINISTER OF INTERIOR

In the Supreme Court sitting as a High Court of Justice before the President, Justice Meir Shamgar, the Deputy-President, Justice Miriam Ben-Porat, and Justice Menahem Elon, in the matter of *Shoshana (Susan) Miller*, Petitioner, versus *The Minister of Interior and another*, Respondents (H.C. 230/86).

Personal Status—Administrative Law—Registration of Religion of Reform Jews— Jewish Law—Law of Return, 1950, sections 2, 3A, 19B, 27—Population Registry Law, 1965.

The Petitioner converted to Judaism in the United States within the framework of the Jewish Reform Movement. She had taken a conversion course under the supervision of a rabbi in which she studied Jewish religious commandments, the philosophy and history of the Jewish People, and the Hebrew language, and she also underwent immersion in a ritual bath. At the conclusion of the whole process, she received a conversion certificate. She came to Israel in October, 1985, and was given a certificate under the Law of Return of 1950 as an olah, i.e, a Jew who had come to settle in Israel. She then went to the Ministry of Interior to receive her identity card, introduced herself as Jewish, and presented her conversion certificate.

The official refused to register her as Jewish, and referred her to the Rabbinical Court to receive confirmation of her conversion. The Petitioner averred that the official had also suggested that she be registered as a Christian, or that the registration of her religion remain blank. She was later informed that the Respondents were prepared to register her, as to le'om (national group) and religion, as "Jewish (Converted)".

She was not prepared to accept this, and applied to the High Court of Justice for an order on the Respondents to register her as Jewish without the addition relating to her conversion.

The first judgment of the court was given by Justice Meir Shamgar. The Respondents, he said, had relied on precedents of the Supreme Court under which the question whether or not a person had converted to another religion was to be decided by the tests laid down by that religion. Since the registration officer could not decide whether the Petitioner's conversion was valid or not, it was only right, the Respondent submitted, that that question should be decided by the most competent organ in the state, namely, the Rabbinical Court.

The Respondents also argued that the particulars in the register and in an identity card were not only a matter of statistics, for they afforded information to every other authority in the state. The registering authority, therefore, was fully entitled, and even obliged, to warn, in particular, the Registrar of Marriages and Divorces, that the Petitioner was a convert, in order to enable that official to make the necessary inquiries.

The President then analyzed in detail the relevant provisions of the Population Registry Law of 1965. Section 2 prescribed which personal details of a resident were to be registered, including national group and religion. These details had been laid down by the legislature, and were not left to the discretion of the registering officer. Under section 25 of the Law, an identity certificate was to contain the particulars of registration laid down by the Minister of Interior, with the approval of the Law, Constitution, and Justice Committee of the Knesset, and under section 27, nothing could be entered in the certificate otherwise than in accordance with a Law, or with regulations of the minister similarly approved. Justice Shamgar then cited sections of the Law dealing with altering particulars in the register, and pointed out that these sections referred to alterations relating to events after the original registration, and not before.

The President went on to refer to decisions of the Supreme Court whereby a person to be registered as a Jew was one so recognized under section 4B of the Law of Return, namely, the child of a Jewish mother, or a person who was "a converted Jew and had no other religion".

He also cited sections 3A and 19B of the Registration Law, and held that a person claiming to be a Jew was to be registered as such unless some of the counter-indications specified in section 3A were found to exist. After examining other sections of the Law, Justice Shamgar held that, since the legislature had laid down clearly what particulars were to be registered, neither the Minister of Interior nor any registration officer had the power to make additions to the particulars specified in the Population Registry Law. Such additions could only be authorized by regulations made under the Law with the approval of the Knesset Law Committee.

In conclusion, the President cited an extract from a judgment of former Chief Justice Agranat, who said, in another context: "The great event of the statehood of the Jewish People in the land of its birth, did not occur in order to drive a wedge into the people who dwell in Zion, and divide it into two peoples, Jews and Israelis. Such a division — should it, Heaven forbid, ever occur — would contradict the national aspirations for which the state was established, and would mean the frustration of those aspirations, and the undermining of the unity of the Jewish People as a whole".

For the above reasons, the President proposed that the court order the Respondents to register the Petitioner simply as a Jew.

Justice Menahem Elon agreed that the registering authority had no power to add the word "converted" to the word "Jew". He held that this addition also had no place under the Halacha (Jewish law).

He cited the following passage from a 1984 precedent of the Supreme Court dealing with an election petition:

"The Jewish People does not 'seek souls' to attract members of other peoples to its ranks (Micah, IV, 5; Maimonides, Melachim 8, 10), but once the son of another people has joined the Jewish People, he becomes a member of that people, both as to his rights and obligations.

'Ye shall have one statute, both for the stranger, and for him that is born in the land' (Numbers, IX, 14); 'Neither let the alien, that hath joined himself to the Lord, speak, saying 'The Lord will surely separate me from His people . . . For My house shall be called a house of prayer for all peoples' (Isaiah, LVI, 3-7). And not only from now onwards, but also as regards the past; for this was the reply of Maimonides to Ovadia the convert: "Anyone who converts does so for ever, and he who joins his name to that of the Holy One, Blessed be He, is, as is written in the Tora, a pupil of Abraham our father, may peace be upon him, and they are all children of his household . . . and there is no distinction between them and us in any respect whatever.

And do not treat your ancestry lightly; if we are related to Abraham, Isaac and Jacob, you are related to Him who created the world (Maimonides, Responsa, Edition Freimann, 369)".

The Talmud points out, Justice Elon resumed, that the Tora warns against afflicting the stranger in 36 passages — referring to any form of causing him pain, whether in speech, action, or judicial records. There were two principal factors at play. The first was the historical memory of the Jewish People:

"Love ye therefore the stranger; for ye were strangers in the land of Egypt" (Exodus XXIII, 9).

In his above reply to Ovadia, Maimonides wrote, "You must realize that the majority of our fathers who went out to Egypt were idolators, intermingled with the gentiles, and learned their ways, until the Holy One, blessed be He, sent our teacher Moses — may peace be upon him — the father of all prophets, and separated us from other peoples, and brought us under the wings of the Divine Presence, ours and that of all strangers, and gave us all one law".

The other factor, Justice Elon continued, was our particular sympathy towards one who has left the social and spiritual surroundings in which he was born and grew up, was educated, and lived his life, and entered a different social and spiritual environment, assuming different obligations and a different way of life. As it is written, "Also thou shalt not oppress a stranger; for ye know the heart of a stranger, seeing ye were strangers in the land of Egypt (Exodus XXIII, 9)".

Justice Elon then cited further authorities in the Halacha, and concluded by saying that there was no doubt that by adding the word "convert" in brackets to the nationality and religion of the Petitioner, we should be differentiating between her and everyone else. We have been warned, he said, not to act in this way.

The Deputy-President agreed with her colleagues.

For the above reasons, the petition was allowed, and an order made accordingly.

Advocate Arnold Spaer and Advocate Anat Green appeared for the Petitioner, and Advocate Renato Yarak for the Respondents.

Judgment given on December 2, 1986.

RECOGNIZING PRIVILEGE

CITRIN AND NEVO v. ISRAEL BAR DISCIPLINARY COURT

In the Supreme Court before the President, Justice Meir Shamgar, in the matter of *Ben-Zion Citrin and Yifat Nevo,* Applicants, versus *The Disciplinary Court of the Israel Bar and others,* Respondents (Miscellaneous Applications 298/86. 368/86).

Administrative Law—Freedom of Expression—Press Privilege Recognised—Decision of Chamber of Advocates Disciplinary Court Set Aside—Chamber of Advocates Law, 1961—Commissions of Inquiry Law, 1968—Penal Law, 1977— Evidence Ordinance (New Version), 1971, section 1(a).

The Applicants, who are journalists, appeared before a Disciplinary Court of the Bar to testify in proceedings against two advocates charged with self-advertisement in contravention of the ethical standards laid down by the chamber. The charges were based upon newspaper articles published by the Applicants, relating to two specific incidents in which the names of the advocates, and in one case also their photographs, appeared.

The Applicants refused to disclose the source of their information, claiming privilege. The court, however, rejected this claim, and fined the Applicants for refusing to testify without justification. The Applicants then applied to the President of the Supreme Court to annul the fines on the basis of the privilege referred to above.

In giving judgment, Justice Shamgar dealt firstly with the statutory provisions in the Chamber of Advocates Law of 1961, the Commissions of Inquiry Law of 1968, and the Penal Law of 1977, dealing with the power of the disciplinary court to impose the fines referred to, the duty to report thereon to the President of the Supreme Court, and the power of the President or a justice of that court to annul or reduce the fine.

The two central issues which arose, he said, were whether the questions relating to the source of the Applicants' information were relevant, as required by section 1 (a) of the Evidence Ordinance (New Version) of 1971, and whether the claim of privilege advanced by the Applicants was justified.

On the issue of relevancy, it was clear that the main question before the court was whether the publications in question were induced by the Applicant or by someone else. It followed, therefore, that the source of the Applicants' information was a relevant factor.

Proceeding to deal with the question of privilege, Justice Shamgar referred to the provisions of the Evidence Ordinance relating to the privilege imposed in the interests of the state and the community, and that protecting a witness from incriminating himself.

He referred also to the privilege enjoyed by lawyers, medical practitioners, psychologists and clerics, pointing out that the privilege relating to lawyers and medical practitioners was that of the client and the patient, and not of the lawyer or doctor. If, therefore, the client or patient waived the privilege, the lawyer or doctor would not be protected.

He also mentioned that the privilege relating to doctors, psychologists and clerics was not absolute, the court being empowered to overrule the privilege if, in its opinion, the doing of justice required that the disclosure objected to was to be preferred to the interest sought to be protected from disclosure.

It was noteworthy that there was no statutory privilege for a journalist, but counsel had argued that such a privilege was recognized as if it were part of the common law, operating beyond the limits of the relevant statutory provisions.

Since the question of a journalist's privilege had not yet arisen before the Supreme Court, Justice Shamgar continued, he would deal shortly with some developments on this subject in countries having a similar legal system.

It had been argued in the English courts, as it was contended here, that the public had an interest in a journalist acquiring his information, and that he would be unable to do this unless his informant were confident that his identity would not be disclosed.

Thus, Lord Chief Justice Parker had said, "... I have without the slightest hesitation come to the conclusion that in regard to the press, the law has not developed and crystallized the confidential relationship in which they stand to an informant into one of the classes of privilege known to the law ...".

"It would remain open to this court to say in the special circumstances of any particular case that public policy did demand that the journalist should be immune ...".

Lord Denning has also dealt with the privilege claimed by journalists and professional advisers standing in a confidential relationship to their clients. Pointing out that under English law, only communications to a lawyer were privileged, he added:

"The judge will respect the confidences which each member of these honourable professions receives . . . and will not direct him to answer unless not only is it relevant but also it is a proper and, indeed, necessary question in the course of justice to be put and answered.

"A judge is the person entrusted, on behalf of the community, to weigh these conflicting interests — to weigh on the one hand the respect due to confidence in the profession and on the other hand the ultimate interest of the community in justice being done . . .".

Here Lord Denning was considering a case connected with spying, and the court held that the public interest required disclosure of the journalist's source of information. But he discussed the question of journalistic privilege again in a subsequent case dealing with a strike of steel workers. There, too, he held that the public interest required disclosure of the sources relied upon by Granada Television in reporting on the strike, and repeated the principles already laid down, saying:

"The public has a right of access to information which is of public concern and of which the public ought to know. The newspapers are the agents, so to speak, of the public to collect that information and to tell the public of it. In support of this right of access, the newspapers should not in general be compelled to disclose their sources of information . . . The reason is because, if they were compelled to disclose their sources, they would soon be bereft of information which they ought to have. Their sources would dry up . . .

"Nevertheless, this principle is not absolute. The journalist has no privilege by which he can claim, as of right, to refuse to disclose the name. There may be exceptional cases in which, on balancing the various interests, the court decides that the name should be disclosed . . . Have we any scales by which to hold the balance? Have we any yardstick by which to determine which cases are exceptional?

"It seems to me that the rule (by which a newspaper should not be compelled to disclose its source of information) is granted to a newspaper on condition that it acts with a due sense of responsibility. In order to be deserving of freedom, the press must show itself worthy of it. A free press must be a responsible press. The power of the press is great. It must not abuse its power. If a newspaper should act irresponsibly, then it forfeits its claim to protect its sources of information".

Following these quotations from Lord Denning's judgments, Justice Shamgar added that in 1981 the British parliament passed the Contempt of Court Act, under Section 10 of which: "no court may require a person to disclose, nor is any person guilty of contempt of court for refusing to disclose, the source of information contained in a publication for which he is responsible, unless it be established to the satisfaction of the court that disclosure is necessary in the interests of justice or national security or for the prevention of disorder or crime".

In the United States, Justice Shamgar continued, there is no federal statutory provision covering this subject. However, Wigmore summed up the position thus:

"The communications must originate in a confidence that they will not be disclosed. This element of confidentiality must be essential to the full and satisfactory maintenance of the relation between the parties. The relation must be one which in the opinion of the community ought to be seriously fostered. The injury which would inure to the relation by the disclosure of the communications must be greater than the benefit thereby gained for the correct disposal of litigation".

Justice Shamgar then referred to the leading decision of the U.S. Supreme Court on this subject, in which the court considered the cases of three journalists who refused to testify as to the sources of their information relating to drug trafficking and other criminal conduct.

The journalists relied on the First Amendment to the U.S. Constitution, under which Congress shall make no law, *inter alia*, "abridging the freedom of speech, or of the press".

In the majority decision in that case it was held that "the great weight of authority is that newsmen are not exempt from the normal duty of appearing before a Grand Jury and answering questions relevant to a criminal investigation".

However, the court went on to emphasize that the duty to disclose sources of information was not absolute, and would be imposed only where the public interest to be served by disclosure was "paramount" and "compelling".

Justice Shamgar posed the question whether the fact that journalists were not mentioned in the Israeli Evidence Ordinance cited above, led to the conclusion that such a privilege did not exist. He then quoted from an article by the American Justice Jackson that "perhaps even more than by interpretation of its written word, this court has advanced the solidarity and prosperity of this nation by the meaning it has given to these great silences of the constitution". He held that despite the omission in the

Evidence Ordinance, the existence of journalistic privilege must be tested in the context of the fundamental freedoms and our basic constitutional concepts.

Justice Shamgar then referred to decisions of the Israel Supreme Court, including the case of *Hanna Klopper-Naveh* (H.C. 372/84 — *The Jerusalem Post*, October 22, 1984), in which it was held that freedom of expression was a prerequisite to the existence and smooth working of democracy.

The freedom to voice opinions and the unfettered exchange of views were conditions precedent to the existence of a political and social regime under which a citizen could judge, fearlessly and through studying the facts, what to the best of his understanding was required for the benefit and welfare of the community and the individual, and for ensuring the existence of a democratic regime and the political framework within which it functioned. It was stressed in that case, he said, that the media played an all-important role in voicing opinions and exchanging views. They enabled the meaningful publication of information in every sphere of life, and the conduct of open and public debate on ideas and conceptions. The interest of journalists to protect their sources of information stemmed from their desire to protect the freedom of the press.

On the other hand, Justice Shamgar continued, there was the duty to testify. Lord Chief Justice Parker once said that "Any privilege which exists constitutes a shackle on the discovery of the truth and an impediment on the true administration of the law".

The duty to testify was one of the cornerstones of the legal process, and served not only the interests of the litigants, but also of the public. As the English judge Lord Hardwicke said: "The public has a right to every man's evidence".

The above analysis, said Justice Shamgar, showed that there were two conflicting public interests, and a balance had to be struck between them. Recognition of the privilege prevented the disclosure of the truth, while failure to recognize the privilege damaged the important public interest of the free flow of information to the press.

The inevitable conclusion was that a journalist's privilege was not absolute, while the power to compel him to answer was also limited. The rule was, therefore, that a journalist's right to claim privilege in respect of his sources of information was to be recognized, subject to the power of the court, in its discretion, to order him to disclose such sources in proper cases.

In regard to the exercise by the court of its discretion, said Justice Shamgar, it must be borne in mind that freedom of expression enjoyed a special status in our law. Indeed, the Supreme Court had already held that freedom of expression and a statutory provision limiting that freedom were not of equal force, and wherever the language so permits, freedom of expression will be preferred.

It followed, therefore, that the right not to disclose sources of information must not be unduly restricted. An order to disclose sources should be made only when such evidence is relevant to the proceedings according to the accepted legal tests, and in addition to, and apart from, this requirement, when such evidence *is vital and important for doing justice in a matter of substance*. Not every trial would justify disclosure while, on the other hand, in a trial dealing with a felony or serious crime or civil wrong having severe consequences, the court would be justified in refusing to recognize the privilege. However, even in cases of drug trafficking or housebreaking, the court was obliged to consider each case specifically, and decide whether the demands of justice, in that particular case, outweigh the recognition of the privilege in question.

Justice Shamgar then considered whether the Disciplinary Court was justified in refusing to recognize the privilege claimed by the Applicants in the particular cases before it. In doing so, he examined the relevant sections of the Chamber of Advocates Law, and the rules of the Chamber relating to unethical conduct. He also examined recent developments in England in regard to self-advertisement by lawyers, quoting the recommendations of the Monopolies and Mergers Commission of 1976, and the Royal Commission on Legal Services (the Benson Commission) of 1978,which led to a relaxation of the ban on self-advertisement. He referred also to a 1977 decision of the U.S. Supreme Court leading to the same result.

In conclusion, Justice Shamgar held that in the present case, the sources of the Applicants' information were relevant, since there was a logical and real connection between the charges of self-advertisement and the answer to the question whether it was the advocates concerned who had injured the newspaper articles.

The second and principal question, he said, was whether the circumstances justified the freedom of the press having to yield before the requirement of doing justice.

With all his appreciation of the Bar's legitimate efforts to advance and maintain proper disciplinary norms, he could not be convinced that this was a case justifying non-recognition of the privilege, and compelling the Applicants to disclose their sources.

This was not a case of a serious crime having drastic consequences, or causing a serious breach of public order. The disciplinary proceedings in question could not tilt the scales in favour of disregarding a journalist's privilege, which expresses the maintenance of the freedom of the press, imposed by the basic principle of the freedom of expression.

For the above reasons, the fines imposed on the Applicants were set aside, the court declaring that the privilege claimed by them should have been recognized, and that they were justified in refusing to disclose their sources of information.

Advocates Haim Stanger, Avi Horwitz and Mibi Mozer appeared for the Applicants, and Advocates Shimon and Arnon Ben-Ya'acov for the Respondents.

The judgment was given on April 7, 1987.

THE RIGHT TO EXPRESS DANGEROUS IDEAS

KAHANE v. THE BROADCASTING AUTHORITY

In the Supreme Court sitting as a High Court of Justice before Justice Aharon Barak, Justice Gavriel Bach, and Justice Shoshana Netanyahu, in the matter of *Rabbi Meir Kahane MK and the Kach Movement*, Petitioners, versus *The Broadcasting Authority and others*, Respondents (H.C. 399/85).

Administrative Law—Freedom of Expression—Refusal of Broadcasting A ithority to Broadcast Inflammatory Matter—Broadcasting Authority Law, 1965, sections 3, 4, 8—Penal Law, 1977, section 144.

On August 1, 1984, the Broadcasting Authority decided that "in order to ensure that the state media should not be used as a platform for incitement against citizens and for declarations harmful to the State of Israel and in conflict with the principles in the Declaration of Independence . . . interviews with Meir Kahane, or the quotation of his declarations, and information and reports connected with his activities . . . shall be examined in accordance with the above principles, and only information which is clearly newsworthy and does not offend against those principles and the Broadcasting Law and its spirit, may be broadcast".

Under this decision, the Authority declined to broadcast any information relating to Rabbi Kahane which was not "clearly newsworthy". The Petitioners applied to the High Court of Justice to set aside this decision, contending that it imposed an unjustified limitation on their right to freedom of speech and expression.

The first judgment of the court was given by Justice Aharon Barak.

The Respondents, he said, relied on section 3 of the Broadcasting Law of 1965, which set forth the duties of the Authority, and included, *inter alia*, the promotion of the objects of state education as defined in section 2 of the State Education Law of 1953.

Counsel for the Respondents emphasized that this section spoke of "freedom, equality, tolerance, mutual assistance, and love of mankind" — values which were in direct conflict with the outlook and opinions of the Petitioners. Counsel for the Petitioners, on the other hand, relied on section 4 of the Broadcasting Authority Law, under which the Authority was obliged to ensure that room would be found for the appropriate expression of different views and opinions in the community, and that it would broadcast reliable information.

The question that now arose was what scope should be allowed for opinions which were offensive and inflammatory, which propagated hatred and strife, and which were based on race, or national and ethnic origin. He would assume, as Petitioners' counsel had done (since the matter had not been proved in the present proceedings), that the material in question was of this kind.

Justice Barak then analyzed the nature of freedom of expression. Referring to numerous authorities, he quoted the following remarks of U.S. Justice Brandeis, who had attempted to rest this freedom on a "broad ideological base".

"Those who won our independence . . . believed that freedom to think as you will and to speak as you think are means indispensable to the discovery and spread of political truth; that without free speech and assembly discussion would be futile; that with them, discussion affords ordinarily adequate protection against the dissemination of noxious doctrine; that the greatest menace to freedom is an inert people; that public discussion is a political duty; and that this should be a fundamental principle of American government . . .

"Believing in the power of reason as applied through public discussion, they eschewed silence coerced by law — the argument of force in its worst form. Recognizing the occasional tyrannies of governing majorities, they amended the constitution so that free speech and assembly be guaranteed".

Justice Barak stressed the importance in this context of the mass media. Thus, the American authority Professor Barron had said: "In the era of mass communication, the words of the solitary speaker or the lonely writer, however brave or imaginative, have little impact unless they are broadcast through the great engines of public opinion — radio, television and the press".

Citing other American, Canadian, European and Israeli precedents, Justice Barak then discussed what he described as the three intrinsic bases of the right to freedom of expression, namely: the desire to discover the truth; the need of every man to achieve personal fulfilment; and the demands of a democratic regime.

In regard to truth, he quoted, *inter alia*, Justice Oliver Wendell Holmes: "But when men have realized that time has upset many fighting faiths, they may come to believe even more than they believe the very foundations of their own conduct, that the ultimate good desired is better reached by free trade in ideas — that the best test of truth is the power of the thought to get itself accepted in the competition of the market, and that truth is the only ground upon which their wishes can be carried out".

Dealing with the right of the citizen to be fully informed, Justice Barak quoted the following extract from a judgment of Justice White, of the U.S. Supreme Court:

"It is the right of the viewers and listeners, not the right of the broadcasters, which is paramount . . . It is the right of the public to receive suitable access to social, political, aesthetic, moral and other ideas and experiences, which is crucial here".

Regarding the demands of a democratic regime, the U.S. Supreme Court had said, "Speech concerning public affairs is more than self-expression; it is the essence of self-government". On the same lines, Justice Cardozo had said: "Of that freedom one may say that it is the matrix, the indispensable condition, of nearly every other form of freedom".

Justice Barak went on to emphasize that freedom of expression did not mean the right to express only ideas generally accepted, but also dangerous, aggravating and deviant ideas which the community hated, and from which it recoiled. Thus Justice Jackson of the U.S. Supreme Court had said: "Freedom to differ is not limited to things that do not matter much. That would be a mere shadow of freedom. The test of its substance is the right to differ as to things that touch the heart of the existing order".

Israel's Supreme Court, said Justice Barak, had recognized the right to produce a play — which is one forum of free expression — which was "a disgusting mixture of eroticism, politics and all forms of deviation". The court had pointed out that the way to confront this type of expression was by education and explanation, not by suppression.

The rule permitting the expression even of racist ideas applied with even greater force to a political party participating in parliamentary life. The Petitioners were permitted to participate in the election, and received more than 20,000 votes. How, in a democratic regime, can a body which was permitted to participate in the elections be prevented from expressing its ideas after the elections?

That did not mean that society in general, or the court in particular, supported racism; but if a racist political opinion were suppressed, the danger would arise of where to draw the line between permissible and forbidden political opinions.

It was also true that recent history provided sufficient examples of anti-democratic movements which had exploited freedom of expression to destroy democracy. This danger had to be borne in mind, although it was not decisive.

So far, Justice Barak continued, he had dealt with the "intrinsic" nature of freedom of speech in Israel, i.e., that according to our constitutional concepts, every utterance, whatever its content, is covered by that freedom.

The next question was whether there were any "extrinsic" limitations on freedom of expression. Did that freedom permit the publication of material which was libelous or abominable, or disclosed state secrets, or was calculated to influence judges? Was this freedom absolute or relative?

The accepted view in Israel, and other democracies, was that it was relative. Each state imposed its own limitations. Freedom of expression did not mean unbridled license. In Israel, there was as yet no constitution to lay down limitation. Apart from individual statutes which limited this freedom, it was for the courts — in Israel, the Supreme Court — to define these limits.

Freedom of expression was not the only basic freedom. In a democratic society other basic freedoms had to be considered, such as the dignity of the individual, rights to property, the purity of the judicial process, and public welfare and security. The court was also obliged to consider the sensitivities of the individual, or of a group of individuals. All these features together constituted the social order.

It was evident that under Israeli law, these freedoms, too, were protected. It was the duty of the court, therefore, to strike a balance between freedom of expression and the preservation of the social order. In this conflict, the latter was to be preferred, but the questions still arose as to what degree of damage to the social order justified a suppression of freedom of speech, and what was the extent of the probability of such damage being caused.

Justice Barak then reviewed extensively Israeli and other precedents on these questions, again citing Justice Brandeis:

"To justify suppression of free speech there must be reasonable ground to fear that serious evil will result if free speech is practised . . . There must be reasonable grounds to believe that the evil to be prevented is a serious one . . . Prohibition of free speech and assembly is a measure so stringent that it would be inappropriate as the means for averting a trivial harm to society".

The Supreme Court had held that the danger to the social order had to be "real and serious". A minor infraction did not justify restriction of the freedom of expression.

As to the probability of damage, our precedents justified the view that freedom of expression should be limited only where there was a "near certainty" of real damage to the social order. In this regard, a theoretical possibility was not sufficient. On the other hand, our law did not require a "clear and present danger" of damage, as the test had been expressed in the U.S. Moreover, restriction of freedom of expression must be the last resort. Only where no other course was possible was this step justified.

Justice Barak also emphasized that the damage to the social order was not limited to harming security or creating violence. It included harm to the dignity of the individual, or the sensitivities of a religious or ethnic minority. For example, the prevention of a demonstration by the Petitioners would be justified if it were designed to be held in Arab areas.

Justice Barak then referred to the Penal Law (Amendment No. 20) of 1986, under which new provisions relating to racism were added to section 144 of the Penal Law of 1977.

Under these provisions, publication of material with the purpose of inciting racism was a criminal offense.

In his view, the Broadcasting Authority would certainly be entitled to refuse to broadcast material which would make it guilty of a criminal offense. Freedom of expression did not mean freedom to break the law.

On the other hand, the fact that the material was of a racist character, and might indicate an offense by others, would not justify a refusal to broadcast it unless the broadcast would create a "near certainty" of harm to the social order.

The question whether others had committed an offense was for the courts to decide. *A priori* refusal to broadcast was not the function of the Respondents. As the Supreme Court of the United States had said:

"A free society prefers to punish the few who abuse rights of speech after they break the law than to throttle them and all others beforehand. It is always difficult to know in advance what an individual will say, and the line between legitimate and illegitimate speech is often so finely drawn that the risks of freewheeling censorship are formidable".

Justice Barak went on to deal with the powers of the Broadcasting Authority, and the manner in which it was to exercise them. It had stated that the material in question would in all cases be recorded, and then brought before the appropriate bodies for decision as to whether it should be broadcast or not.

It was for the Authority to decide what political opinions could be broadcast, but it was not open to doubt that expression must be given to the views of any political party represented in the Knesset.

The Authority would then be required to decide whether, in its opinion, there was a "near certainty" of damage to the social order. In such an event, and only then, would it be entitled to refuse a broadcast. In the decision of the Authority which was the subject of the present petition, the critical question of the possible effect of a broadcast had not even been raised. A blanket refusal to broadcast material unless it was "clearly newsworthy" was wholly unacceptable.

In conclusion, Justice Barak dealt with the court's review of the Authority's decisions. The Authority, he said, had to interpret the Broadcasting Law, and act within its powers. It must exercise its discretion in each case *ad hoc*, after having laid down a scale of priorities in the broadcast of political opinions, and giving an opportunity to a political party to reply to criticism of its policies. In regard to the interpretation of the Law, the final decision rested with the court.

In reviewing the exercise by the Authority of its two other specified functions, the court would act as it did when reviewing the decisions of any other administrative authority. It would inquire, therefore, whether the authority had acted in good faith, had considered all the relevant factors, had not considered extraneous matters, and had acted fairly and without discrimination.

Justice Barak emphasized that his legal conclusions should in no sense be understood as agreement with the views and conceptions of the Petitioners. Their opinions repelled him, but he insisted on their right to express them.

For the above reasons, Justice Barak proposed that the decision of the Authority which was the subject of the petitions be set aside.

Justice Gavriel Bach agreed that the decision of the Authority be set aside, since it involved a general ban on the broadcast of the Petitioners' opinions unless they were "clearly newsworthy".

He could not agree, however, with Justice Barak's reasoning in regard to expressions inciting hatred between different sections of the population on the basis of race, nationality, or ethnic origin. Nor could he agree that even where Rabbi Kahane's utterances contained clear racial incitement, and the Authority believed, in good faith, that their publication would involve a criminal offense, they were entitled to refuse the broadcast only if there was a "near certainty" of harm to the social order.

There was no need, in Israel, with the tragic and traumatic background of our people, to emphasize the utterly destructive influence of the incitement of racial hatred. No other form of expression can so effectively create violence, stir the lowest and most vile instincts in human beings, and lead to the degradation of sections of the population against whom the propaganda is direct.

He agreed with what was written in the introduction to the United Nations' Universal Declaration of Human Rights: "Among the values of democratic regime is 'recognition of the inherent dignity and of the equal and inalienable rights of all members of the human family".

"Racist speech", Prof. David Kretzmer of the Hebrew University has written, "is not merely speech which advocates abrogation of this recognition. It is speech which in itself is an affront to the inherent dignity of man. It is not clear why speech must be allowed in a democracy when it clashes with this basic value".

Justice Barak had said, continued Justice Bach, that "harm to the social order" could also include an offense against the sensitivities of the community, or part of it. Could one conceive of racial incitement the publication of which would not offend public sensitivities, or at least those of that section of the public affected? In his view, the protection of incitement of this kind on the basis of freedom of expression was unjustified and artificial.

Justice Barak had gone even further and had held that the Authority was obliged to publish material which, in its opinion, constituted a criminal offense, provided it itself did not commit an offense.

This, too, was going too far. If the Authority published material which constituted an offense, it would become party to that offense. Indeed, the same would apply, if the Authority refused to publish material which was libelous, or would support a claim for damages, or constitute a breach of contract.

There was a difference, said Justice Bach, between some government agency, or the court, preventing a person from publishing something he wishes to publish, and compelling the Broadcasting Authority to publish something it does not wish to publish. Justice Bach then analysed some of the authorities relied upon by Justice Barak, and expressed the view that they did not justify his conclusion.

In summing up, Justice Bach held that racial, nationalistic or ethnic incitement offended the majority of the population, and inevitably offended those against whom it was directed. There was undoubtedly a "near certainty" that the publication of such incitement would have this effect. For this reason alone, the Authority would be justified in refusing to allow the broadcast.

Moreover, even if, theoretically, there could be cases of such incitement whose publication did not create a "near certainty" of damage to the social order, the Authority would be justified in refusing the broadcast if it believed, reasonably and in good faith, that the publication involved a criminal offense, that is to say, was not merely an objective broadcast of news.

Justice Bach added that there were many matters of public interest in regard to which there was no fear of the commission of a criminal offense, or of a "near certainty" of damage to the social order. There was no reason to deprive the Petitioners of their right to participate in broadcasts relating to such matters.

Justice Shoshana Netanyahu agreed to the proposed order. She expressed no opinion as to whether the racist utterances of the Petitioners constituted a criminal offense, and it was clear, she said, that in agreeing to the order, she did not intend to oblige the Authority to commit an offense.

Aharon Papu appeared for the Petitioners, and Renato Yarak for the Respondents.

Judgment given on July 27, 1987.

Note: The following Supreme Court precedents cited in the judgments were reviewed in *The Jerusalem Post* on the dates indicated: (H.C. 243/82 — April 24, 1983, *supra* p. 5; H.C. 153/83 — Aug. 19, 1984; E.A. 2/84 — May

31, 1985; H.C. 372/84 — Oct. 22, 1984; H.C. 742/84 — Nov. 25, 1985; H.C. 73/85 — Sept. 29, 1985, *supra* p. 32; H.C. 14/86 — Feb. 23, 1987; H.C. 669/ 86 — Dec. 18, 1986).

SUPREME COURT: GIVE RIGHT OF APPEAL IN THE TERRITORIES

ARJUB v. IDF COMMANDER IN JUDEA AND SAMARIA

In the Supreme Court sitting as a High Court of Justice before the President, Justice Meir Shamgar, Justice Dov Levin, and Justice Eliezer Goldberg, in the matter of *Jamal Ahmad Jaber Arjub and another*, Petitioners, versus *The Commander of the Israel Forces in Judea and Samaria, and others*, Respondents (H.C. 87/85).

Military Law—Administrative Law—Right of Appeal from Decisions of Courts Martial in Occupied Territories—Conventional and Customary International Law—Order Relating to Security Directives, 1970, section 43—Military Justice (Military Courts Appeals) Amendment Law, 1963—International Covenant on Political and Civil Rights, sections 4(1), 14(5)—Hague Regulations, 1907, Article 43—Fourth Geneva Convention, 1949, Articles 66, 73.

Under section 43 of the Order relating to Defense Instructions of 1970, there is no right of appeal from the decision of a court martial in the administered territories, but a convicted person may apply for relief against a verdict or sentence to the area commander. The Petitioners, who were being tried by court martial, petitioned the High Court of Justice to intervene in the proceedings on the ground that their being deprived of a right of appeal in the event of their conviction, was unlawful.

The first judgment of the court was given by Justice Meir Shamgar. The Petitioners had argued, he said, that a right of appeal in criminal proceedings was a basic right in a democracy, similar to that, for example, of freedom of speech. They had emphasized, in this context, that under the Military Justice (Military Courts Appeals) Amendment Law of 1963, an appeal did lie from the decision of a court martial in Israel itself.

They had also contended that the absence of a right of appeal infringed section 14 (5) of the International Covenant on Political and Civil Rights, under which: "Everyone convicted of a crime shall have the right to his conviction and sentence being reviewed by a higher tribunal according to law".

It was also an infringement, they argued, of Article 43 of The Hague Regulations of 1907, under which: "The authority of the power of the state having passed *de facto* into the hands of the occupant, the latter shall do all in his power to restore, and ensure, as far as possible, public order and safety, respecting at the same time, unless absolutely prevented, the laws in force in the country". Since an appeal in criminal proceedings existed under Jordanian law, they argued, Israel, as the occupying power, was obliged to recognize that right.

The Petitioners also relied on Article 66 of the Fourth Geneva Convention of 1949, under which the military courts of the occupying power must sit in the occupied country, and courts of appeal should preferably sit in that country.

They relied, too, on Article 73 of that Convention, under which: "A convicted person shall have the right of appeal provided for by the laws applied by the court".

Finally, they argued that the denial of the right of appeal was unreasonable.

The Respondents stated that although they had weighed carefully all the arguments in favor of a right of appeal, they had decided not to introduce such a right. Their reason was the practical necessity of making the war against terrorism more effective, and shortening and simplifying legal proceedings. They also stressed the vital importance of courts martial in strengthening the army in its task.

They denied that there had been any infringement of international law, and argued that the court would not interfere in legislation of the principal legislature — in this case the Military Commander — as distinct from subsidiary legislation. They also contended that in considering primary legislation, the question of reasonableness did not arise.

The President went on to consider whether a right of appeal was one of the basic rights in a democratic regime which existed independently of legislation. After reviewing Israeli, English and American authorities, his conclusion was that such a right had to be provided for specifically by statute.

The accepted view in England was that "the creation of a right of appeal is an act which requires legislative authority. Neither the inferior nor the superior tribunal nor both combined can create such a right".

In the United States, too, "Appeal has not been held to be a matter of constitutional right under the due process clause, but in all jurisdictions, appellate review is generally available in some form from the judgments of trial courts".

Quoting from the *Yale Law Journal*, Justice Shamgar also noted, that, "in modern continental countries, the right of appeal is usually elevated to the constitutional level".

In Israel, too, he pointed out, the right of appeal, in the framework of the ordinary courts, is recognized by statute in section 17 of the Basic Law: the Judicature.

Dealing with the situation under public international law, Justice Shamgar held that section 14 (5) of the International Covenant on Political and Civil Rights could not assist the Petitioners. Israel had not adopted that Covenant and, in any case, it could not be regarded at this stage as part of customary international law. Moreover, section 4 (1) of the Covenant provided specifically: "In time of public emergency which threatens the life of the nation and the existence of which is officially proclaimed, the states parties to the present covenant may take measures derogating from their obligations under the present Covenant to the extent strictly required by the exigencies of the situation . . .".

Indeed, in dealing with a case relating to Ireland, the European Court of Human Rights had recognized the existence of a "public emergency threatening the life of the nation" on the basis of "the situation in that country in 1956-57".

Article 43 of The Hague Regulations of 1907, Justice Shamgar continued, did not oblige Israel to institute the right of appeal claimed by the Petitioners. The duty of the occupying power under that article to respect "the laws in force in the country" referred to the laws applied by the normal civilian courts in civil and criminal cases, and not to those applied in a system of military courts established by the occupying power.

An example of the application of Article 43 was an order by the military commander of Judea and Samaria replacing the right of appeal to the Court of Cessation in Amman which existed in those areas, and which obviously could not be exercised under the occupation. In establishing military courts, the military commander was not acting under local law, but under Public International Law, so Article 43 was irrelevant.

In regard to Article 66 of the Fourth Geneva Convention of 1949, Justice Shamgar held that this provision did not mean that an occupying power was required to create an appellate system of occupation courts, but provided where they should sit if they do exist. He relied for this conclusion on various authorities, including the official interpretation of that provision by the International Committee of the Red Cross. Referring to Article 73 of the Convention, Justice Shamgar pointed out that the same article provided that "where the laws applied by the court make no provision for appeals, the convicted person shall have the right to petition against the finding and sentence to the competent authority of the occupying power". Section 43 of the Respondents Order now attacked made specific provision for such a petition. In this connection, the President referred to the *English Manual of Military Law*, edited by Sir Hersch Lauterpacht, and to the *Legal Guide to the American Army on the Law of Land Warfare*, both of which make it clear that there is no right of appeal to a court, and that a right of petition to the competent authority is sufficient.

The result was, said Justice Shamgar, that there was no provision in conventional international law requiring the establishment of courts of appeal.

In regard to customary law, he continued, the authority Kelsen had pointed out that the acceptance of a custom as part of the law depended on its being recognized by a decisive majority of states. This had not been proved, and in this regard Kelsen wrote: "If there is no norm of conventional or customary international law imposing upon the state . . . the obligation to behave in a certain way, the state is under international law free to behave as it pleases; and by a decision to this effect, existing international law is applied to the case".

The arguments of the Petitioners based upon international law, therefore, failed.

The question of reasonableness did not enter into the matter, the President said. Moreover, it was well known that the High Court of Justice did not intervene in matters in which its decision would be purely academic, as in the present case. For the above reasons, therefore, the petition should be dismissed.

Despite his decision on the law, Justice Shamgar continued, he was strongly of opinion that the right of appeal should be introduced in the administered territories, even if restricted to legal points. Dealing at length relating to that right, he stressed that it had existed in the Israeli army for very many years, and was provided for, *inter alia*, in the Military Justice

Law of 1955. Indeed, Israel had introduced this right before either England or the U.S.

Its inclusion in legal procedures in the territories would only strengthen the administration of justice in these areas.

It was perhaps understandable that the introduction of an appeal procedure immediately after the occupation would have been difficult; but more than 20 years had elapsed since then, and the authorities should now act to bring such procedures into conformity with those existing in Israel itself.

As the Supreme Court had once stressed, "Life does not stand still, and no power, whether an occupier or not, fulfills its duty if it 'freezes' its legislation, and fails to advance it with the times".

The Respondents had stressed the importance of the war on terrorism, and the necessity of expediting legal proceedings. This was certainly an important consideration, but he saw no conflict with the military effort. Moreover, he rejected the concept that everything had to be sacrificed on the altar of saving time. Legal procedures served a basic purpose: the doing of justice and ensuring that justice be seen to be done. The power, effectiveness and influence of legal proceedings are not measured only by the element of speed. A legal proceeding should be completed within a reasonable time, but it is not a race against time.

Justice Shamgar suggested, therefore, that the Respondents adopt the approach which he now recommended.

Justice Dov Levin concurred. Having regard to the length of time since the occupation, and the common features of life in the territories and Israel itself, it was entirely unreasonable, he said, to apply different legal procedures in the territories from those applied in Israel.

There was no reason at all why a person accused of terrorist activity in, for example, Kfar Sava, should have a right of appeal which would be denied to a terrorist in Kalkilya. It was imperative, therefore, that this question be urgently reconsidered by the authorities concerned.

Justice Eliezer Goldberg agreed with his colleagues. It was accepted in the U.S. that: "Review procedure is not a necessary part of a legal system, required by due process, nor is the right of appeal an inherent or inalienable right".

Moreover, as had been pointed out by Prof. Menahem Elon, such a procedure did not exist under the Halacha (Jewish law) and, indeed, the establishment of the Rabbinical Court of Appeals in Israel had been the subject of much controversy.

Nevertheless, and with due regard to the military considerations advanced by the Respondents, he agreed that an appeal system should be introduced in the territories. The fear of undue delays in the legal process could be avoided by proper procedural safeguards.

He agreed, therefore, with the President's recommendations, but would not accept his suggestion that the right of appeal be limited to legal points.

The petition was dismissed.

Darwish Nasser appeared for the Petitioners, and Renato Yarak for the Respondent.

The judgment was given on February 7, 1988.

YESHIVA STUDENTS' MILITARY EXEMPTION NEEDS CONTROL

RESSLER v. MINISTER OF DEFENCE

In the Supreme Court sitting as a High Court of Justice before the President, Justice Meir Shamgar, former Deputy-President Justice Miriam Ben-Porat, and Justice Aharon Barak, in the matter of *Advocate Yehuda Ressler (Major in the Reserves) and others*, Petitioners, versus *The Minister of Defence*, Respondent (H.C. 910/86.)

Military Law—Administrative Law—Exemption of "Yeshiva" Students from Military Service—Not So Unreasonable as to Justify Intervention by Court— Defence Service Law (Consolidated Version), 1986, section 36.

Under Section 36 of the Defence Service Law (Consolidated Version) of 1986,"The Minister of Defence may, by order if he thinks fit to do so for reasons connected with the size of the Regular Forces or Reserve Forces of the Defence Army of Israel, or for reasons connected with the requirements of education, defence settlement of the national economy, or for family reasons or other reasons, exempt a person of military age from the duty of regular service, or reduce the period of his service; exempt a person of military age from reserve service . . .; and on the application of a person of military age, or another person who will be liable for defence service, exempt, such person for such period as he may fix, from reporting for service . . . and from registration, medical examination, or from defence service, or from the continuation of such service if he has already started to serve".

The Petitioners, all reserve officers, prayed the court to set aside the Respondent's order exempting yeshiva students from defence service. They argued, first, that in view of the principle involved, such exemption should be granted, if at all, by the Knesset itself, and not by administrative order of a minister. Secondly, they argued that the minister's grounds were discriminatory and unreasonable; the purpose of the above Law, they contended, was to promote security, and not yeshiva study.

It was argued on behalf of the Respondent that the petitioners had no legal standing to approach the court, and also that the petition was non-justiciable, since it dealt with a subject of public controversy which should be resolved by the political authorities, and not by the court.

The considerations of the minister had also been placed before the court. He had weighed respect for the historic spiritual obligation of those teaching and studying the Tora to pursue their task continuously, a principle regarded as sacred by part of the Jewish people, both in Israel and in the Diaspora; the difficulties which would face extremely Orthodox yeshiva students in serving in the army, and at the same time observing strictly their religious practices; the fact that the emotional conflicts created for such students would seriously impair the value of their military service; and lastly, the deep public sensitivity in Israel to this ideological conflict, and the necessity of striking a delicate balance at governmental level in this kind of situation.

The first judgment of the court was given by Justice Aharon Barak. He reviewed the proceedings of the Knesset in connection with the problem now arising, and also referred to previous decisions of the Supreme Court on the matter. All the previous petitions, he said, had been dismissed on the ground that the Petitioners had no legal standing.

He then reviewed in detail the previous decisions of the Supreme Court and the opinions of leading scholars both in Israel and in England and the United States, citing also the work of Dr. Ze'ev Segal, the locus classicus in Israel on this topic.

As an example of the conflict of judicial opinion in this regard, he cited an opinion of Justice Witkon that the more the petition savours of public controversy, the more must the court insist on the Petitioner showing that he has suffered some real injury in a personal right of his, as against an opinion of Justice Berenson that the more important the petition from the public point of view, the more will the court incline to give the Petitioner a hearing.

In the present case, Justice Barak held, the Petitioners had *locus standi* even according to the classical view that they must show that a personal right of theirs had been infringed. They had filed affidavits by Col. Wald and Col. Bahat, of the Personnel Division of the Ministry of Defence, who had averred, on the basis of details of the situation, that there was a direct relationship between the exemption of yeshiva students from regular and reserve service, and the length of time the Petitioners had to do reserve service. This was sufficient to give them the required standing. Moreover, said Justice Barak, they would have standing even under other heads recognized by the more liberal school, namely, that the petition dealt with an important constitutional topic, and also touched upon the preservation of the rule of law.

Justice Barak then analysed in detail the argument that the petition before the court was non-justiciable.

After citing numerous authorities, both Israeli and others, he reached the conclusion that the matter before the court fell clearly within section 15 of the Judicature Law, under which the court was empowered to deal with matters not within the jurisdiction of any other court, and with which it found it desirable to deal in the interests of justice. Under this section, the court reviewed the actions of administrative authorities performing duties imposed upon them by law.

In the present case, the court was called upon to review the actions of the Minister of Defence under section 36 of the Defence Service Law. Indeed, there were cases which were non-justiciable, in which the court was of the opinion that they were not appropriate for judicial decision, but this was not one of them. The fact that the present case was one of political controversy was not sufficient reason for not dealing with it.

In this regard, Justice Barak cited the opinion of Justice Murphy of the United States Supreme Court that "It is essential that there be definite limits to military discretion . . . The military claim must subject itself to the judicial process of having its reasonableness determined and its conflicts with other interests reconciled. What are the allowable limits of military discretion, and whether or not they have been overstepped in a particular case, are judicial questions".

Justice Barak also cited an opinion of Chief Justice Marshall of the U. S. Supreme Court, that "We have no more right to decline the exercise of jurisdiction which is given, than to usurp that which is not given".

Turning to the powers of the Minister of Defence, Justice Barak held that the exemption of yeshiva students from defence service fell within the minister's authority under section 36 above. It fell partly under the ground of a reason connected with the size of the reserve forces, and fully under the grounds of reasons connected with the requirements of education, and other reasons.

The expression "other reasons" did not mean any reason which the minister thought sufficient. These words must be interpreted objectively, having regard to the legislative purpose of the section in question. There was no ground for confining the words "other reasons" to reasons of security alone. They also included religious reasons. It was on the basis of this ground that exemption from service had been granted to new immigrants and members of minority communities, and also to members of the Druse community. There was no reason, therefore, not to include the exemption of yeshiva students in the same category.

It had been argued, said Justice Barak, that an exemption from service so far-reaching should have been included in the Law itself, and not left to the discretion of the minister. He agreed that it would be more desirable that basic provisions of this kind be stated clearly in the statute, and not be left to a minister's discretion in terms so general as "other reasons". On the other hand, there was no adequate ground for not applying the law as it was. The legislature had decided to leave the matter in the minister's hands, and it was for the court to give effect to this decision.

Finally, Justice Barak dealt with the Petitioners' argument that the exemption complained of was so unreasonable that the court should set it aside. It was one thing, they argued, to exempt a few hundred students, as was the situation when this problem was first considered. It was quite a different thing, however, to exempt 17,017 students, as was the situation now. To this the Respondent replied that he had weighed all the relevant considerations, and was satisfied that the exemption was justified, and would not affect security to the extent that it should be withdrawn. He also submitted that the court would not substitute its discretion for his, and that his decision was not so unreasonable that the court would interfere.

The main consideration under section 36, Justice Barak continued, was that of security. Much importance, therefore, attached to the number of students affected by the exemption, and there was a limit beyond which the minister was not entitled to go. In his opinion, Justice Barak said, the Petitioners had not shown that this limit had been exceeded. The question was not what the court would have decided had the discretion been in its hands, but whether the minister was entitled to reach the decision he took.

Justice Barak could not hold that no reasonable minister would have reached such a decision. The court's power of review was confined to the question of whether the minister, after weighing all the relevant considerations, had reached a reasonable conclusion. He could not say that that was not the case.

It was possible, he noted, that the situation now considered could change. The matter had to be continually reviewed.

Justice Miriam Ben-Porat concurred. Dealing in the main with the question of *locus standi*, she said she tended to agree with the more liberal approach, and not to demand in every case that some right of the Petitioner himself be infringed. On the other hand, the court had to be wary, and not open the doors too wide to would-be litigants.

Justice Ben-Porat agreed with Justice Barak that the Petitioners had not shown that the minister's decision was so unreasonable as to be invalid. She also emphasized that the judge's personal opinion was quite irrelevant, and agreed that the situation could be reached where the number of yeshiva students exempted from service rendered the decision of exemption unreasonable.

The President of the court agreed that the petition be dismissed for the legal reasons already stated. It was sometimes appropriate, he said, that the judge content himself with stating his legal conclusion, and saying nothing more. On the other hand, there were cases, standing on the boundary of reasonableness, where that was not enough, and where the judge should also express his opinion on the merits of the question at issue. This was such a case.

The existing situation, said Justice Shamgar, in which some yeshiva students were exempted from military service, while others were serving, and had served, in all Israel's wars, was quite unacceptable. It raised serious questions of public and personal ethics, which remained unresolved. He voiced this opinion, he said, so that the legal result should not obscure the national and human values involved.

In examining the present system of exempting a portion of yeshiva students from service — which, in effect, meant both regular and reserve service — Justice Shamgar stressed that this was a problem of progressive seriousness, as the number of students exempted grew each year.

It was necessary, therefore, to define a reasonable annual limit for exemptions, which would ensure the maintenance of a proper level of security in the army; to ascertain the effect of the exemptions on the numbers of soldiers enlisted, and on the length of their regular and reserve service; to determine what tests should be applied for granting exemptions, so that it should not be left to each individual to decide whether he prefers Tora study to military service; and to decide what steps should be taken to supervise the implementation of the arrangements made. This was not a closed list, the President said, for the whole subject had to be reviewed continuously.

For the above reasons, the petition was dismissed.

The first Petitioner appeared for all the Petitioners, and Nili Arad, the Director of the High Court Division of the State Attorney's Office, for the Respondent.

The judgment was given on June 12, 1988.

PRESS PRIVILEGE MAY BE OVERRULED

"TIME" MAGAZINE v. MINISTER OF DEFENCE

In the Supreme Court sitting as a High Court of Justice before Justice Aharon Barak, in the matter of *"Time" Magazine and others*, Petitioners, versus *The Minister of Defence and others*, Respondents. (H.C. 172/88).

Administrative Law—Freedom of Expression—Seizure by Soldiers of Photographer's Film to Assist in Murder Investigation— Seizure Lawful, but Films to be Returned—Order Relating to Security Directives (Judea and Samaria) No. 378 of 1970.

Following the murder of a soldier in Bethlehem, photographic films of the incident taken by press photographers were seized by a soldier and retained by the authorities. On the application of the Petitioners, the High Court of Justice issued an order nisi directing the Respondents to show cause why the films should not be returned. The court also issued a temporary injunction preventing the films from being developed. Subse-

quently the injunction was cancelled. The films were eventually returned
to the Petitioners and, by consent of the parties, the order nisi was set aside.

Giving the final judgment of the court setting aside the order nisi, Justice
Aharon Barak said that the films had been seized to assist in tracing the
murderer. The photographers had been informed at the time that the films
would be returned to them after their examination by the army. After the
temporary injunction was issued, the Respondents had asked the court to
cancel it. They then pointed out that some of the films had been damaged
while being seized, and others had already been developed and returned
to the petitioners. Three films, however, had not yet been developed, and
they applied for leave to develop them.

In seizing the films, Justice Barak said, the soldier concerned had acted
under Order Relating to Defence Instructions (Judea and Samaria) No. 378
of 1970, issued by the military commander of that area. That order empowered a soldier to seize articles "which may be evidence" of the commission
of an offence.

The question that arose was whether the soldier had acted lawfully. It
had been argued that the seizure of the films was a serious infringement
of freedom of expression and of the rights of the press, and of the right of
the public to receive information.

Referring to the decision of the Supreme Court in the case of *Citrin* v.
The Disciplinary Court of the Israel Bar (M.A. 298/86, *The Jerusalem Post* of
May 3, 1987, *supra* p. 41), Justice Barak said it was not necessary for him to
define the boundaries between freedom of expression and the public interest in investigating a crime. It was also unnecessary for him to define the
exact scope of the discretion to be exercised in seizing media material as
evidence in court.

(It was held in *Citrin's* case that, as a rule, a journalist's right to claim
privilege in respect of his sources of information was to be recognized. An
order to disclose the information, however, was to be given if it was
relevant, and vital and important for doing justice in a matter of substance,
such as one dealing with a felony or serious crime, or a civil wrong having
serious consequences. A.F.L.)

It was sufficient for him to point out, said Justice Barak, that freedom of
expression and of the press was not enough to prevent the disclosure of
material, such as films, which was reasonably required by the competent
examining authorities for the investigation of serious crimes. This approach
ensured the striking of a proper balance between the freedom of the press

and the apprehension of offenders, and was consistent with the principles of an enlightened democracy.

If this was the proper conception as regards the examining authority in Israel, it would certainly apply to a soldier in the occupied territories. Neither the murderer nor the murder weapon had been found, and it was reasonable to assume that the films, taken soon after the occurrence, would assist the investigation.

For the above reasons, said Justice Barak, he had held that the seizure of the films, and their being developed immediately, were lawful acts.

Dr. Yisrael Leshem appeared for the Petitioners, and Nili Arad, Director of the High Court Division of the State Attorney's General Office, for the Respondents.

The judgment was given on July 10, 1988.

KIDNEY TRANSPLANT DISALLOWED

ATTORNEY-GENERAL v. A.B.

In the Supreme Court sitting as a Court of Civil Appeals before the former Deputy-President, Justice Miriam Ben-Porat, the Deputy-President, Justice Menahem Elon, Justice Aharon Barak, Justice Moshe Bejski and Justice Gavriel Bach, in the matter of *The Attorney-General and others*, Appellants, versus *A.B. and others*, Respondents. (L.A. 698/86, 151, 184/87).

Personal Status—Refusal of Court to Permit Transplant of Mentally Defective Minor's Kidney—Jewish Law—Capacity and Guardianship Law, 1962, section 68(b).

The Respondent, A.B., is the father and legal guardian of his mentally defective son, aged 39. He looks after his son in the family home, and attends to all his needs with the utmost devotion.

A.B., aged 65, suffers from a kidney disease, and undergoes dialysis at home every eight hours. In order to improve his condition with the object of being able to care for his son more effectively, he wished to receive an implant of one of his son's kidneys.

Since his son is completely unable to understand the situation and give his own consent to the transplant, A.B., as the son's guardian, consented in his stead, and applied to the District Court in Beersheba to confirm the arrangements made.

The District Court made the order sought but the Attorney-General and Akim (the Association for the Rehabilitation of the Mentally Handicapped) applied to that court to reopen the case in order to hear further evidence. The case was reopened, but the court confirmed its previous order. The Attorney-General and Akim then appealed to the Supreme Court.

The first judgment of the Supreme Court was given by Justice Menahem Elon. Dealing with the statutory provisions applicable, he referred to the relevant sections in the Capacity and Guardianship Law of 1962, citing particularly section 68 of that Law, under which "(a) The Court may, at any time, on the application of the Attorney-General or his representative or of an interested party or of its own motion, take temporary or permanent measures which seem to it appropriate for protecting the interests of a minor, a legally incompetent person, a ward or a person in need of guardianship, either by appointing a temporary guardian or a guardian ad litem, or otherwise. The court may also do so on application of the minor, the legally incompetent person, the ward or the person in need of guardianship himself.

"(b) Where the application is for a direction to perform surgery or to take any other medical measure, the Court shall not issue the direction unless it is satisfied, on the basis of a medical opinion, that the measure is necessary in order to protect the physical or mental well-being of the minor, legally incompetent person, or ward."

In discussing the legislative history of section 68, Justice Elon pointed out that the words "or permanent" in sub-section (a) had been added to the original section mainly to cover cases of insane persons who were unable to consent to operations having permanent effect.

Sub-section (b) had also been added to the original Law, he said, having regard specifically to transplant cases. The Knesset had so acted following a court decision permitting a transplant of bone marrow from a minor to one of her sisters, since it was in the minor's interest to do so, and also since bone marrow was a self-renewing substance.

That was not the case, of course, with a kidney transplant, but subsection (b) of section 68 was sufficiently wide to empower the court to make the order now considered. It had to be satisfied, of course, that the transplant was necessary in the interests of the minor, incompetent person, or ward. In the words of an American court, it must be "conclusively demonstrated that it will be of significant benefit to the incompetent." It was not necessary, however, that the transplant should be of direct medical benefit to the protected person. Indirect benefit, as was argued in the present case, was sufficient.

Justice Elon then discussed the Halacha relating to the question before the court. It was a cardinal rule, he said, that one who could save another person, and did not do so, offended the precept that "*neither shalt thou stand idly by the blood of thy neighbour*" (Leviticus 19:16). It was clear that a person was obliged to help another where there was no risk to himself.

The question was, however, whether he was obliged, or even permitted, to do so at the risk of his own life. The question of transplants had been considered by halachic authorities, and the conclusion was that even where there would be no danger to the donor, a person could not be obliged to donate one of his organs to another. It was clear, therefore, that if a normal person could not be obliged to donate an organ, an incompetent person could not be forced to do so.

The theory of "substituted judgment" had also been considered within the framework of the Halacha, namely, that it would be permissible to oblige the incompetent person to do what a normal person would have done in the same circumstances. Justice Elon, however, rejected this conception.

Returning to section 68(b) above, Justice Elon said the court in the present case, had to be convinced on the basis of objective medical opinions, that the son's interests would be adversely affected unless the transplant were performed. It would have to be satisfied that there was no alternative, and that the matter could not be delayed.

Reviewing English and American authorities, he added that the theory of "substituted judgment" had been considered in those countries too, but he agreed with those who did not accept it. He shared the opinion that "it must be clearly established that the surgical intrusion is urgent, that there are no reasonable alternatives, and that the contingencies are minimal".

Justice Elon then dealt at length with the facts of the case, considering the possible advantages, and disadvantages, physical and mental, for the father and the son, and the available alternatives to the transplant proposed.

In this regard, he considered the possibility of a transplant from another member of the family, or from a deceased donor. He also cited medical authorities dealing, *inter alia*, with transplants from members of the same family, and the factor of the father's age in respect of the prospects of success of the operation, its effects on his life expectation, and the degree to which his effectiveness as his son's guardian would be improved.

In the result, he held that the conditions laid down in section 68(b) had not been established and that the application to the District Court should therefore have been dismissed.

In conclusion, Justice Elon said that there was no doubt as to the father's sincerity, and his genuine belief that the transplant would not harm his son but, on the contrary, would be to his benefit. The court, however, was obliged, both legally and morally, to consider the problems in all its aspects — the transplant of a vital organ not self-renewable from a "donor" who had no idea what was being done to him, and what was being extracted from his body.

Much had been written about the family, social and psychological pressures associated with transplants within the family. Even in the cases of normal people, there was often doubt if the donor was really a person *"whose heart maketh him willing"* (Exodus, 25:2). The present case, however, was not the case of a "donation" at all, but a clear example of compulsion, touching the very foundations of the cultural and spiritual foundations of the fabric of our society.

The court is the "father" of legally incompetent persons who cannot think and act for themselves. That does not mean that the court is a better father than the Respondent, who is devoted heart and soul to his son's welfare; but it does mean that it is obliged to see the problem in all its aspects and weigh all the elements, applying the tests which the law imposes upon it.

We repeat our recommendation, at the time of giving our decision, that everything be done to arrange an early transplant from a deceased donor, to enable the father to continue helping his son as effectively as possible.

Justice Gavriel Bach concurred, since he was not convinced that the son would derive clear and meaningful benefit from the transplant proposed.

Justices Aharon Barak, Miriam Ben-Porat and Moshe Bejski also concurred, pointing out that the court's decision should be regarded as confined to the particular facts of the present case only, and not regarded as a precedent of general application.

For the above reasons, the appeal was allowed, and the decision of the District Court set aside.

Senior Assistant State Attorney Dr. Yosef Bar-On and Zerah Rosenbloom appeared for the Appellants, and Nissim Mazur and Tahar Shahaf for the Respondents.

The reasons for the judgment were given on July 3, 1988.

THE LIMITS TO CENSORSHIP

SHNITZER v. CHIEF MILITARY CENSOR

In the Supreme Court sitting as a High Court of Justice before Justice Aharon Barak, Justice Ya'acov Maltz, and Judge Shulamit Wallenstein, in the matter of *Meir Shnitzer and another*, Petitioners, versus *Yitzhak Shani, Chief Military Censor, and another*, Respondents (H.C. 680/88).

Administrative Law—Freedom of Expression—Censorship of Newspaper Article— Military Law—Military Censor's Decision Set Aside—Defence (Emergency) Regulations, 1945, Regulation 87(1).

The newspaper *Ha'ir* requested the censor to authorize the publication of an article containing, *inter alia*, criticism of the functioning of the head of the Establishment for Intelligence and Special Duties (the Mossad), and the date of his replacement. The censor refused, and the Petitioners applied to the High Court of Justice for an order directing the censor to give the authority sought.

The judgment of the court was given by Justice Aharon Barak.

Military censorship, he said, existed by virtue of the Defence Emergency Regulations of 1945, under Regulation 87(1) of which: "The censor may by order prohibit generally or specifically the publishing of matters the publishing of which, in his opinion, would be, or be likely to be or become, prejudicial to the defence of Palestine or to the public safety or to public order."

A number of newspapers had reached an agreement with the censor regarding his supervision of their publications. *Ha'ir*, however, was not a party to that agreement. The legality of the censor's actions in respect of that paper, therefore, were to be tested directly on the basis of the regulations mentioned.

Those regulations, Justice Barak continued, were issued by the High Commissioner, and were part of the legislation of the British Mandate. Under section 11 of the Law and Administration Ordinance of 1948, they became part of the law of Israel, subject, however, "to such modifications as may result from the establishment of the State and its authorities."

As the Supreme Court had held, that was not a mere technical condition, but one of considerable substance. A colonial and autocratic regime was replaced by a democracy, by the rule of the people acting through the majority, and upholding the rights of the individual. This change naturally led to a new conception of the law, and its application by the courts.

It had been argued in the Supreme Court, Justice Barak said, that the above regulations were inconsistent with the maintenance of a democratic regime, but that argument had been rejected. Attempts had also been made in the Knesset to abolish the regulations in their entirety, but those attempts had also failed.

Meanwhile, portions of the regulations had been repealed, and replaced by Israeli legislation. Those regulations not repealed, however, were part of Israeli law, and were to be interpreted against the background of the basic freedoms which that law recognized.

The primary factors to be considered in interpreting the Defence Regulations, Justice Barak continued, were the security of the state, public safety, and public order. Where the regulations conflicted with the basic freedoms recognized in a democratic regime, the court had to strike a balance between the inconsistent values.

Justice Barak then examined several Supreme Court precedents dealing with the conflict between state security and other basic values in different situations.

The court had adopted the judicial interpretative principle that freedom of expression could be limited in the interests of state security and public order only where there was a "near certainty" of real, serious damage to security if the expression were permitted.

He also cited an opinion of the scholar Flinn that "On matters affecting the national interests, the people must be provided with all the pertinent information, so that they can reach intelligent responsible decisions. The first constitutional principle is that a self-governing people must have a thorough knowledge and understanding of the problems of their government in order to participate effectively in their solution . . .

"In the absence of strong and effectual governmental checks and balances in the areas of national defence and international affairs, the only effective restraint on executive power lies in a well-informed citizenry. Without an alert, free, and diligent press there cannot be a well-informed citizenry. Only if the government is vigorously and constantly cross-examined and exposed by the press can the public stay informed and thereby control their government."

It was true, Justice Barak continued, that the censor's discretion was subjective. The regulation spoke of matters "which, in his opinion" were prejudicial to state security.

This did not mean, however, that the discretion was absolute. It had to be exercised within the provisions of the enabling Law and for the objective purposes of that Law. The authority concerned, here the censor, had to act in good faith, without caprice, and on the basis of relevant considerations alone. In choosing between the various possibilities, he had to base himself on reliable and convincing facts, and his assessment of the situation had to be reasonable.

Justice Barak then cited several Supreme Court precedents dealing with judicial review of administrative decisions by the courts, referring particularly to cases involving state security.

There was nothing special about state security, he said, when considering judicial review. Judges were not security officials, and should not interfere with matters of security. They were also not administrators, but they reviewed the administrative acts of the executive.

Their review was directed to the legality and reasonableness of the acts of the authority concerned, and in this respect the censor, and other security authorities, were in no special category.

He mentioned, in this regard, that the view he expressed was now also accepted in England, the House of Lords having departed from the well-known decision in *Liversidge* v. *Anderson*, decided during World War II, in which a contrary ruling was given (see 1942 A.C. 206; 1980 A.C. 952). Indeed, because of the extreme importance of security matters, the Supreme Court had emphasized the necessity for special care in reviewing security decisions.

Justice Barak then proceeded to consider the censor's decision in this particular case.

It was not disputed, he said, that any publication which would lead to identifying the head of the Mossad would be correctly disallowed. The censor had argued, however, that any negative criticism of the head of the Mossad, and the efficiency and consequences of his performance, and legitimizing the publication of such matters in Israel (as distinct from overseas), would damage the ability of the Mossad to operate at all levels, including the security-political area.

The censor had contended that it would also hamper the relations between the Mossad and similar organizations outside Israel, and would affect security officials working in the field. He distinguished between criticism of the Mossad itself and criticism of the functioning of the head of the Mossad. The latter, he submitted, would damage the security of the state.

The above reasoning of the censor, said Justice Barak, was unacceptable. No near certainty of real damage to the security of the state would be caused by published criticism of the functioning of the head of the Mossad. That was only a remote possibility of which the court would not take account.

On the contrary, criticism of persons occupying public office was desirable in a democratic society. Of course, criticism was not pleasant, and was sometimes damaging, and that applied to the head of the Mossad, or the prime minister, or any other public functionary.

Unpleasantness, however, was not a ground for stifling criticism in a democratic society based on the exchange of ideas, and public debate. Freedom of expression included freedom to criticize, and to harass those in power with troublesome questions.

A democracy, said Justice Barak, was a regime of balance and control. This was a consequence of the reciprocal relations between the executive, the legislature, and the judiciary. The state comptroller was charged with the duty of criticism, but there were also other, non-official organs. Among these, a vital part was played by the press.

The press had the duty of exposing irregularities, and protesting against them. It must therefore be allowed to perform its functions. Only in extreme cases of a near certainty of real danger to the state was the restriction on publishing information in the press justified.

It was difficult to conceive a case in which the publication of criticism, as distinct from facts, could create a near certainty of real danger to state security. The Supreme Court of the United States had said that "Any system of prior restraints of expression comes to this court bearing a heavy presumption against its constitutional validity." It was for the censor to show that the restriction on publication which he had imposed was justified. In the present instance, he had not done so.

The censor's objection to publishing when the successor of the present head of the Mossad would assume his duties, Justice Barak continued, was also based on the premise that such publication would lead to the disclosure of the head's identity, particularly outside Israel.

The court could not accept this submission, he said. It was true that it was for the censor to decide whether the publication would create a "near certainty" of real danger to state security. At the same time, the decision had to be reasonable, and the court was of opinion that the censor's fears were unreasonable.

In conclusion, Justice Barak said that the court had no doubt whatever as to the military censor's good faith. He had a difficult task, which he had to discharge under difficult conditions. It was clear, of course, that a democracy was entitled, and also obliged, to defend itself. A democratic state could not exist without security. At the same time, it must be remembered that security meant not only the army. Democracy was also security. Our strength lay in our moral force, and in our adherence to democratic principles, even when surrounded by great danger.

Security was not a goal in itself, but a means to a goal. The goal was a democratic regime, a regime of the people recognizing the freedoms of the individual.

Freedom of expression occupied an honoured place among these freedoms. Everything possible must be done, therefore, to prevent security considerations impinging on freedom of expression. The censor was obliged to bear these matters in mind in discharging his duty.

For the above reasons, the petition was allowed, and the censor ordered to grant the authorization requested.

Shlomo Lieblich appeared for the Petitioners, and Nili Arad, Director of the High Court Department of the State Attorney's Office, appeared for the Respondents.

The judgment was given on January 10, 1989.

A STADIUM AT LAST

ZUCKER AND OTHERS v. MINISTER OF THE INTERIOR

In the Supreme Court sitting as a High Court of Justice before Justice Aharon Barak, Justice Avraham Halima, and Judge Hanoch Ariel, in the matters of *Dedi Zucker, Mayor Teddy Kollek, and the Manahat Jerusalem Football Stadium Jerusalem Ltd.*, Petitioners, versus *The Minister of the Interior and others*, Respondents (H.C. 581, 832, 849/87).

Administrative Law—Intervention by Supreme Court in Administrative Decision— Unreasonable Refusal to Confirm Town Planning Scheme—Planning and Building Law, 1965, section 134(b)(1).

The idea of establishing a football stadium in Jerusalem was first mooted in 1973. A grandiose project was conceived for the erection in Shuafat of a center of Olympic proportions, of which the stadium would form only a part. Preliminary work on the site was begun, but as a result of pressure by the haredi community,* the project was abandoned.

After further consideration, it was decided to freeze the Shuafat project and build a municipal stadium in Katamon. This project was rejected by the District Town Planning Commission in May 1983, after the filing of 1,200 objections, including those of the Interior Ministry, local residents, and the Council for a Beautiful Israel.

Thereafter a new project was conceived for the erection of a stadium in the suburb of Manahat, and a planning scheme was prepared for its implementation. This scheme is known, under the Planning and Building Law of 1965, as Local Outline Scheme No. 3420.

On March 8, 1984, the District Commission decided to authorize the deposit of Scheme 3420, and notice thereof was given in *Reshumot*, the Government Gazette, on August 30, 1986.

A number of other projects in the same area are also contemplated, including a commercial center, diverting the existing railway line, laying down a road, building a Beit Halohem, (a soldiers' center), and establishing a zoo. However, no general overall outline planning scheme has yet been prepared.

Neither the Ministry of the Interior nor the Council for a Beautiful Israel opposed Scheme 3420. However, more than 1,000 objections were filed, mainly by residents of Bayit Vegan, and some by residents of nearer suburbs. On January 13, 1985, the Local Planning Commission recommended to the District Commission to reject the objections; but on April 14, 1985, the latter appointed a sub-committee to hear the objectors.

The sub-committee held 30 meetings, the last of which took place on February 22, 1987. During this period of 21 months, the Deputy Attorney-General, following a complaint by the Manahat stadium company, remonstrated with the District Commissioner on the ground that the long delay frustrated its fulfilling its duty under the law.

Eventually, on April 21, 1987, three years after Scheme 4320 was deposited, the District Commission confirmed it, with some modifications, by a majority of twelve to two.

One of the dissenters in the District Commission then appealed to the National Planning Commission, but on July 19, 1987, the appeal was dismissed.

* Ultra Orthodox.

Under section 134 (b) (1) of the 1965 Law, modifications to a local outline scheme authorized by the District Commission require the confirmation of the Minister of the Interior. The minister delegated this power to the Director-General of the ministry, who declined to give the confirmation required. Three petitions were then presented to the High Court to secure the confirmation.

The judgment of the court was given by Judge Hanoch Ariel. The Director-General, he said, had stated in detail his reasons for not confirming Scheme 3420. These reasons fell under three heads: specific defects in the scheme; the manner in which the site of the stadium had been selected; and the need for a general outline scheme for the whole area before the scheme relating specifically to the stadium was confirmed.

Judge Ariel then examined the Respondents' contentions as to defects in Scheme 3420 from three aspects — noise, parking and transport — and held that, on the material before the court, these defects had not been established.

In dealing with the question of the selection of the site, the argument was that the planners had proceeded on the basis that the site would be the one already chosen, while the possibility of other sites was not considered. After examining the facts in some detail, Judge Ariel found that this argument, too, had not been substantiated.

The Respondents' main argument (which, on the face of it, said Judge Ariel, seemed reasonable) was that as a rule, although not necessarily always, a general scheme relating to the whole area should be approved before a scheme relating to a specific project.

He wished to emphasize that the Respondents had described the general undertaking as "enormous," extending over 9,000 dunams, even though they were not speaking of a plan covering the whole of this area. Testing the necessity of a general scheme in these circumstances was extremely difficult.

The Petitioners had argued that proper consideration had been given to the other projects planned in the vicinity, and that the absence of a confirmed general scheme should not defer the confirmation of the specific scheme now being considered.

After reviewing the attention given by the planners to the other projects contemplated, Judge Ariel rejected the Respondents' argument that these had not been properly considered. On the contrary, everyone concerned, including the members of the District Commission, had been aware of the details of the other projects, and had given this aspect full weight.

The Supreme Court had already held, Judge Ariel continued, that the preparation of a general scheme was not always to be a condition precedent for the confirmation of a scheme for a specific project. The court had then said that while understanding the general requirement that prior preparation of a general scheme ensured better harmony between the various projects contemplated, the timing of the different stages was a matter for the planning authorities. If they decided not to wait for a general scheme, the court would not force them to do so. The court in that case had also pointed out that the investors had been dealing with the matter for nearly five years.

Judge Ariel then quoted Supreme Court precedents considering the circumstances in which the court would set aside administrative decisions of the executive on the ground of unreasonableness. It had been held, he said, that unreasonableness in itself was sufficient ground for the court's interference, even if there were no question of caprice, or absence of good faith, or failure to consider all the relevant factors.

Turning to the facts of the present matter, Judge Ariel held that the Director-General's decision was unreasonable, and should be set aside.

The question of the stadium had occupied the attention of the authorities for many years, and the Respondents had failed to show what damage would be caused if the scheme in question were now confirmed, and implemented.

The demand of the Director-General that the whole project await the preparation of a general scheme took insufficient account of the time and effort already devoted to the stadium project, and also took insufficient account of the time that was likely to elapse before such a general scheme was prepared and confirmed. This remained unlimited, perhaps "until the coming of Elijah." At best, his refusal of confirmation could hold up the stadium project for several more years, without justification.

For the above reasons, the petitions were allowed, and the Director-General was ordered to give the confirmation sought.

Itamar Hacohen, Yitzhak Eliraz and Naomi Weil appeared for the Petitioners, and Menahem Mazuz and Renato Yarak appeared for the Respondents.

The judgment was given on January 9, 1989.

DEPORTATION AND SECRECY

SHAKSHIR v. IDF COMMANDER IN WEST BANK

In the Supreme Court sitting as a High Court of Justice, before Justice Gavriel Bach, in the matter of *Balal Shakshir*, Applicant, versus *The Commander of the IDF Forces in the West Bank*, Respondent (H.C. 765/88: Application 497/88).

Evidence—Refusal to Disclose to Deportee—Administrative Law—Partial Disclosure Ordered by Supreme Court—Defence (Emergency) Regulations, 1945, Regulations 111(4), 112(1), 112(8)—Evidence Ordinance (New Version), 1971, sections 44(a), 46(a)—Criminal Procedure Law (Consolidated Version), 1982— Emergency Powers (Arrest) Law, 1979.

On August 17, 1988, the Respondent issued an expulsion order against the Applicant under regulation 112(1) of the Defence (Emergency) Regulations of 1945. The case was then considered by an advisory committee under regulations 111(4) and 112(8) of the Regulations, which confirmed the Respondent's decision. The Applicant then petitioned the High Court of Justice to set the expulsion order aside.

Part of the evidence submitted to the advisory committee was regarded by the Respondent as secret, and was therefore not disclosed to the Applicant or his counsel. In his reply to the Applicant's petition to the court, the Respondent repeated his submission of secrecy, and supported his refusal to disclose the evidence by filing a certificate of the Defence Minister under section 44(a) of the Evidence Ordinance (New Version) of 1971.

Under that section, "A person is not bound to give, and the court shall not admit, evidence regarding which the Prime Minister, or the Defence Minister, by certificate under his hand, has expressed the opinion that its giving is likely to impair the security of the state . . . unless a judge of the Supreme Court, on the petition of a party who desires the disclosure of the evidence, finds that the necessity to disclose it for the purpose of doing justice outweighs the interest in its non-disclosure."

The Applicant moved the court to allow the disclosure of the evidence in question, requesting that the application be heard by a judge other than those hearing the main petition. The application was referred to Justice Bach.

In his decision, Justice Bach said that he had first received the representatives of the Attorney-General and the General Security Service in the absence of the Applicant and his counsel, and they had given him a general review of the relevant material.

This procedure was made available to him under section 46(a) of the above Ordinance. He then conducted a hearing with the participation of both parties. Thereafter he had again received the representatives of the state, and had examined all the evidence, document by document, bearing in mind the arguments of counsel for both parties.

The Supreme Court had already held that in order to justify concealing evidence from a person awaiting expulsion, the court must be convinced that the relevant authorities fear, honestly and in good faith, that the disclosure of the evidence involves revealing information which is liable to constitute a real security risk, or is liable to reveal and jeopardize secret sources of information, and that that fear is reasonable. He had repeated this principle in the context of criminal proceedings in the *Vanunu* case (M.A. 64/87—*The Jerusalem Post*, Sep. 28, 1987).

Some of the alleged subversive activities of the Applicant were stated in the expulsion order, and others had been stated by the authorities in the course of the hearing. Thirty out of some 100 documents had been disclosed to the Applicant. In regard to the others, the fear was that their disclosure would reveal sources of information, and seriously impair state security. The Applicant was not satisfied with this situation, and requested that all information be disclosed.

He had some understanding of the feelings of the Applicant and his counsel, said Justice Bach. In fact, keeping the Applicant ignorant of a large part of the information against him caused a measure of discomfort to counsel for the state as well. The expulsion of a person from his home was a serious and painful matter.

On the other hand, the present legal position was created by the harsh Defence Regulations of the Mandate, and also by the emergency situation in the state, and particularly in the territories it occupied.

Applicant's counsel had pointed out that in considering the disclosure of secret information in criminal cases, the court had held that no consideration of security could justify impairing an accused's defence to the extent of causing the possible conviction of an innocent person (*Livni*, M.A. 838/84, *The Jerusalem Post*, Jan. 14, 1985, and *Vanunu*, M.A. 64/87, *The Jerusalem Post*, Sep. 28, 1987). Counsel had urged that the court should apply the same test in cases of expulsion, since the non-disclosure of part of the evidence seriously impaired the deportee's ability to answer the charges.

It was true, Justice Bach said, that section 44(a) made no distinction between criminal cases and other cases to which it applied. However, there were basic differences between criminal cases and those of expulsion.

In the former, there was a presumption of innocence in the Defendant's favour, and the secret evidence generally related to marginal matters in the case. Moreover, section 74 of the Criminal Procedure Law (Consolidated Version) of 1982 entitled the Defendant to see the evidence against him, save where such disclosure was prohibited by law. He was unable, therefore, to accept counsel's argument on this point.

The legislature had made some provision to protect a person who was to be expelled. It had constituted the advisory committees, presided over by a jurist, which were empowered to examine all the evidence, including what was regarded as secret by the authorities. In addition, there was the right to petition the High Court of Justice.

Another form of protection was the practice now accepted by the court of itself examining all the relevant material, with the consent of both parties. Applicant's counsel in the present matter had preferred the examination of the documents by a single judge.

It had been suggested, Justice Bach continued, that in deciding what material, if any, may be disclosed, the court must strike a balance between the public interest and the interest of the individual. He himself had already said in the *Vanunu* case that he does not accept this approach. Protecting the individual from injustice is no less a public interest than protecting the community as a whole, and protecting the whole community indirectly serves the interest of the individual.

While giving full weight to the situation of the Applicant, it was clear, on the facts brought before him, that disclosure of some of the sources of information which the Respondent sought to protect would cause serious damage to the security of the state, and endanger human life. On the other hand, it was only those sources of information, hitherto not disclosed, which, in his view, should be disclosed to the Applicant. This disclosure would be made in addition to the disclosure of evidence to which counsel for the state had agreed at an earlier stage in the proceedings.

In conclusion, Justice Bach suggested that the legislature consider introducing into the framework of expulsions a provision similar to that in section 6(c) of the Emergency Powers (Arrests) Law of 1979, dealing with administrative detention. Under that section, the court is empowered, without the consent of the parties, to examine the secret material, without disclosing it to the detainee or his counsel, in order to decide what portion, if any, may be disclosed.

For the above reasons, the application was allowed in part, and portions of the evidence against the Applicant formerly withheld were to be disclosed to him and his counsel.

Avigdor Feldman, Lea Tsemel, and Abed Asli appeared for the Petitioner. Assistant State Attorney Malchiel Blass appeared for the State.

The decision was given on February 2, 1989.

UNFAIR DELAY

GAZIT INVESTMENTS v. REHOVOT TOWN PLANNING COMMISSION

In the Supreme Court sitting as a High Court of Justice before the President, Justice Meir Shamgar, Justice Ya'acov Maltz, and Judge Shula Wallenstein, in the matter of *Gazit Concilium Investments and Development Company Ltd.*, Petitioner, versus *The Rehovot Local Town Planning Commission*, Respondent (H.C. 100/88).

Administrative Law—Delay in Considering Town Planning Scheme—Decision Ordered by Fixed Date—Planning and Building Law, 1965.

The Petitioner (hereinafter called the company) acquired three plots of land in the center of Rehovot with the intention of expanding an unfinished building which had already been erected there. The company then lodged with the Respondent a detailed planning scheme under the Planning and Building Law of 1965 to cover the additional building operations not included in the original scheme relating to the unfinished building. This new scheme was confirmed by the District Town Planning Commission on August 25, 1976.

According to the Respondent, errors were subsequently discovered in the scheme which had been approved and, moreover, the company built in contravention of the scheme. As a result, legal proceedings were instituted against the company in 1980, and the demolition of the additions ordered by October 9, 1982.

Thereafter the company lodged a new scheme, which was considered by both the Local and District Commissions, but was not approved.

On November 18, 1984, the company lodged yet another scheme, which was transmitted by the Respondent to the District Commission on February 11, 1985, with the recommendation that it be approved after consideration by the legal adviser, and the finding of a solution to the parking problem.

However, on November 19, 1986, the Respondent decided to reconsider this latest scheme. The company then applied to the High Court of Justice to set aside this decision.

The company's application was considered by the court on February 16, 1987. At that hearing, the company withdrew its application on the basis that the Respondent would appoint a special sub-committee to consider the company's latest scheme, and report to the plenum. The sub-committee reached its decision on January 10, 1988, and the Respondent's chairman called a meeting of the full commission for February 21, 1988.

According to the Respondent, the company and its legal advisers were invited to the above meeting of the plenum, and were requested to present their arguments, despite the fact that they had appeared before the sub-committee on May 27, 1987, and June 7, 1987, and had then presented documents, and stated their case in detail. The company denied that it had received any formal invitation to the February 21 meeting.

In its present application, the company asked the court itself to examine the contentions of the parties regarding the scheme.

The judgment of the court was given by Justice Meir Shamgar.

It was not disputed, he said, that the proceedings relating to the company's schemes had lasted far too long. The sub-committee had not approved the company's last scheme, but had prepared an alternative one. There was nothing wrong in that. However, the long-drawn-out consideration of this matter, a known indication of inefficiency, was unreasonable.

Whether the question related to one scheme, or alternative schemes, a matter such as this must be decided without unnecessary delays, and without burdening the citizen who requires the decision of the authorities. A planning authority must realize that it receives its jurisdiction and powers in order to serve the public interest, which includes the consideration of the citizen's applications within a reasonable time.

If a citizen infringes a scheme, legal proceedings may be instituted against him. That in itself, however, is no justification for such a prolonged consideration of a scheme. Citizens applying to the planning authorities have different approaches to upholding the law, and differing interests in regard to planning schemes. However, in order to give a fair decision, each application must be considered on its merits.

The court would not place itself in the shoes of the planning commissions and deal with the schemes on their merits, nor would it order the company's applications to be placed at once before the District Commission, as the company had requested. The latter was entitled to have before it the opinion of the local commission, as the law required.

In the result, the court ordered the Respondent to hear the company, or its counsel, within 30 days and to give its decision within 30 days from the hearing.

The matter would then be referred to the District Commission. The court would not fix a time limit for the final decision of the District Commission.

The Respondent was ordered to pay the company's costs.

Yitzhak Yehiel and Gershon Darnes appeared for the Petitioner, and Zvi Terlo and Shlomo Segev appeared for the Respondent.

The judgment was given on March 6, 1989.

WHAT IS MORAL TURPITUDE?

UDAH v. JALJULIA LOCAL COUNCIL

In the Supreme Court sitting as a High Court of Justice, before Justice Aharon Barak, Justice Gavriel Bach and Judge Shulamit Wallenstein, in the matter of *Wagi'a Udah*, Petitioner, versus *Talal Raabi, Chairman of the Local Council of Jaljulia, and another*, Respondents (H.C. 251/88).

Constitutional Law—Forfeiture of Seat on Local Council—"Moral Turpitude"— Local Councils Order (A), 1950—Penal Law, 1977, section 432.

Under section 101(7) of Local Councils Order (A) of 1950, an elected council member who has been convicted, within five years of his becoming a member, of a crime involving moral turpitude, shall be disqualified from continuing his membership. Under section 105(a) of the Order, where it appears to the chairman of a council that a member has become disqualified under section 101, he shall inform the member that his seat on the council has become vacant.

The Petitioner, a member of the local council of Jaljulia, and a company under his control, were convicted of passing a cheque without cover, in contravention of section 432 of the Penal Law of 1977. The first Respondent then sent the Petitioner a notice under section 105(a) above, and the Petitioner moved the High Court of Justice to set it aside, on the ground that it had been issued unlawfully.

The judgment of the court was given by Justice Aharon Barak. The fate of the application, he said, depended on the meaning of the expression "moral turpitude." This expression was vague, and its application to different sets of circumstances was unclear. Not every crime involved moral turpitude.

After reviewing precedents of the Supreme Court and other authorities, Justice Barak held that the distinction between crimes involving moral turpitude and those which did not, was not to be found in the formal elements constituting the offence. The test was the circumstances in which the crime was committed.

The decisions of the Supreme Court seemed to reveal some differences of opinion on this subject, Justice Barak continued.

Justice Haim Cohn had held that the test as to whether moral turpitude existed or not was the opinion of "the reasonable man."

Justice Moshe Landau was said to have differed from this view. According to him, it was not the conditions in the market of municipal politics which should set the standard of morality required. In his opinion, it was intended in section 101(7) that the court should set the standard.

In his opinion, said Justice Barak, the above two opinions were only two aspects of the same approach. The "reasonable man" was the court, and the reasonableness required was none other than the balance between the different social values and principles appropriate to a democratic and enlightened society.

A crime "involving moral turpitude," therefore, was one in which the circumstances of its commission showed that the criminal had been guilty of a serious moral lapse. The nature of that lapse was to be judged by the legislative context in which the expression appeared.

The Local Councils Order dealt with the disqualification of a person from being a member of a local council, and the moral turpitude spoken of, therefore, was connected with the demands of an enlightened society regarding those holding public office. The emphasis was on conduct revealing corruption, or necessarily showing a moral lapse.

The central conception was that the elected holder of public office in an enlightened society, who needs the confidence of the public, must maintain a proper standard of moral behaviour, both in his private and in his public conduct, to enable him to continue in office.

In this context, therefore, a crime "involving moral turpitude" was one in connection with which the moral conduct of the public official concerned was so base that he was no longer fit to hold public office. As had been held in one case, he must be unfit to be in the society of honest men, and unfit to be responsible for decisions on which the safety of the community depends.

In the present case, Justice Barak continued, the circumstances of the offence were not disclosed in the indictment, and no evidence was presented, since the Petitioner admitted that he had passed a cheque without cover, as was alleged against him.

In arguing on the question of sentence, however, the Petitioner's counsel had explained that his client had made a verbal arrangement with the manager of the bank, enabling him to have an overdraft which would have covered the amount of the cheque in question.

Unfortunately, the manager had been changed, and the new manager, who belonged to a political group opposed to the Petitioner, denied that any such arrangement existed. Petitioner's counsel explained that the Petitioner had decided to plead guilty, since he saw no prospect of successfully contradicting the statement of the new manager that no arrangement for an overdraft was made.

Counsel had now pointed out, said Justice Barak, that the Petitioner had made immediate arrangements to cover the cheque, after being informed that it had been dishonoured.

For the purposes of the present application, Justice Barak said, it must be assumed that the Petitioner's versions was true. In these circumstances, the real issue was of a civil nature, and no question of moral turpitude was involved.

It appeared, Justice Barak continued, that the Petitioner had other previous convictions for passing cheques that were dishonoured. These took place more than five years before he became a member of the council, and the court had had no opportunity of seeing the records of those convictions.

However, counsel had stated that in those instances, too, the dishonour had occurred despite an arrangement for an overdraft with the bank manager. In the absence of any information to contradict this statement, no inference against the Petitioner, from the point of view of the relief he now sought, could be drawn.

For the above reasons, the petition was allowed, and the notice sent to the Petitioner by the chairman of the council was set aside, with no order as to costs.

Advocate Yeshayahu Etgar appeared for the Petitioner, and Advocate Ya'acov Lerer appeared for the Respondents.

The judgment was given on February 20, 1989.

THE RIGHT TO INHERIT

ALON v. MENDELSON

In the Supreme Court sitting as a Court of Civil Appeals before the President, Justice Meir Shamgar, Justice Eliezer Goldberg, and Justice Ya'acov Maltz, in the matter of *Sarah Alon*, Appellant, versus *Freda Mendelson*, Respondent (C.A. 107/87).

Personal Status—Right of Inheritance of Putative Wife—"Common Household"— Succession Law, 1965, section 55.

Under section 55 of the Succession Law of 1965, "Where a man and a woman, though not being married to one another, have lived together as husband and wife in a common household, then, upon the death of one of them, neither being then married to another person, the deceased is deemed, subject to any contrary direction expressed or implied in the will of the deceased, to have bequeathed to the survivor what the survivor would have inherited on intestacy if they had been married to one another."

The Appellant, the only remaining child of the deceased, Moshe Shmueli, a widower who died in 1984, applied to the District Court of Tel Aviv for an order declaring her to be the sole heir of her father. The Respondent opposed the application on the basis that she was the reputed wife of the deceased, and entitled, therefore, to inherit half his estate under section 55 above. The court upheld the Respondent's claim, and the Appellant appealed to the Supreme Court.

The judgment of the court was given by Justice Meir Shamgar.

The Supreme Court had already held, he said, that section 55 contained two elements: a relationship such as that between husband and wife, based on love and affection, devotion and fidelity; and a joint household, not for purposes of convenience, but as is accepted between married couples. The test to be applied as to whether these elements have been proved is flexible, depending on the concrete circumstances of each case.

Section 55 was based on the assumption that where the two elements mentioned existed, and the deceased left no will, he regarded the survivor as his heir. The court had said, in this context, that there was no intention of adding a third element in section 55, namely, proof that the deceased had resolved, specifically or impliedly, that the survivor should be his heir. The question was whether the relationship between the parties gave a basis for the assumption that such was the case.

Justice Shamgar then reviewed the evidence upon the basis of which the District Court had ruled in the Respondent's favour. That court had heard the evidence not only of the Respondent herself, but also of friends and neighbours.

The couple had lived together for six years, until the deceased's death, and during the last four years they had lived in the Respondent's apartment. Although the relationship between them had started with the Respondent, a niece of the deceased's wife, assisting him in his home, it subsequently became closer. For this reason the deceased went to live in the Respondent's flat. They attended social functions together, and travelled together overseas.

At a certain stage, the Appellant stopped visiting her father, from which the District Court had concluded that she resented the close relationship between the couple. The Respondent ran the home, and they ate their meals together. They conducted their financial affairs separately, but the Respondent paid monies into the deceased's account when necessary.

Finally, although the deceased's brother had asked him to make a will leaving his whole estate to the Appellant, he had not done so.

Appellant's counsel, Justice Shamgar continued, had raised three main arguments against the District Court's decision.

He had contended that the original relationship, under which the Respondent had been only a household help to the deceased, had persisted until the deceased's death; that the element in section 55 of the couple having "lived together as husband and wife" had not been established; and that since the couple had each managed his and her own financial affairs separately, they had not lived together "in a common household."

There was no basis for interfering with the District Court's finding on the first point, said Justice Shamgar.

As to the second point, he cited Supreme Court authority on the meaning of "lived together as husband and wife." It embraced three elements: *torus*, intimate relationship; *mensa*, support; and the emotional factor, "love, brotherhood, peace and fellowship."

These elements were not capable of clear definition, and even the absence of one of them did not necessarily mean that the condition in the section was not satisfied.

There was no direct evidence in the present case that the couple had engaged in intimate relations. However, the District Court was entitled to conclude, on the evidence before it, that the relationship between the couple was such as to create the possibility of such relations, subject, of course, to physical disabilities, as distinct from emotional difficulties which would have prevented it.

With regard to the third argument, Justice Shamgar said, the expression "a common household" did not necessarily mean a pooling of the couple's resources. As the Supreme Court had held, it meant a sharing of the common dwelling — food, drink, lodging, clothing, and the other features of everyday life. The evidence in the present case supported the conclusion that this condition had been proved.

The result was, said Justice Shamgar, that the decision of the District Court was correct, and the appeal, therefore, would be dismissed.

Ben-Zion Tzinani appeared for the Appellant, and Musari Goldenberg appeared for the Respondent.

Judgment was on April 27, 1979.

'THE LAST TEMPTATION OF CHRIST':
THE CASE FOR FREEDOM OF SPEECH

UNIVERSAL CITY STUDIOS v. FILMS CENSORSHIP BOARD

In the Supreme Court sitting as a High Court of Justice before the
President, Justice Meir Shamgar, Justice Aharon Barak, Justice Shlomo
Levin, Justice Eliezer Goldberg, and Justice Ya'acov Maltz, in the
matter of *Universal City Studios Inc. and others*, Petitioners, versus *The
Films and Plays Censorship Board and others*, Respondents (H.C. 806/88)

*Administrative Law—Freedom of Speech—Censorship—Banning of Film Set
Aside—Penal Law of 1977, section 173.*

The Petitioners applied to The Films and Plays Censorship Board to
permit the screening in Israel of the film "The Last Temptation of Christ."
The application was refused, and the Petitioners applied to the High Court
of Justice for an order directing the Board to grant the permit sought.

The first judgment of the court was given by Justice Meir Shamgar. The
film, he said, was made in Morocco, based on a book by the Greek writer
Nikos Kazantzakis, and produced by Martin Scorsese. It describes the life
of Jesus from the time of his stay in Jerusalem — including his baptism in
the River Jordan, his being joined by his apostles, his miracles, and the
spreading of his doctrines — until his crucifixion.

The film contains realistic overtones, and expresses the open and clear
intention of the author and producer to introduce human characteristics
into the personality of Jesus, as against the accepted conception of believers
in the Christian faith. At the same time, the film is dominated by a deeply
Christian theme, an outstanding example of which is the description of the
miracles. While, therefore, it contains deviations from accepted Christian
doctrine, the producers can reply that many accepted works of art depict
the same features and have been the subject of many theological and
philosophical disputes.

Those opposed to screening, Justice Shamgar continued, relied particularly on a section showing a kind of hallucination, an erotic scene in which
the hero of the film takes part. It depicts the reflections of Jesus on an
alternative form of living to being the victim of crucifixion. This is one of
the sections describing the efforts of Satan to tempt Jesus, from which the
film derives its title.

His description of the film, the President added, was not intended to furnish any rigid or complete identifying or typifying indications of the ideas or descriptions which it contained. His sole purpose was to emphasize the cleavage of opinion as to its being screened in Israel.

The Censorship Board was of the opinion, Justice Shamgar said, that "the screening of the film, which deals with the very foundations of Christianity, will be deeply offensive to the religious feelings and faith of the Christian community." The question thus arose as to the criteria to be applied by the court in reviewing the Board's decision.

The basis of the court's enquiry, he said, was the great principle of freedom of speech, which was the source, *inter alia*, of the freedom of artistic creativity in the field of both literature and the visual arts. It made no difference whether the creation was a written theoretical philosophical analysis, or a play, or other visual medium.

For us, it is clear and simple that a man is entitled to give public expression to his ideas and thoughts, including his interpretation of events in the past, the present and the future, without restraint. This is the central feature of the freedom of human thought, and man's ability to achieve self-expression.

Freedom of speech flows from the doctrine that the law may not prevent a man from behaving as he wishes except for some positive reason relating to damage, or possible damage, which may be caused to another. Freedom of speech, therefore, cannot be absolute, but must be exercised so as not to damage another, or disturb public order.

Justice Shamgar then cited Supreme Court precedents dealing with the restriction of the right of free speech, including cases in which the banning of a film or play was discussed.

The Board was entitled to ban a film whose screening would disturb public order. The court had held that "public order" was a wide term, "the definition of which is difficult, and changes according to the context. It includes an impairment to the existence of the state, its democratic regime, the public welfare, morality, religious sentiments, a man's good name, ensuring fair judicial process, and other similar features concerning public order."

At the same time, the court had accorded freedom of speech a special status among the basic freedoms. The court had once held, for example, that "bad taste" would be a ground for banning a film, but he doubted whether the court would rule so today.

"Bad taste" was a subjective expression, and neither the Board nor the court was a guardian of good taste. According to the proper criteria, only a serious, significant and extreme impairment of public order would justify the restriction of free speech. The court had to strike a balance between competing freedoms, and only a far-reaching, deep and blatant impairment could limit freedom of speech.

Justice Shamgar also cited a well-known passage from a judgment of Justice Louis Brandeis, of the United States Supreme Court:

"Fear of serious injury cannot alone justify suppression of free speech and assembly. Men feared witches and burnt women. It is the function of speech to free men from the bondage of irrational fears. To justify suppression of free speech there must be reasonable ground to fear that serious evil will result if free speech is practised. There must be reasonable ground to believe that the danger apprehended is imminent. There must be reasonable ground to believe that the evil to be prevented is a serious one."

On the basis of the above considerations, the court had adopted the rule that only a "near certainty" that freedom of speech, in a particular, concrete case, would impair the security of the state, or public order, would entitle the competent statutory authority to restrict that freedom.

It was true, Justice Shamgar continued, that serious offence to religious sentiment could justify the banning of a film. The circumstances of the present case, however, did not justify such a ban. The Christian world was in itself pluralistic, and the court would have to be convinced that the literary and artistic subjective expressions of Kazantzakis and Scorsese are so offensive to Christian belief as to justify their suppression in Israel.

The fact that the film might arouse opposition, or even disgust, among some viewers, was not sufficient. It could not be overlooked that Jesus is portrayed in the film in a positive and sympathetic manner, and that his superhuman powers are a basic concept of the author and producer. In fact, it is only the Jewish fighters against Rome, and that section of the simple people of Jerusalem and its surroundings who did not follow Jesus, who are described negatively. That, of course, was not sufficient ground to ban the film.

His main consideration, the president continued, was the fact that the vast majority of the Christian world would view the film in the countries of the West and not in the cinemas of Israel. It was completely illogical that a film that was so offensive to the Christian community that it should be banned in Israel was screened widely in Christian countries such as Italy, Spain, Germany and France.

It had been argued that the level of culture and sophistication of the Christian community in Israel was below that of the communities in the West. This argument had unacceptable undertones, and was quite unconvincing. It was an insult to the Christian community in Israel, and had no factual basis whatever. There was no reason to think that the Christians of Nazareth are of a lower cultural level than those of Calabria.

Since there was no "near certainty" of a serious and far-reaching impairment of public order in the screening of the film, which alone could justify its being banned, the decision of the Censorship Board could not be supported.

Justice Shamgar proposed, therefore, that the application be allowed, and the decision of the Board be set aside.

Justice Aharon Barak concurred. Citing several Supreme Court precedents, he emphasized that freedom of expression gave democracy the breath of life. Without that freedom, democracy would lose its soul. That freedom, therefore, enjoyed a special status. It ensured the existence of a democratic regime, and thus secured the existence of other basic rights.

Every discussion of freedom of expression, Justice Barak said, raised two questions: what was included in that freedom, and what protection was afforded by the law to what was expressed?

The Supreme Court had already explained that the process of democracy was one of investigating the truth, and that "the principle of freedom of expression serves as a means and an instrument for the purpose of investigating that truth, for only by considering all points of view, and a free exchange of all opinions, is the truth likely to be reached."

Freedom of expression, therefore, covers all opinions, popular and unpopular, acceptable and arousing opposition, offensive to religious belief, and even abominable.

As the court had held, however, freedom did not mean unbridled licence. There were circumstances in which freedom of expression had to be curbed. This occurred, in some cases, because of the content of what was expressed, such as matter that is defamatory, or obscene, or *sub judice*.

In other cases, freedom of expression had to be curtailed because of the necessity to protect other basic freedoms. In those cases, the court had to find a balance between the "competing" freedoms. Moreover, this had to be done by the application of objective tests. The matter was not to be decided by the subjective feelings of the members of the statutory body concerned, in this case the Censorship Board, nor by the individual feelings of the judges.

In the present case, Justice Barak continued, the question arose whether religious sentiment was a value which the law should protect. In his opinion, it was. Indeed, under section 173 of the Penal Law of 1977, offending religious sentiment was a crime. The Censorship Board, therefore, was entitled to take this factor into consideration.

As Justice Felix Frankfurter had said, "To criticize or assail religious doctrine may wound to the quick those who are attached to the doctrine and profoundly cherish it. But to bar such pictorial discussion is to subject non-conformists to the rule of sects."

The Supreme Court had held, said Justice Barak, that only a "near certainty" of "hard, serious and severe" damage to another basic value would justify the restriction of free expression. The court, therefore, had to ask itself, objectively, whether a reasonable censorship board could find, in the present case, that such a "near certainty" existed. In his opinion, it could not. Counsel for the Respondents had conceded that in the circumstances of this case, no criminal offence had been committed. Moreover, the very fact that the film was shown in many Christian countries, in some of which censorship of films existed, showed that the film was not so offensive as to justify its being banned in a democratic regime which recognized freedom of expression, and was built on tolerance towards opposing views.

Justice Barak agreed, therefore, to the granting of the order sought.

Justice Shlomo Levin agreed, mainly on the grounds advanced by Justice Barak. He added that the Board's decision had been based, partly, on the possible political damage that would be caused to the State if the film were screened, but he disagreed that such damage would be caused.

Justice Eliezer Goldberg agreed. There was no need in the present case, he said, for the court to assess the reasonableness of the possibility of damage to another basic right if the film were screened, for the court could decide itself, by what it saw and heard, if such a possibility existed. There was no doubt, in this instance, that showing the film would offend a section of those believing in the Christian faith.

The central question was whether there was an irreconcilable conflict between freedom of expression and the offence to religious sentiment, which demanded a solution by the court. He in no sense underestimated the offence which would be caused to some viewers of the film; but neither the gravity nor the extent of that offence made him question the words of the wisest of all men: "*There is no man that hath power over the spirit to imprison the spirit.*" (Ecclesiastes 8:8.)

Justice Goldberg concurred, therefore, in the judgment of the President.

Justice Ya'acov Maltz also agreed with the legal analysis of the President, and with his conclusion.

He had found only one passage, he said, which was seriously offensive. It portrayed an imaginary conversation between Jesus and Paul, in which the latter said: "If you had not already been crucified, I myself would have crucified you."

Justice Maltz said he had considered proposing the showing of the film with the excision of that passage. However, he had concluded that, against the background of the film as a whole, the passage would not create a near certainty of damage to state security, or public order.

Justice Maltz also agreed, therefore, to the granting of the application.

For the above reasons, the petition was allowed, and the banning of the film set aside.

Dov Peri and Shaul Stratzker appeared for the Petitioners, and Nili Arad, Director of the High Court Division of the State Attorney's Office, appeared for the Respondents.

The judgment was given on June 15, 1989.

RELIEF FROM TAXATION

KFAR VERADIM v. MINISTER OF FINANCE

In the Supreme Court sitting as a High Court of Justice before Justice Dov Levin, Justice Avraham Halima, and Justice Theodore Orr, in the matter of *Kfar Veradim and Eli Eliyahu*, Petitioners, versus *The Ministers of Finance and Defence and the Knesset Finance Committee*, Respondents (H.C. 678, 803/88).

Income Tax—Administrative Law—Unjust Discrimination—Recognition of Tax Exemption Wrongly Withheld—Income Tax Ordinance (New Version), 1961— Income Tax Regulations (Tax Exemptions in Settlements of the Northern Border), 1985.

On November 4, 1985, the Minister of Finance published the Income Tax Regulations (Tax Exemptions in Settlements of the Northern Border), 1985. The regulations were published under section 11 of the Income Tax Ordinance (New Version), whereby the minister is empowered, with the confirmation of the Knesset Finance Committee, to make regulations granting a tax exemption on the income of a resident in the area of a new settlement, or a development area, as defined in the regulations.

The regulations were issued after discussions in the Ministerial Economic Affairs Committee and the government, in which it was decided to grant an exemption of 10 per cent on the taxable income of residents of settlements on Israel's northern border. In the result, the exemption is granted to settlements on what is known as the "frontier line." These settlements are set out in a list prepared by the IDF,* and include two categories — those in the framework of regional brigades, and those regarded as an attractive target for enemy terrorist activity and artillery shelling.

Except for Shavei Zion, because of its proximity to Nahariya which is regarded as a terrorist target, and four settlements of the minorities, because of their proximity to the border, only the residents of settlements included in the list enjoy the exemption.

The settlements of Kfar Veradim and Ein Ya'acov, of which the Petitioner Eli Eliyahu is a member, are not included in the list, and therefore are also not covered by the above regulations. The application of these two settlements to the Minister of Finance to be included in the regulations having been refused, the Petitioners applied to the High Court of Justice for relief.

The judgment of the court was delivered by Justice Theodore Orr.

Petitioners' counsel, he said, had argued that the Minister of Finance, who alone was empowered by section 11 of the Income Tax Ordinance to make the regulations in question, had not weighed the matter himself, but had transferred his authority to the Minister of Defence. The IDF had compiled the list of frontier settlements, and the Finance Minister had simply accepted it as his own.

Counsel had also argued that the minister's refusal to include Veradim and Ein Ya'acov in the list was based on unjust discrimination, was unreasonable to the extent of being capricious, and amounted to his having acted beyond his powers.

In reply to the petition, Justice Orr continued, the Minister of Defence had argued that the regulations had been issued by the Minister of Finance, who alone was responsible for their provisions. The IDF had acted merely in an advisory capacity, and there was therefore no basis for the petition against him.

---

* Israel Defence Force.

The Minister of Finance had argued that he was entitled to be assisted by the IDF in preparing the list of frontier settlements. These carried an exceptional defence burden, which also involved the investment of financial resources, and it was only proper that they should enjoy some exemption from income tax. He had also contended that Veradim and Ein Ya'acov did not answer the criteria for inclusion in the list, and that their exclusion was logical and reasonable and did not constitute unjust discrimination.

The argument that the Finance Minister was not entitled to rely on the list prepared by the IDF, could not be accepted. The question whether a particular northern settlement bore an exceptionally heavy defence burden, with all the economic and personal effort involved, was connected with the knowledge and expertise of the defence authorities in the area. Just as the minister would be entitled to establish an advisory committee to help him reach a decision, he was entitled to rely on a list compiled by experts, provided he was satisfied that they acted in good faith, and on the basis of clear criteria open to review.

It was not simple to find the real reason for the exclusion of the two settlements in the voluminous correspondence between the Petitioners and the two ministers. The replies to the Petitioners were often delayed, and the answers given vague and inconsistent. It must be remembered that the citizen had nothing before him but the reply of the authorities, and vagueness and inconsistency could lead him — and sometimes even the court — to doubt the truth of what he had been told.

In the present case, however, he had decided that the Minister had consistently applied the policy of basing himself on the IDF list. It remained, therefore, to examine whether the two settlements had been justifiably excluded, or whether they had been the victims of unjust discrimination.

Justice Orr then cited Supreme Court precedents on the subject of discrimination, emphasizing that not all discrimination was unjust. Unjust discrimination meant a different attitude towards equals. It implied unfairness in giving different treatment to those entitled to the same treatment. It meant treating people differently out of caprice, without justification, in the absence of any real, reasonable difference in their circumstances.

Counsel for Veradim, said Justice Orr, had argued that Meona which, from the defence point of view, was in exactly the same position as Veradim, had been included in the list. He himself had come to the conclusion that there was no ground for treating Veradim differently from Meona, and that the argument of unjust discrimination in this case was therefore justified.

On the other hand, he held that the exclusion of Ein Ya'acov was justified.

The Minister of Defence, said Justice Orr, was right in arguing that the IDF had acted in an advisory capacity only, and that there had been no ground, therefore, for filing a petition against him.

For the above reasons, the petition against the Minister of Finance in regard to Veradim was allowed, and the minister was ordered to include it in the list of settlements enjoying tax exemption. The petition relating to Ein Ya'acov, and the petitions against the Minister of Defence, were dismissed.

Mishael Cheshin, Zvi Agmon and Meir Hefler appeared for the Petitioners, and Senior Assistant State Attorney Uzi Fogelman appeared for the Respondents.

The judgment was given on July 18, 1989.

CONTROLS ON DEMOLITION

A.C.R.I. v. IDF COMMANDERS OF
CENTRAL AND SOUTHERN COMMANDS

In the Supreme Court sitting as a High Court of Justice before the President, Justice Meir Shamgar, the Deputy-President, Justice Menahem Elon, and Judge Shulamit Wallenstein, in the matter of *The Civil Rights Association in Israel, and others*, Petitioners, versus *The IDF Commanders of the Central and Southern Commands*, Respondents (H.C. 358/88).

Administrative Law—Demolition or Sealing of House—Right of Occupier to be Heard—Hague Regulations, 1943, Regulation 43—Fourth Geneva Convention, 1949, Article 64—Defence (Emergency) Regulations, 1945, Regulation 119— Law and Administration Ordinance, 1948, section 11—Proclamation Relating to Law and Administration (No. 2), 1967.

The Petitioners applied to the High Court of Justice for an order directing the Respondents to enable the occupier of a house to be demolished or sealed off under Regulation 119 of the Defence (Emergency) Regulations of

1945; to present his arguments to the competent authority before the demolition or closing off is effected; to afford him an additional period of 48 hours to petition the court if his representations are unsuccessful; to allow him to contact a lawyer immediately if he so desires; and directing the Respondents to inform the occupier of the house of his above rights.

The judgment of the court was given by Justice Meir Shamgar. He began by quoting the above regulation, emphasizing the passages in italics, as follows:

"(1) *A military commander* may by order *direct the forfeiture to the Government of Israel of any house*, structure, or land from which he has reason to suspect that any firearm has been illegally discharged, or any bomb, grenade, or explosive or incendiary article illegally thrown, detonated, exploded, or otherwise discharged, or of any house, structure or land situated in any town, village, quarter or street, *the inhabitants or some of the inhabitants of which he is satisfied have committed, or attempted to commit, or abetted the commission of,* or been accessories after the fact to the commission of, any offence against these Regulations *involving violence or intimidation or any Military Court offence.* And when any house, structure or land is forfeited as aforesaid, *the military commander may destroy the house,* the structure, or anything in or on the house, the structure or the land.

"Where any house, structure or land has been forfeited by order of a military commander as above, the Minister of Defence may, at any time by order remit the forfeiture, in whole or in part, and thereupon, to the extent of such remission, the ownership of the house, structure or land, and all interests and easements of the persons who would have been entitled to the same if the order of forfeiture had not been made, and all charges on the house, structure or land, shall revive for the benefit of the person who would have been entitled thereto, if the order of forfeiture had not been made.

"(2) Members of Government Forces, or of the Police Force, acting under the authority of the military commander, may seize and occupy, without compensation, any such property in any such area, town, village, quarter or street, as is referred to in subregulation (1), after eviction without compensation of the previous occupiers, if any."

Citing several Supreme Court precedents, Justice Shamgar held that the above regulations were part of the law of Israel by virtue of section 11 of the Law and Administration Ordinance of 1948, under which the existing law remains in force subject to other Israeli enactments, and subject to such modifications as may result from the establishment of the State and its authorities.

They also became part of the law in Judea and Samaria, he said, by virtue of similar Jordanian legislation as to the continuation in force of British Mandatory legislation in Jordan. Since there had been no material change in the law in the Gaza Strip since the time of the Mandate, the regulations remained in force there as well.

The Petitioners argued, Justice Shamgar continued, that military commanders acting under emergency regulations are obliged to apply the principles of natural justice recognized in Israeli law in the same way as any other executive authority. Those principles demand that an individual whose person or property will be affected by an administrative act of the authorities is entitled to an opportunity to state his case before action is taken against him. The fact that the above regulations, or emergency regulations under section 9 of the above Ordinance, do not contain provisions stipulating this right of the person affected, does not mean that the right does not exist.

The Petitioners also argued that the delay in taking action which they now urged would prevent the military commander from acting rashly, possibly because of his own sense of outrage at the terrorist act committed, or because of his desire to assuage public anger.

The Petitioners also contended that the insistence of the army authorities on acting immediately was intended to frustrate any attempt to apply to the court for assistance, since it was known that the High Court of Justice does not intervene in matters which have become purely academic. The Petitioners emphasized particularly that the demolition of a house was final and irreversible.

The Respondents replied that, in many cases, an opportunity was afforded to the occupier of the house to make his representations, or to apply to the court. They also stated that the occupier could consult a lawyer, if he so wished.

On the other hand, they pointed out that there was nothing in the regulation to require them to delay taking action, and that in exceptionally serious cases, or where the commander is of the opinion that the circumstances demand a speedy and effective deterrent, no opportunity would be given to the occupier to state his case. Such circumstances include, today, the throwing of petrol bombs.

Justice Shamgar added that the court had suggested that the army should, in the first instance, be satisfied with sealing the house, postponing the demolition, if this be ordered, until the occupier had stated his case, or applied to the court. Counsel for the Petitioners, he said, had accepted the suggestion, but the Minister of Defence had rejected it.

The President then referred to the Proclamation Relating to Law and Administration (No. 2) of 1967, under which the law which existed in the Gaza Strip, and in Judea and Samaria, on June 5 and 6, 1967, respectively, continued to apply.

This Proclamation gave expression to the principles of public international law as included also, *inter alia*, in Regulation 43 of The Hague Regulations of 1943, and Article 64 of the Fourth Geneva Convention of 1949.

At the same time, he continued, the Supreme Court had held that the legality of actions of military officials is also tested by the principles of Israeli administrative law.

This did not mean that that law applied to the occupied territories and their inhabitants. What it meant was that military officials in the above areas, like Israeli executive officials everywhere, must act according to the legal standards demanded of such officials in Israel itself, namely, the standards of fair and proper administration.

These military officials, therefore, did not discharge their duty only by applying public international law. They were under the additional duty of applying the administrative norms laid down by the court, including the duty — save only in the most extreme cases — of giving a hearing to those affected by their actions.

Justice Shamgar also cited a passage previously quoted by the court from his essay on "Legal Concepts and Problems of the Israeli Military Government" that:

"From the normative point of view, the rule of law in the territories found its expression in the adoption of two main principles of action: (1) The prevention of the development of a legal vacuum by the *de facto* observance of customary international law and the humanitarian rules included in The Hague Rules and the Fourth Convention and, furthermore; (2) The supplementation of the above-mentioned rules and provisions by the basic principles of natural justice as derived from the system of law existing in Israel, reflecting similar principles developed in Western democracies."

It was not to be understood from what was said above, he continued, that the local law in the territories was to be regarded as automatically amended to conform to the rules of natural justice applied by the court. The law remained as it was, and could only be changed by legislative action.

Justice Shamgar then reviewed the general obligations of the military commander citing, *inter alia*, the work of Sir Hersch Lauterpacht on *The Law of War on Land*.

He pointed out that the prevention of violence was a necessary condition for the preservation of security and public order. There could be no security without law enforcement, and enforcement would be ineffective without a deterrent element.

One of the legal sanctions contained in the local law was Regulation 119. Its application was within the discretion of the military commander, and the court would examine if that discretion was exercised lawfully; if the commander had weighed all the circumstances correctly; and if the degree of application of the regulation was commensurate with the seriousness of the act complained of.

Everyone agreed that Regulation 119 was a harsh and serious punishment, and its deterrent effect did not detract from its severity. One of its central features, in the case of demolition, was that it was irreversible, so that any consideration after the event would have only a very limited effect.

It was of great importance, therefore, according to our legal conceptions, that the person affected be enabled to state his case before the action is taken, in order to acquaint the commander with facts and arguments which he may have overlooked.

There were military operational circumstances, Justice Shamgar continued, which precluded prior judicial review. For example, a military unit may be required, in the course of an operation, to remove a barrier, or overcome opposition, or react immediately to a military or civilian attack. Or there may be other conditions in which the competent military authority finds it necessary to take immediate operational action.

In all other circumstances, however, ways must be found to afford the person affected a right to be heard.

Since the establishment of the Military Administration in 1967, the President continued, the High Court of Justice had never closed its doors against complaints or appeals of the residents of Judea, Samaria and Gaza, and had treated them in exactly the same way as anyone else who had approached the court. There was no legal or other justification for a policy whereby, especially in cases where the actions of the authorities are irreversible, the court should close its doors and refuse to hear arguments against the acts of the Military Administration.

For the above reasons, the court ordered (1) that except in cases of immediate operational necessity, as described above, an order under Regulation 119 should contain a notification permitting the person affected to consult a lawyer to state his case, within a prescribed period, before the military commander, and thereafter, if he so wishes, and within a prescribed period, to petition the court before the order is implemented; (2) that the State be allowed, if it so wishes, to apply to the court to advance the hearing of a petition lodged as aforesaid; and (3) that in urgent cases, a house may be sealed off — as distinct from demolished — before the hearing of the appeal or petition. In such a case, the person concerned must be informed that his right to a hearing before the military commander, and thereafter to petition the court, is not affected.

Yehoshua Shofman appeared for the Petitioners, and Nili Arad, Director of the High Court Division of the State Attorney's Office, appeared for the Respondents.

The judgment was given on July 30, 1989.

REFORM RABBIS AND MARRIAGE LAW

MOVEMENT FOR PROGRESSIVE JUDAISM v. MINISTER FOR RELIGIOUS AFFAIRS

In the Supreme Court sitting as a High Court of Justice before the President, Justice Meir Shamgar, the Deputy-President, Justice Menahem Elon, Justice Shlomo Levin, Justice Dov Levin, and Justice Eliezer Goldberg, in the matter of *The Movement for Progressive Judaism in Israel, and others*, Petitioners, versus *The Minister for Religious Affairs and the Council of the Chief Rabbinate of Israel*, Respondents (H.C. 47/82).

Administrative Law—Refusal to Register Reform Rabbis as Marriage Registrars—Jewish Religious Law—Chief Rabbinate of Israel Law, 1980, section 2(6)—Rabbinical Courts Jurisdiction (Marriage and Divorce) Law, 1953, section 2.

On February 15, 1980, the Petitioners applied to the Minister for Religious Affairs to recognize two Reform rabbis as "registering authorities" for the celebration and registration of marriages under the Marriage and Divorce (Registration) Ordinance of 1919. The Minister replied that he could only grant the application if the Chief Rabbinate Council first confirmed the candidates' eligibility to be so recognized. The Petitioners did not agree that the Council's opinion was necessary, but they nevertheless approached that body too to agree to their request.

The Council in its reply referred to section 2(6) of the Chief Rabbinate of Israel Law of 1980, under which one of the Council's functions is "the conferment upon a rabbi of eligibility to serve as a rabbi and marriage registrar." The Council added that the conditions for eligibility were the same as those required for the appointment of a rabbi of a town or community, namely, that the candidate's life-style was appropriate, and that he had passed examinations in Talmud and rabbinical responsa. Moreover, eligibility was granted only to one who functioned as a community rabbi, and after consideration of the needs of that particular community.

Since the Applicants did not fulfil these requirements, their application could not be granted. The Petitioners then approached the High Court of Justice for relief.

The hearing before the court was postponed from time to time in an effort to find an agreed solution to the dispute, but without success. In the meantime, the Council filed further documents, stressing that it was influenced by halachic* considerations alone, particularly in the light of section 2 of the Rabbinical Courts Jurisdiction (Marriage and Divorce) Law of 1953, under which "Marriages and Divorces of Jews shall be performed in Israel in accordance with Jewish religious law." The Petitioners also filed further material, explaining their refusal to comply with the Council's requirements.

The first judgment of the court was given by Justice Menahem Elon, who dealt first with Supreme Court precedents in the time of the British Mandate relating to the 1919 Ordinance. It had been held clearly that the authority registering the marriage was the same authority that celebrated the marriage, and the court had then laid down that:

"As regards Jews, the rabbi entitled to be recognized by the District Commissioner as registering authority is the rabbi designated by the competent religious authority of the Jewish community (i.e., the organized Jewish Community — A.F.L.) and persons who are not members of the Jewish community, whether organized as a congregation or not, have no statutory right to have their own rabbis officiating as registering authorities

---

*   Jewish Law.

... To an outsider the law as stated may appear to be hard on those persons who, for one reason or another, have elected to opt out of the Jewish community. The answer to that objection is that, good or bad, that is the law... On the other hand, one cannot overlook the danger — to which the Respondents themselves must be alive no less than anyone else — if it is held that any group of persons can organize themselves into a congregation for religious purposes . . . appoint rabbis, and thus become registering authorities. The main object of the Ordinance would then be defeated, and the purpose of keeping the celebration of marriages and divorces within the framework of law and good order, undermined."

Justice Elon then pointed out that after the establishment of the State, the function of the District Commissioner as the civil authority under the above Ordinance had been assumed by the Minister for Religious Affairs. The requirement of the prior agreement of the Council, however, remained in full force and, indeed, had been specifically incorporated into the law of Israel by section 2 (6) of the Chief Rabbinate of Israel Law of 1980. The same result flowed from section 2 of the Rabbinical Courts Jurisdiction Law of 1953, quoted above. He also referred, in this regard, to the rules laid down by the Chief Rabbinate in 1950, known as "The Jerusalem Ban," under which every rabbi or other person in Israel is prohibited from solemnizing marriages "unless he has been authorized and appointed to perform this function by the writ and signature of the chief rabbis of the towns of Eretz Yisrael." The Supreme Court had held that these rules, too, formed part of Israeli law.

The Petitioners had argued against the above conclusion, continued Justice Elon. They had contended that once the State was established, not only was the Minister not obliged to refer the matter to the Chief Rabbinate Council, but he was not permitted to do so. From the point of view now discussed, however, the Minister was in no different position from the District Commissioner in the time of the Mandate. Our sages had taught that he who has no understanding of divorce and marriage should not meddle in them. The Minister was a secular authority, and was responsible for enforcing the Registration Ordinance both from the administrative and the religious aspects.

The celebration of marriages under Jewish religious law sometimes raised many complex and involved questions which the Minister was not qualified to resolve, and it was for this reason that he was obliged to seek the confirmation of the body that was qualified, namely, the Council. In any case, even if it were correct — and it was not — that there was no obligation to consult the Council, the Minister was clearly entitled to seek its opinion, and act upon it if he were satisfied that it was sound.

The Petitioners had argued that since they had applied to the Minister for the confirmation sought before the Chief Rabbinate Council Law had been passed, they were entitled to his ruling without reference to the Council's opinion. This, too, was incorrect, said Justice Elon, for as he had held, the Minister was also obliged to refer the matter to the Council before the Law was passed.

Apart from that, however, it was clear from precedents of the Supreme Court, which he cited, that the only right the Petitioners may have had before the Law was passed was to have their application considered by the competent authority. That authority now, as far as the religious aspect was concerned, was the Chief Rabbinate Council. It was inconceivable that the court would now order the Minister to weigh and decide the Petitioners' qualifications, when the legislature had laid down specifically that this was to be done by the Council, and not by the Minister.

The Petitioners had argued that the Minister's refusal to recognize them was based on unjust discrimination. There was no basis for this assertion. The Minister had stated that he was satisfied that the Council's refusal to grant the Petitioners' eligibility was based purely on halachic considerations, and there was no reason to doubt that this was correct. On the administrative side, the Minister had pointed out that the rabbis qualified to celebrate marriages far outnumbered those required for that purpose. As a rule, only rabbis of towns and settlements were authorized in this regard, and the Petitioners had not shown that there was any objective need for their recognition under the Ordinance. No unjust discrimination, therefore, had been established.

The Petitioners had argued that the Minister had also acted in other cases without the confirmation of the Chief Rabbinate Council, and they cited the recognition of the late Rabbi Ya'acov Landau of Bnei Brak, two rabbis of the Haredi* community in Jerusalem, and the rabbi of the Karaite community.

In regard to the late Rabbi Ya'acov Landau and the rabbis of the Haredi community, said Justice Elon, the Council had in fact given its consent. The case of the Karaite community, however, could not be compared with other cases. Citing Supreme Court precedent, he dealt with the particular features of the Karaites, which justified the Minister in treating them differently from other communities. Moreover, there was no basis for treating the Reform community in the same way as the Karaites. Finally, Justice Elon

---

*   Ultra Orthodox

pointed out that the court would not order a competent authority to act unlawfully in one case because it had acted unlawfully in others.

It had been contended by the Petitioners that the decision of the Respondents offended against freedom of religion and conscience guaranteed in the Declaration of the Establishment of the State. On this basis they argued that the Chief Rabbinate Council should be regarded as the Council of the Orthodox community alone. They had also argued that the expression "Jewish religious law" (Din Tora) in section 2 of the Rabbinical Courts Jurisdiction (Marriage and Divorce) Law of 1953 was used in two different senses, and that the Supreme Court itself had recognized the validity of marriages performed otherwise than in accordance with the Halacha.

After reviewing the proceedings in the Knesset relating to the passing of the Chief Rabbinate Council Law, the Deputy President stressed that the suggestion had been raised to call the Council the "Orthodox Chief Rabbinate Council in Israel." This suggestion, however, had been rejected, and it was therefore now beyond doubt that the Council enjoyed the authority conferred upon it by the Law of 1980 in regard to the whole Jewish community.

It must be emphasized, he said, that the celebration and registration of marriages were matters affecting the State and the whole community. They were organized in a legal framework according to the Halacha, and the public welfare demanded that they be centralized in the hands of one halachic authority only.

In regard to the argument relating to the meaning of the term "Jewish religious law," Justice Elon dealt at length with Supreme Court precedents in which recognition had been given to marriages performed otherwise than according to Halacha. The clear position was that the court had indeed recognized such marriages as valid ex post facto, since they were so recognized also by the Halacha. They had been recognized by the court only for the purpose of registration in the Population Register, but the court had never held that Jewish religious law was changeable, and subject to two different meanings. Such a conception, he added, would introduce chaos, and expose married couples to risk and damage which could be irreversible.

In conclusion, Justice Elon quoted at length from the material submitted to the court by the Petitioners explaining their approach to the Halacha. The basic difference was that the Petitioners regarded the Halacha as changeable, and accepted the premise that it was open to be accepted or rejected according to the conscience and belief of a particular group. This conception, of course, stood in direct contradiction to the Orthodox view that the Halacha was binding.

In the result, said Justice Elon, there was no escape from the conclusion that the Petitioners sought the recognition of marriages and divorces contrary to the provisions of the law of Israel. This the court could not accept, bound as it was to uphold the law as it is.

For the above reasons, Justice Elon proposed that the petitions be dismissed.

Justice Shlomo Levin dealt, in the main, with the legal questions which arose.

In regard to the Marriage and Divorce Registration Ordinance, the Supreme Court had said, in the time of the Mandate, that "It is difficult to conceive a more sketchy, unsatisfactory or inept piece of legislation, dealing as it does with such an important matter." It was true that the court had ruled, by majority decision, that a rabbi competent to celebrate and register marriages was one recognized by the appropriate body of the Jewish community. Thus, those belonging to Knesset Yisrael and the minority belonging to Agudat Yisrael were recognized. As to the rest, who were an insignificant minority, there was nothing to be done.

It was only natural, Justice Levin continued, that when, on the establishment of the State, the Minister for Religious Affairs took over the functions of the District Commissioner, he should consult the appropriate religious authority in cases of doubt as to the competence of one or other rabbi to celebrate marriages. There was also no objection to his doing so as a matter of routine. The acts of an unqualified rabbi in this context could lead to the most serious consequences for those getting married, bearing in mind particularly that even the Chief Rabbinate Council's confirmation, if accepted by the Minister, would not help the couple if some irregularity in their marriage were subsequently discovered.

Nevertheless, the undisputed right of the Minister to consult the Council did not mean that he was obliged to do so. In his opinion, Justice Levin said, the Minister's intimation to the Petitioners that the law required him so to consult, was mistaken. The Minister was a secular authority, and the responsibility of recognizing registration under the Ordinance was his alone. In this respect, therefore, he differed from the opinion of the Deputy President.

In his view, Justice Levin continued, neither the "Jerusalem Ban" nor section 2(6) of the Chief Rabbinate of Israel Law supported the view that the Minister was legally required to consult the Council. The Jerusalem Ban was aimed at secret marriages, and had no application to marriages which were open, and celebrated by a rabbi recognized by a competent State authority. As to section 2(6), Mr. David Glass, the then chairman of the Law and Constitution Committee of the Knesset, had stressed, in presenting the Law, that it was "a photograph of the existing legal situation." Since the existing legal situation did not require the Minister to consult the Council, the Law introduced no change.

The most serious argument advanced by the Respondents, Justice Levin continued, was that based on section 2 of the Rabbinical Courts Jurisdiction Law. They had stressed that the Rabbinical Courts, which exercised exclusive jurisdiction in matters of marriage and divorce, applied Jewish religious law, which was different from that which would be observed by Reform rabbis in celebrating marriages.

The Petitioners had declared that they would apply Din Tora,* but a study of the material they had placed before the court showed that their Din Tora was different from that applied by the Rabbinical Courts. They relied on decisions of the Supreme Court recognizing the validity of marriages for purposes of subsequent registration only, as justifying the celebration of marriages against Din Tora. In reply to the question which body would be consulted in regard to halachic questions which might arise, they had designated "The Council of Progressive Rabbis in Israel."

It followed, Justice Levin said, that even taking into account the limitations the Petitioners had imposed upon themselves, there was a collision between two normative conceptions as to the marriage ceremony, its content and meaning. This feature could lead, in practice, to a conflict between two different marriage systems, and involve married couples in litigation and even lead to their marriage being nullified. These are dangers which can be expected in advance.

In regard to matters such as these, the Petitioners could not rely on the few exceptional cases in which the Supreme Court had found a secular solution relating to registration of marriages between a Cohen (a member of the priestly sect) and a divorced woman, which could not have been validly celebrated within the accepted norms.

In the light of the above considerations, said Justice Levin, the Minister was justified in acting as he did in the interests of the public welfare, and for this reason he agreed that the petition be dismissed.

Justice Meir Shamgar said that in view of the existing legislation, as explained by Justice Elon, and the considerations relied upon by Justice

* Jewish Law.

Shlomo Levin, there was no possibility of allowing the petition. Various suggestions had been raised during the hearings to resolve the problems which arose, and the proceedings had been postponed from time to time to enable a settlement to be reached. It appeared, however, that the problems raised by the Petitioners could be resolved by the legislature alone.

Justice Dov Levin concurred in the judgment of the Deputy President. He stressed that there was only one Din Tora. It was not the law of the State, and applied only to the extent that the legislature so decided. It was desirable, however, that there be one body only to give an authoritative ruling as to what the religious law was in particular circumstances.

It had to be remembered, Justice Levin continued, that the decisions of the Minister for Religious Affairs were subject to judicial review. If, therefore, he acted out of opposition to this or another stream in Jewish life, and not on the basis of objective considerations, the court would interfere.

He recognized the importance to the Jewish people of the part played by the various streams of Jewish life, and it was vital that a solution be found to the problems that arose between them. This could be achieved by an attitude of goodwill, without provoking opposition to existing entrenched conceptions on the one hand, and the rejection in advance of any different conception or different religious authority on the other.

Justice Eliezer Goldberg also agreed to the dismissal of the petition. He said that when questions of "religion and state" are brought to court, the court should confine itself to matters of law alone. It was not for the court to decide between different attitudes of faith, and different conceptions of life.

The one legal question at the basis of the petition was the designation of "Jewish religious law" applied by the Rabbinical Courts under section 2 of the Rabbinical Courts Jurisdiction Law of 1953. The court had already held that this law included not only the written law, but "the totality of the responsa dealing with the law of personal status in the laws of Israel."

Since the Petitioners themselves had declared that they would celebrate marriages in a manner that did not conform with "Jewish religious law" as applied by the Rabbinical Courts, no fault could be found with the Minister's decision refusing to recognize them as "Marriage Registrars" under the Ordinance in question.

For the above reasons, the petition was dismissed.

Hannan Meltzer and Uri Regev appeared for the Petitioners, and Renato Yarak and Nili Arad, Director of the High Court Division of the State Attorney's Office, appeared for the Respondents.

The judgment was given on July 24, 1989.

FREEDOM OF EXPRESSION

AVNERI v. SHAPIRA

In the Supreme Court sitting as a Court of Civil Appeals before Justice Aharon Barak, Justice Eliezer Goldberg, and Judge Eliyahu Matza, in the matter of *Arye Avneri and others*, Petitioners, versus *Avraham Shapira and another*, Respondents (C.A. 214/89).

Administrative Law—Freedom of Expression—Defamation—Civil Procedure— Interim Injunction—Defamation Law, 1965, section 14—Civil Procedure Rules, 1984, Rule 122—Civil Wrongs Ordinance (New Version), 1968, sections 71- 74—Contracts (Remedies for Breach of Contract) Law, 1970.

The Appellant Avneri, a journalist, wrote a book about the Respondent Shapira, an industrialist and, at the relevant time, leader of the Agudat Yisrael faction in the Knesset and chairman of the Knesset Finance Committee. Shapira had not seen the book. He alleged, however, on the basis of various sources, including declarations by the Appellant and extracts of the book which had been published, that it contained defamatory matter which would damage his good name. He therefore filed a claim against the Appellant in the District Court of Tel Aviv, and also applied for a temporary injunction restraining the publication of the book until the claim was decided.

Avneri argued that the matter to be published was true, and that its publication was in the public interest. He was entitled, therefore, to the defence provided by section 14 of the Defamation Law of 1965.

In dealing with the application for a temporary injunction, the court gave a decision suggesting that Avneri provide Shapira and the court with copies of the book so that the matter could be dealt with on the basis of the actual facts in issue. Avneri, however, refused to accept this suggestion on the ground that it would constitute prior censorship, and he also applied to the Supreme Court for leave to appeal against the decision. This application was dismissed, and the District Court later issued the temporary injunction which Shapira had requested. (The proceedings described above were reported in *The Jerusalem Post* of December 12, 1988.)

The road was now open for the District Court to deal with Shapira's claim itself, and in the course of preliminary proceedings it ordered Avneri to produce the book for inspection by Shapira and the court. Arguing again that this would mean prior censorship, Avneri refused to comply with the order. The court, acting under rule 122 of the Civil Procedure Rules of 1984, then struck out Avneri's defence and, at Shapira's request, issued a permanent injunction against the publication of the book. Avneri then appealed to the Supreme Court.

The judgment of the Supreme Court was delivered by Justice Aharon Barak, who dealt first with the jurisdiction of the court to issue injunctions relating to the publication of defamatory matter. After citing Israeli, English and American authorities, he held that whatever the position might be elsewhere, Israeli courts had that jurisdiction. Defamation was a civil wrong, and section 7 of the Defamation Law imported some provisions from the Civil Wrongs Ordinance (New Version), including sections 71-74, which empowered the court to grant injunctions.

Although there was jurisdiction, there still remained the question of how that power was to be exercised.

The grant of an injunction, Justice Barak continued, was a matter of discretion. In the past, this concept was based upon the equitable nature of the remedy of an injunction in English law. However, since the link between English and Israeli law had been broken,* and in view of statutory developments in Israel, the victim of a civil wrong should be regarded as entitled to an injunction.

Under the Contracts (Remedies for Breach of Contract) Law, of 1970, a party injured by a breach of contract was entitled to an injunction, and there was no logical reason why the victim of a civil wrong should be treated differently. The court should seek "legislative harmony" in interpreting and applying the law. There were differences between the remedy of an injunction in relation to contracts and in relation to civil wrongs. In the field of contracts, an injunction was a principal remedy, while in regard to civil wrongs it was subsidiary.

Although the party injured by a civil wrong had a right to an injunction, Justice Barak said, this right, like all other rights, was not absolute. The court had a discretion whether or not to issue an injunction. It had to consider, in the case of defamation, whether the defamatory material was known or not; the stage which had been reached in the proceedings; and whether or not the liability of the Defendant had already been established.

It also had to consider the public interest, and where the defamatory material had not yet been published, it had to consider not only the Plaintiff's right to his fair name and reputation, but also the basic rights of the Defendant, including the right to freedom of expression.

---

* See Foundations of Law Statute, 1980.

In regard to public interest, the English authority Spry had spoken of "the extent to which third persons or the public generally may be interested in the truth of those [the defamatory] statements"; and the American Restatement on Torts (civil wrongs) had stated that "One of the public interests most frequently encountered in the determination of the appropriateness of injunction against tort is that in the freedom of speech and of the press."

In exercising its discretion, Justice Barak continued, the court had to strike a balance between two basic interests. One interest was the right of a man to his good name. Quoting many sources, including Ecclesiastes, Maimonides and Shakespeare, Justice Barak described this right as basic to our regime of law which was, in the words of an American court, "a concept at the root of any decent system of ordered liberty." The other interest was the right of free speech, which included defamation.

These two interests were in continual competition. As Justice Moshe Landau had said, "This is a conflict between the freedom of a citizen and his right. He enjoys the freedom to say what is on his heart, and to hear what others have to say; and, as against this, he has the right not to be injured in his honour and good name." The stronger the defence of a man's good name, the greater the damage to freedom of speech.

Citing several authorities, Justice Barak then dealt with the nature of freedom of speech, and its place among other basic freedoms. Although Israel had no formal constitution, freedom of speech was recognized as occupying a foremost place among the basic freedoms. Not all freedoms were of equal importance, and the court had to resolve the conflict between them in the light of all the circumstances.

In the case of freedom of speech, some assistance was given by the legislature. The Defamation Law itself, by providing some defences to a claim of defamation, gave some indication of the balance to be found. Moreover, the court had a discretion as to issuing temporary injunctions, and also as to the disclosure of documents prior to trial. However, the legislature provided only the starting point. It was then for the court, by interpretation so as to give effect to the wishes of the legislature, and in consideration of all the recognized basic freedoms, to strike the balance sought.

In according pride of place to freedom of expression, Justice Barak continued, special consideration must be given to matters of public concern, and to those relating to persons holding public office.

This had been well expressed by the U.S. Supreme Court in saying:

"An individual who decides to seek governmental office must accept certain necessary consequences of that involvement in public affairs. He runs the risk of closer public scrutiny than might otherwise be the case. And society's interest in the officers of government is not strictly limited to the formal discharge of official duties . . . The public's interest extends to anything which might touch on an official's fitness for office . . . The first remedy of any victim of defamation is self-help — using available opportunities to contradict the lie or correct the error, and thereby to minimize its adverse impact on reputation. Public officials and public figures usually enjoy significantly greater access to the channels of effective communication and hence have a more realistic opportunity to counteract false statements than private individuals normally enjoy."

Justice Barak then considered the granting of temporary injunctions to restrain the publication of defamatory material in advance, where the publisher averred that he had a good defence to the action against him, such as that the allegations against the Plaintiff were true, and were made in good faith.

After citing several authorities, and examining the law in many countries, his conclusion was that unless it could be shown that the defence raised was worthless and completely unfounded, no prior injunction should be issued.

In this regard he also quoted the opinion of Lord Denning that "the court will not prejudice the issue by granting an injunction in advance of publication . . . There are some things that are of such public concern that the newspapers, the press, and indeed everyone, is entitled to make known the truth, and to make fair comment on it. [The Defendants] admit that they are going to injure the Plaintiff's reputation, but they say they can justify it . . . We cannot prejudge this defence by granting an injunction against them."

Although we were not bound by English precedents, Justice Barak said, we should be guided by them, since we also accepted the basic concepts upon which they were founded.

One must not go from one extreme to another, he warned. There could perhaps be highly exceptional circumstances — such as, for example, where security considerations are involved — in which the granting of a temporary injunction would be appropriate. The rule was that a temporary injunction, which meant prior censorship of the matter to be published, should not be issued.

Shapira's counsel had argued that in the present context, different considerations applied to a book than to the press. He did not accept this distinction. Both a book and a newspaper report enjoyed the protection of freedom of expression, and there was no difference, as far as granting a temporary injunction was concerned, between the two situations.

Justice Barak then discussed the difficulties facing the judge who had to balance conflicting basic freedoms. He had to display understanding, restraint, and care. He had to overcome his personal opinions, and give expression to the basic concepts of an enlightened society. He laid the basis upon which the whole system of law, and the rights of the individual, would be built. We were on the threshold of erecting our own national edifice. We were an ancient people, and a young state.

If there were any room for doubt, said Justice Barak, he would place freedom of expression above protecting the individual's good name. If we allowed any erosion of freedom of expression, the results would be unforeseeable. The injury to the victim of defamation was understandable, but every choice between the basic freedoms involved this result.

In conclusion, Justice Barak held that the District Court had erred in suggesting that the book should be made available in advance for scrutiny by Shapira and the court. It had erred in granting a temporary injunction, in striking out Avneri's defence, and in entering judgment in Shapira's favour.

For the above reasons, the appeal was allowed.

Advocates S. Lieblich and J. Miller appeared for the Appellants, and Advocates A. Zichroni and Wangelnik appeared for the Respondents.

The judgment was given on October 22, 1989.

Note: The following precedents cited in the above judgment were reported in *The Jerusalem Post* on the dates indicated: H.C. 152/82, February 27, 1983; E.P. 2/84, May 31, 1985; H.C. 399/85, August 3, 1987, *supra* p. 47; H.C. 680/88, January 20, 1989, *supra* p. 71.

FAIRNESS FOR DEMJANJUK

SHEFTEL v. ATTORNEY-GENERAL AND OTHERS

In the Supreme Court sitting as a High Court of Justice before Justice Gavriel Bach, Justice Avraham Halima and Justice Theodore Orr, in the matter of *Advocate Yoram Sheftel*, Petitioner, versus *The Attorney-General, Dov Yudkovsky and Noah Klieger*, Respondents (H.C. 223/88)

Administrative Law—Criminal Procedure—Publication of Court Proceedings Likely to Influence Trial—Attorney-General's Decision Not to Prosecute Set Aside—Nazi and Nazi Collaborators Law, 1950—Courts Law (Consolidated Version), 1984, section 71(a)—Criminal Procedure Law (Consolidated Version), 1982.

The third Respondent, a journalist, wrote a number of articles in the newspaper *Yediot Aharonot*, edited by the second Respondent, in connection with the trial, in the District Court of Jerusalem, of John (Ivan) Demjanjuk. Demjanjuk was charged with a number of grave offences under the Nazi and Nazi Collaborators Law of 1950. He was convicted, and sentenced to death, and his appeal to the Supreme Court is pending.

The articles in question were published during the trial, and reflected Klieger's own opinions about the evidence, the witnesses, the conduct of the prosecution and the defence, and the comments of the court. Himself a victim of the Holocaust, Klieger was highly critical of the defence, and openly expressed his support for the prosecution's case.

The Petitioner, Demjanjuk's counsel in the trial, lodged a complaint with the police, alleging that Yudkovsky and Klieger had contravened section 71(a) of the Courts Law of 1984 (Consolidated Version), under which "A person shall not publish anything concerning a matter pending in any court if the publication is calculated to influence the course or outcome of the trial." He submitted extracts from the articles in which, he contended, Klieger displayed a clear inclination to attack the credibility of Demjanjuk and his witnesses, and to show that, despite his denials, Demjanjuk was "Ivan the Terrible" of Treblinka, had committed the crimes imputed to him, and had no defence.

The police rejected the complaint on the ground that no criminal offence had been committed, and the Petitioner then appealed to the Attorney-General under section 64 of the Criminal Procedure Law (Consolidated Version) of 1982.

The Attorney-General dismissed the appeal, stating that "having regard to all the circumstances, including the wide coverage given to the Demjanjuk trial, and the deep emotional stress involved in reporting the proceedings in that case, I have decided not to instruct the police to continue the investigation of your complaint."

The Petitioner then applied to the High Court of Justice to order the Attorney-General to indict the second and third Respondents for an offence under section 71 of the Courts Law, that is to say, contravening the rule of "*sub judice*."

The first judgment of the court was given by Justice Gavriel Bach.

The Respondents, he said, had argued that the petition should be dismissed, since the Petitioner had come to court "with unclean hands," having himself induced publications in contravention of section 71 above. However, since the petition related to the rights of a Defendant in a criminal trial, the court had decided not to deal with that argument, but to rule on the merits of the application itself.

The Attorney-General had conceded in his reply to the petition, Justice Bach continued, that Klieger's articles were, *prima facie*, in contravention of section 71 of the Courts Law. He had, however, furnished the grounds for his decision, which were, in part, additional to what he had already stated in dismissing the Petitioner's appeal.

He had pointed out, first, that the purpose of section 71 was to ensure the purity of the judicial process, and that there was no objective fear that the publications complained of would frustrate that purpose.

Secondly, he had referred again to the wide publicity given to the trial, and the acute emotional strains connected with the case. In weighing the interest of preserving the purity of the judicial process against the interest of freedom of expression he had, in these circumstances, preferred the latter.

Thirdly, he had also taken into account Klieger's personal circumstances. The latter had himself been in a concentration camp during the Holocaust, and his articles had given expression to his own experiences in this context. The sole ground for the Attorney-General's decision, therefore, said Justice Bach, was the absence of any public interest in pursuing the investigation which the Petitioner demanded.

Justice Bach did not completely reject a person's being the victim of the Holocaust as a ground for closing a criminal file against him, even if the charge were one of contempt of court. If, for example, such a victim were guilty of a spontaneous outburst in court, he would not, basically, disagree with the opinion that no public interest would be served by his being prosecuted. On the other hand, he was doubtful if closing the file, as against taking the victim's situation into account as a mitigating factor, would be justified where the victim was a journalist who published dozens of articles which could influence the course of the trial, and its outcome.

In the present case, however, said Justice Bach, he did not need to decide this point. The fact that Klieger suffered in the Holocaust was certainly no ground for not continuing the enquiries in regard to the complaint against Yudkovsky. He was the editor of the paper and well knew Klieger's past. If he instructed Klieger to cover the trial and, what was more important, continued to publish the articles knowing that Klieger could not control himself and show more latitude, Klieger's sufferings could surely not protect Yudkovsky from an investigation "in the public interest."

The Attorney-General's ground that there was no objective fear that the articles would damage the purity of the judicial process was, on the face of it, surprising. Once he agreed that, *prima facie*, an offence against section 71 above had been committed, he was estopped from raising this ground. How could one hold, without an investigation, that the purity of the judicial process would not be affected? It must certainly not be assumed that the purity of the judicial process had in fact been damaged. Proof of this, however, was not necessary for an indictment under section 71. It was sufficient if the publication could produce this result.

This ground, moreover, had no basis in reality. The newspaper in question enjoyed one of the largest circulations in the country. If its readers were told, article after article, that the Defendant in the case, despite his denials, was indeed the sadistic murderer described by the prosecution witnesses, and that the defence witnesses were confused and unreliable, could it be said with certainty that the outcome of the case could not be affected, at least as far as the influencing of witnesses was concerned?

He was also far from holding, Justice Bach continued, that a professional judge could never be influenced by a newspaper publication. The Supreme Court had already pointed out that the process of justice was not an accurate machine, and although there was less possibility of influencing professional judges than other persons, the public was obliged not to attempt to influence them in the discharge of their professional duties.

The real danger, however, as he had said, was the possibility of influencing witnesses who had not yet testified, both as to the content of their testimony, and as to the manner of their giving their evidence.

The main ground for the Attorney-General's decision, Justice Bach continued, was his conception that there was no public interest in conducting the investigation sought, because of the deep emotions aroused by a case dealing with Nazi crimes. His reply implied that because of the wide interest in the case, and the many opinions disseminated by the media both in Israel and elsewhere, there was no point in applying the "*sub judice*" rule. He held this view even in a case such as the present, in which he was of the opinion that, *prima facie*, an offence under section 71 of the Courts Law had been committed.

In his view, said Justice Bach, the features mentioned above led to the very opposite conclusion. It was easy to apply the "*sub judice*" rule in ordinary routine cases, to which the public was indifferent. The rule stood its real test where there was an actual fear that public opinion, sympathizing with the defence, or expressing hostility towards the Defendant, was likely, directly or indirectly, to influence the trial or its outcome.

In any event, it was clear that as long as the "*sub judice*" rule was accepted in Israel, and enshrined in section 71 of the Courts Law, it was to be observed. Could there be a case more fitting for the application of the rule than one in which the Defendant faced the death penalty, the acts attributed to him aroused strong feelings, and he argued that he was the victim of false identification?

The Attorney-General's decision implied that in a case in Israel against a Defendant accused of Nazi crimes, there was no public interest in applying the rules laid down by the legislature to ensure the purity of the judicial process.

This conclusion, said Justice Bach, was likely to be interpreted as impliedly supporting the opinion of those who rejected Israel's right to try Nazi criminals. He himself had no doubt that the Israeli legal system was capable of giving such a Defendant a fair trial, and that an Israeli court was the most appropriate forum for trying cases of crimes against the Jewish people. For that very reason there was no reasonable ground for not applying the provisions of the law for protecting the rights of the parties against outside influences, including "trial by newspaper."

In his opinion, therefore, there was no substance in any of the Attorney-General's grounds, either singly or cumulatively.

Justice Bach then reviewed precedents of the Supreme Court dealing with decisions of the Attorney-General.

The Attorney-General could decline to act for various reasons. Where, however, his basis was the absence of public interest, the court would only interfere if his reasons were clearly wrong, or based on irrelevant considerations.

In his opinion, concluded Justice Bach, the grounds of the Attorney-General for not ordering the investigation applied for by the Petitioner were all without substance. For this reason, the court was obliged to intervene. He proposed, therefore, that the Attorney-General be ordered to instruct that the investigation in question be proceeded with.

Justice Avraham Halima concurred in the judgment of Justice Bach.

Justice Theodore Orr dissented from his colleagues.

Citing the Agranat Report of 1962, and Supreme Court precedents, he emphasized that the powers of the Attorney-General in regard to initiating criminal proceedings were very wide. Moreover, the Supreme Court had often stated its reluctance to interfere in the Attorney-General's decisions. The court had at one time held that it would only intervene if his decision were tainted with lack of good faith.

In later judgments, however, different tests had been formulated, and in the present instance Justice Bach had adopted the test that the decision was "clearly wrong, and based on irrelevant considerations." Whatever language was used, however, it was clear that only in the rarest instances would the court intervene.

Justice Orr then cited a number of examples to demonstrate the wide range of considerations which the Attorney-General was entitled to weigh in deciding not to take action. There were factors relating to the suspect himself, such as his having suffered damage as the result of his own crime. Another possibility, connected with the public interest, was the desire not to divulge sensitive material. Or the Attorney-General might decide not to create a forum for the suspect to disseminate his opinions. The Attorney-General was also entitled to lay down criteria for the exercise of his discretion. It was also possible that he would give different decisions in cases featuring the same circumstances, and each decision would be legitimate.

It must be remembered, said Justice Orr, that it was not sufficient for the court to hold that it itself would have decided differently, or that the Attorney-General may have been mistaken. In order for the court to intervene, there must have been some flaw in the decision in question which, on the basis of the accepted tests for the court's interference, would justify that step.

In Justice Orr's opinion, the Attorney-General's decision in the present case was legitimate and reasonable, and free from any flaw which would justify the intervention of the court. The Attorney-General had explained that he had considered every application to take proceedings under section 71 with the greatest care, having regard to the principle of freedom of expression.

Justice Orr agreed with his colleagues that there was no objective danger, in the present case, of damage to the purity of the judicial process. On the other hand, he was not prepared to reject the grounds of the Attorney-General's decision based on considerations of the public interest.

The Attorney-General had also relied, in the present case, on the strong emotional feelings associated with the Demjanjuk trial, and the wide publicity given to the proceedings in the overseas press. In his view, Justice Orr said, these were also factors which the Attorney-General was entitled to take into account. He had no control over publications in other countries, and was entitled to decide not to institute a prosecution regarding only a small portion of the wide publicity given to this particular case.

In conclusion, Justice Orr cited a precedent in which the court had laid down that it "does not sit in the Attorney-General's place, and does not substitute its discretion for his. The court will ask itself whether the Attorney-General's decision was one which a reasonable Attorney-General could reach in the circumstances of the case." In his view, the decision in the present instance fell into that category.

Justice Orr proposed, therefore, that the petition be dismissed.

By majority decision, the petition was allowed, and the Attorney-General was directed to order the investigation sought.

Advocate Bakerman appeared for the Petitioner; Senior Assistant State Attorney Nava Ben-Or appeared for the Attorney-General; and Advocate M. Moser appeared for the second and third Respondents.

The judgment was given on November 11, 1989.

RIGHTS OF DETAINEES

AUDEH AND OTHERS v. IDF COMMANDERS IN JUDEA AND SAMARIA

In the Supreme Court sitting as a High Court of Justice before the Deputy-President Justice Menahem Elon, Justice Theodore Orr, and Judge Eliyahu Matza, in the matter of *Mussah Audeh and two others, and the Association for Civil Rights in Israel*, Petitioners, versus *The Commanders of the Military Forces in Judea and Samaria, and the Gaza Strip*, Respondents (H.C. 670/89).

Administrative Law—Rights of Military Detainees in Occupied Territories— Notification to Relatives of Place of Detention—Order Relating to Security Directives (Judea and Samaria), (No. 378), 1970, section 78(A)(b)—Geneva Convention, 1949.

The first three Petitioners were relatives of persons who had been detained by the army authorities in the occupied territories, and who had not been notified of the place where the detainees were held. They therefore petitioned the High Court of Justice to order the Respondents to give them that information, and to inform them of any other place to which the detainees might be transferred in the future. They also petitioned for a general order directing the Respondents to furnish the above information in every case of detention by the military authorities in the territories.

The first judgment of the court was given by Justice Menahem Elon. The first three Petitioners, he said, had described their efforts to ascertain where their relatives were detained, but without success. Counsel for the Petitioners had informed the court that the Association for Civil Rights was asked from time to time to secure this information for relatives of detainees, and that it was usually given within four days.

Counsel for the Respondents had told the court that the first three Petitioners had been informed of the place of detention of their relatives on August 30, 1989. Their particular problem, therefore, had been solved, and the assistance of the court was no longer required. The court wished to note, however, that the fact that no notice of the detention had been given to the detainees' relatives for about a month and a half should be investigated. The court had good reason to expect that in view of the additional procedures introduced, as later described, such delays would not recur.

Justice Elon then turned to the general obligation of the army to supply relatives with the information now being discussed. Section 78A(b) of the Order Relating to Security Directives (Judea and Samaria) (Number 378), of 1970, provided that if a person was detained, a notification of the detention, and the place of detention, must be given, without delay, to his close relatives, unless the detainee requested otherwise. This provision expressed the basic right of both the detainee himself, and his close relatives, to know his whereabouts, and thus be enabled to render him assistance. It was a natural right, based upon the general principles of justice, and the detainee's dignity as a human being.

For the same reasons, section 78A(c) obliged the authorities to give a similar notification to a lawyer named by the detainee.

The above provisions had been introduced in February 1988, and counsel for the Petitioners had pointed to various deficiencies in the procedures followed, as a result of which the notification did not reach those affected.

Counsel for the Respondents had stressed the difficulties which her clients faced in the prevailing conditions of violence. They had therefore issued detailed administrative instructions in this regard, and only recently further changes and improvements had been introduced to ensure that the notification reached its destination.

Justice Elon went on to deal in some detail with the administrative instructions and later improvements mentioned by counsel. These included the sending of postcards by the detainee, the orderly transmission of notifications from detention centers, the posting of notifications in Arabic on notice boards at central points, and other means of publishing the information in question.

The latest instructions also provided for the necessary notification to be communicated by telephone in exceptional cases, such as where the detainee needed special medicines. They also provided for the establishment of a control unit which would examine to what extent the instructions were being implemented, and would report its findings to the area commander's headquarters within two months of its appointment.

Justice Elon then quoted Article 106 of the Geneva Convention Relative to the Protection of Civilian Persons in Time of War, of August 12, 1949, which provided for the issue of postcards to detainees to enable them to notify their relatives of their detention, and its location. He also stressed the obligation of the authorities to fill in the necessary particulars, and to attend to the mailing of the postcards without delay.

The Court was satisfied, Justice Elon continued, that the latest directives went a long way to improve the system of notification, and Petitioners' counsel had agreed that this was so. Nevertheless, counsel had submitted that there was still room for further improvement, and he had requested, therefore, that the petition be left open to enable the court to enquire whether the expected improvements came up to expectations.

The court was not prepared to leave the matter open, said Justice Elon. The control unit which was shortly to be established would keep the situation under review, and would also be open to suggestions for improving the position. Counsel could therefore direct his proposals to that unit, if he so wished.

Justice Elon proposed, therefore, that the petition be dismissed, and that the Respondents be ordered to pay the Petitioners' costs in the sum of NIS 2,000, with linkage and interest according to law.

Justice Theodore Orr concurred, but there were some features, he said, upon which he desired to comment.

The sons of the first, second and third Petitioners had been detained on July 5, 6 and 13, 1989, respectively, and no notification of the place of their detention had been given. The Petitioners' efforts to receive that information had yielded no results, and they therefore lodged their petition on August 10. It was only on August 30 that the notification was given, and it was to be assumed that the filing of the petition played some part in the giving of this information, at long last, to the detainees' families.

It was true, Justice Orr continued, that in these circumstances the first part of the petition had been fulfilled. He should have thought, however, that it would have been appropriate for the State Attorney to explain to the court what, or who, was responsible for such a long delay in giving the requisite notification. No such explanation had been given, although in all three cases section 78A(b) of the above Order had not been complied with. A detainee had a basic right that his relatives should be informed, so as to be able to assist him, and ensure that his rights were upheld.

Everyone knew how involved and difficult was the task of the authorities responsible for peace and quiet in Judea, Samaria and Gaza, and that detentions were necessary in the discharge of that task. The security legislation in those territories, however, also included obligations which had to be fulfilled, and the test of fulfilling an obligation was its observance.

In view of the latest directives already mentioned by the Deputy President, which were entitled "Notifications of Detention to Detainees' Families and the Red Cross," Justice Orr said he agreed to the dismissal of the petition. The authorities should be given a reasonable opportunity to improve the procedures, as they were trying to do. If it should appear that the new directives were inadequate, or were not properly applied, the door was always open to present a new petition to the court.

Justice Orr then emphasized that it was not sufficient for the authorities to hand a detainee a postcard, and leave him to fill it in. There could be cases in which the detainee, because of his physical or emotional condition, could not be relied upon to fill in the postcard properly, with all the information necessary.

It was the obligation of the authorities to ensure that the postcard was properly completed, and promptly despatched. It was their obligation to give the notification, unless the detainee himself specifically requested otherwise. In this respect, section 78A(b) went further than Article 106 of the Geneva Convention referred to above.

Finally, Justice Orr pointed out that according to the directives now laid before the court, the notification would be given to the relatives by telephone only in exceptional circumstances. Since, however, it was the duty of the authorities to give the notification "without delay," they should consider giving it by telephone whenever possible, and not only in exceptional cases. Justice Orr added that the Minister of Defence had stated that consideration would be given to this possibility in a report to the Speaker of the Knesset on June 29, 1989.

Judge Eliyahu Matza also agreed to the dismissal of the petition, with the imposition of costs on the Respondents. It was to be assumed that the Respondents, in their efforts to improve their procedures, would take the comments of Justice Orr into serious consideration.

For the above reasons, the petition was dismissed, and the Respondents were ordered to pay the costs of the Petitioners in the sum of NIS 2,000, with linkage and interest according to law.

Dan Simon appeared for the Petitioners, and Nili Arad, Director of the High Court Division of the State Attorney's Office, appeared for the Respondents.

The judgment was given on November 21, 1989.

THE MESSIANIC JEWS

BERESFORD v. MINISTER OF INTERIOR

In the Supreme Court sitting as a High Court of Justice before the Deputy-President, Justice Menahem Elon, Justice Aharon Barak, and Justice Avraham Halima, in the matter of *Jerry and Shirley Beresford*, Petitioners, versus *The Minister of the Interior*, Respondent (H.C. 265/ 87).

Administrative Law—Meaning of "Jew"—Refusal to Grant "Oleh" Certificates to "Messianic Jews"—Jewish Law—Law of Return, 1950, sections 4A(a), 4(b).

Under section 1 of the Law of Return of 1950, "Every Jew is entitled to enter Israel as an oleh (a Jew immigrating to Israel)." Under section 4B of the Law, "For the purposes of this Law, a Jew is a person born to a Jewish mother, or one who has converted and is not a member of another faith."

Under section 4A(a) of the Law, "The rights of a Jew under the Nationality Law of 1952, and the rights of an oleh under any other Law, shall also be accorded to the child and grandchild of a Jew, to the spouse of a Jew, and to the spouse of the child and grandchild of a Jew, save where such person was a Jew who had willingly professed another faith."

The Petitioners, who were born Jews, belonged to a group known as "Messianic Jews." They applied to the Respondent for certificates as olim under the Law of Return on the basis of their being Jews who were not members of another faith. Alternatively, they claimed such certificates as the children of Jews who had not willingly professed another faith.

The Respondent refused their request on the ground that, although they were born as Jews, they were members of another faith, and had willingly professed another faith.

The Petitioners then applied to the High Court of Justice to order the Respondent to grant the certificates requested.

The first judgment of the court was given by Justice Menahem Elon, who dealt at the outset with the religious beliefs and practices of the Petitioners, and their relationship with the Jewish community in South Africa and Zimbabwe prior to their aliya. They averred that they had begun to interest themselves in the teachings of Jesus, and his place in the Jewish religion, in 1985. They saw no contradiction between their being Jewish, and their belief in Jesus as the Messiah.

This belief, they urged, characterized a recognized strain in Judaism in the time of the Second Temple: it was legitimate then, and was legitimate now. They were dedicated to the Jewish people, the State of Israel, Zionism, and service in the IDF. They observed the Sabbath, the laws of kashrut, and the Jewish festivals. They regarded themselves as full Jews, had no connection with any other faith, and had undergone no ceremony, such as baptism, of any other religion.

The Petitioners, said Justice Elon, were members of the "Messianic Jews" congregation in Ramat Hasharon, of which one Arye Sorko-Ram was the head. He then cited at length extracts from affidavits and other documents demonstrating the beliefs of Messianic Jews, referring also to their grace after meals and their Passover Haggada,* and he also quoted extracts from Sorko-Ram's diary while serving in the IDF.

Justice Elon then considered whether the Petitioners were "members of another faith," citing Supreme Court precedents — in particular the *Dorflinger* Case — and numerous other legal and religious authorities. He pointed out that in the *Dorflinger* Case,** the court had applied the test of whether the Petitioner there was recognized, by the "other faith," as a member of that faith.

In the present instance, he said, that question presented no difficulty. The Petitioners believed in the divinity of Jesus, in his being the Messiah, who had returned, that he had been sent by God to atone for the sins of Israel and the nations, and that he was the son of God, and king of the Jews.

It had not been proved that they had been baptised, but that was unnecessary. They did not have to belong to a branch of the established church. It was sufficient if they were Christians theologically; and of this there was no doubt. It was true that Messianic Jews were a legitimate Jewish sect in the first century. Since then, however, history had wrought many changes, and that concept had no place today.

It seemed, Justice Elon continued, that the application of the test of what was recognized by the "other faith" was based on the decision of the Supreme Court in the *Rufeisen* Case,*** in which the late Justice Silberg had held that a person who was born a Jew always remained a Jew in the eyes of Halacha, even if he converted to another religion.

This view, however, was wrong, the correct opinion being that, under the Halacha, a willing convert forfeited his legal and social rights expressing his belonging to the family, or the community, or the Jewish people.

---

*   Prayers for home reading on first night of Passover.
**   1979 P.D. II p. 97.
*** Selected Supreme Court Judgments (English) Special Volume, p. 1. 1962 16 P.D. II p. 2428.

It was proper, he said, that the expression "members of another faith" in the Law of Return, should be interpreted in the light of Jewish history and concepts. That Law was based on Jeremiah's vision, "And thy children should return to their own border." It reflected the right of every Jew, wherever he be, to return to the land of his fathers. It could not apply to voluntary members of another faith, as were the Petitioners.

Justice Elon stressed that the court was concerned, in the present case, with the question of who was a Jew for the purposes of the Law of Return. This had no relevance to the question of a person's religion for the purposes of the Rabbinical Courts Jurisdiction (Marriage and Divorce) Law of 1953, in regard to which other considerations could apply.

For the same reasons, said Justice Elon, the Petitioners' alternative claim, based on section 4A(a) of the Law of Return, could not be sustained.

In conclusion, Justice Elon referred to the argument that the refusal of the minister to grant the certificates in question constituted an interference with the Petitioners' freedom of religion and conscience.

This argument had no foundation whatsoever. The Petitioners were free to believe what they wished, and to practise any religion they chose. The court now held that they were not entitled to certificates as olim under the Law of Return — that, and nothing more.

Justice Elon proposed, therefore, that the petition be dismissed.

Justice Aharon Barak concurred, stating, however, that he had reached the same result by a different road.

Reviewing Supreme Court precedents and legal writings, he said that there were three possible tests for the interpretation of the expression: "and is not a member of another faith" in section 4B of the Law of Return. The first was how the "other faith" would regard the person involved, which was the test applied in the *Dorflinger* Case; the second was the test according to Halacha; and the third was the test based on Israeli secular law.

The test of the outlook of the "other faith," although it had been applied by the Supreme Court, was unacceptable, for it led to absurd results. For example, a child born outside Israel to a Jewish mother and a Moslem father would be regarded by the Moslem faith as a Moslem. It was inconceivable that that result, which would bar the entry of the child to Israel under the Law of Return, reflected the intention of the legislature in enacting section 4B.

He would point out, however, that he was concerned here with the Law of Return. The outlook of the "other faith" could play a very different role under the Rabbinical Courts Jurisdiction (Marriage and Divorce) Law, in regard to which other considerations applied.

Justice Barak was also unable to accept the test of Halacha. He emphasized, in this regard, that the definition of a "Jew" in section 4B of the Law of Return, had been added by an amendment in 1970, which was based on the decision of the Supreme Court in the *Rufeisen* Case. In that case a Catholic priest, Brother Daniel, both of whose parents were Jews, claimed an oleh certificate under the Law of Return.

The court rejected the halachic approach, holding — as it now appeared, wrongly — that under the Halacha the Petitioner remained a Jew for all purposes, notwithstanding his having willingly converted to Christianity. The court applied the secular test, and ruled that, according to ordinary, everyday conceptions, a Catholic priest could not be regarded as a Jew under the Law of Return.

It was for the very purpose of giving legislative force to that test that the 1970 amendment was introduced by the Knesset. That purpose of the legislature, although based on error, was nevertheless to be honoured.

Applying the secular test, Justice Barak continued, he was of opinion that the Petitioners were indeed "members of another faith" for the purposes of the Law of Return. As a judge in Israel at this time, asking himself what the average Jew would say regarding persons holding the beliefs, and following the practices, of the Petitioners, his reply was that they were not "Jews" under that Law.

He did not regard their own belief that they were Jews as totally irrelevant, but that was only one factor. Moreover, the court was concerned with the position today, and not 2,000 years ago. The secular test was variable, and could change with the passage of time, and with changes in popular conceptions. At the present time, however, the Petitioners were not entitled to the recognition which they claimed.

The same considerations, said Justice Barak, applied to the Petitioners' alternative claim.

He agreed, therefore, that the petition be dismissed.

Justice Avraham Halima concurred in the result reached by his colleagues.

Yosef Ben Menashe appeared for the Petitioners, and Senior Assistant State Attorney Uzi Fogelman appeared for the Respondent.

The judgment was given on December 25, 1989.

RULE BY DECREE

HERZLIYA MEDICAL CENTER v. MINISTER OF HEALTH

In the Supreme Court sitting as a High Court of Justice before the President, Justice Meir Shamgar, Justice Ya'acov Maltz, and Justice Theodore Orr, in the matter of *Medinvest Medical Center Herzliya, Ltd.*, Petitioner, versus *The Minister and Director-General of the Ministry of Health*, Respondents (H.C. 256/88).

Administrative Law—"Government by Decree"—Minister's Exercise of Emergency Powers Set Aside—Public Health Ordinance, 1940, section 27—Commodities and Services (Control) Law, 1957—Public Health Regulations (Registration of Hospitals), 1966.

The Petitioner, a company registered in Israel, was established by South African and other foreign investors for the development of medical centers and the supply of medical services. It opened the medical center in Herzliya some seven years ago. Until 1988 some 10,000 operations had been performed there, and it had treated some 20,000 patients.

The Petitioner desired to open a similar center in Haifa, and had found a suitable building for the purpose. The lease of the building, and its adaptation as a medical center, had been fully covered by the Petitioner, and no financial assistance from the government, or any other public body, was requested. The total investment, amounting to some $3-5 million, would be provided by private foreign investors, and a sum of some half a million dollars, the transfer of which from South Africa had been authorized by the authorities there, had already been deposited in an Israel bank.

Health Ministry officials examined the building, and detailed plans for its conversion to its new purpose, and found it suitable. Nevertheless, the Ministry refused to issue the necessary license to the Petitioner under the Public Health Regulations (Registration of Hospitals) of 1966, on the grounds, briefly, that there was a surplus of beds in the area, and the fear that the establishment of the center would diminish the medical personnel in public medical institutions. The Petitioner then applied to the High Court of Justice for relief.

The first judgment of the court was given by Justice Meir Shamgar.

The Petitioner, he said, had relied on section 27 of the Public Health Ordinance of 1940 and the regulations thereunder. These, it contended, contained an exhaustive list of conditions necessary for the registration of a hospital under section 25 of that statute. They related to the personnel, premises and equipment required, and had all been fulfilled. They were confined to administrative-organizational matters, and did not cover features such as the number of beds in the area, or the depletion of medical personnel. In refusing the license, therefore, the Respondents had exceeded their powers.

It was true, the Petitioner said, that the license had not been refused under the above Ordinance, but by an order of the minister under the Commodities and Services (Control) Law of 1957, requiring the confirmation of the Director-General of the Health Ministry for, *inter alia*, the establishment of a hospital. This, however, was only a device.

Indeed, the minister, realizing that his powers under the Ordinance might be inadequate, had prepared a Bill to widen his authority. Since, however, the presentation of the Bill to the Knesset had taken too long, he had resorted to the above Law as a stop-gap measure. This stratagem, it was argued, was unlawful and, in addition, the order was unreasonable, and was unlawful on that ground as well. The Petitioner also relied on the basic right of freedom of occupation.

The petition was supported by an affidavit of Professor Moshe Many, the president of Tel Aviv University. In his view, the real problems of the public medicine system were not those raised by the Respondents, but failure to exploit the existing manpower and equipment facilities. The public hospitals could not provide adequate medical services — exemplified, *inter alia*, in the closing of operating theaters and clinics after 2:30 p.m.

The Respondents contended that even the requirements of the Ordinance had not been fulfilled. They also argued that the minister was legally entitled to issue the order referred to. They also filed an affidavit of Dr. Yoram Lotan, the Health Ministry official responsible for the licensing of non-governmental medical institutions. He supported the grounds of refusal stated above, pointing out that the policy against establishing additional general hospitals was applied equally to private and public institutions, such as Kupat Holim* and Hadassah.**

The President then analyzed in some detail the legal arguments raised. He supported the view that the provisions in the Public Health Ordinance, and the regulations thereunder, were exhaustive, and dealt exclusively with administrative and organizational requirements. If, therefore, these requirements were fulfilled, there was no ground for refusing the registration.

---

*   The Health Fund of the General Labor Federation (Histadrut).
**   Hospitals of the Hadassah Medical Organization.

He did not accept the Respondents' contention that even those requirements had not been complied with. It was not necessary that every minute detail should have been carried out. The ministry could confirm the registration in principle, leaving the formal act to be completed when everything necessary had been done. Indeed, it was unreasonable to expect potential investors to complete their part of the transaction, and then possibly be faced with a refusal.

Justice Shamgar then considered the legal status of the minister's order under the Commodities and Services Control Law.

After examining the relevant sections of that Law, and citing numerous Israeli and other authorities and precedents, he held that the minister's order now discussed was valid. At the same time he levelled strong criticism against the Law, pointing out that it blurred the distinction between the legislature and a subordinate authority such as a minister, and conferred upon the latter draconic powers. The Law introduced government by decree, with all the evils that involved.

He was also of the opinion that a minister's order under the Law could even overrule later legislation, unless the order was specifically abrogated by the Knesset.

Under section 3 of the Law, Justice Shamgar continued, the minister was entitled to exercise his powers if "he has reasonable grounds for believing that it is necessary to do so for the maintenance of an essential activity, or the prevention of profiteering and speculation."

It was clear that conducting hospitals was an "essential activity" and the only question that remained, therefore, was whether the minister had exercised his powers correctly in the present case.

His conclusion was that although the minister had not taken into account irrelevant considerations, he had failed to give due consideration to a number of relevant factors which had apparently been completely overlooked, or had not been sufficiently weighed. It had already been stated that "an authority can fail to give its mind to a case and thus fail to exercise its discretion lawfully, by blindly following a policy laid down in advance."

The lines along which a competent authority should weigh the factors involved were laid down by the Supreme Court, *inter alia*, in H.C. 297/82 (see *The Jerusalem Post*, July 24, 1983).

In Justice Shamgar's view, the minister had failed to give due weight to the considerable investment by foreign investors. This was not, of course, an absolute factor, but it was important to weigh whether the damage which would be caused by refusing the license was worth the loss involved. There was also the fact that no public funds would be requested.

Moreover, it was intended to bring doctors as immigrants from overseas. It was also important to prevent local doctors who could not make a living from leaving the country. There was also the factor that there were today long queues of persons awaiting elective operations, and it was clearly in the interests of public health and, indeed, of saving lives, that that situation should be remedied as far as possible.

For the above reasons, Justice Shamgar proposed that the decision to refuse the license be set aside, and that the matter be returned to the Respondents to reconsider the Petitioner's application in the light of the factors he had dealt with.

Justice Ya'acov Maltz concurred.

Justice Theodore Orr agreed with the order proposed by the President. However, after analyzing the relevant provisions of the Control of Commodities Law, he expressed doubts whether a ministerial order under that Law could prevail over subsequent legislation by the Knesset.

The matter was therefore returned to the Respondents for further consideration.

Raphael Dinari and Robert Yohai appeared for the Petitioner, and Senior Assistant State Attorney Menahem Mazoz appeared for the Respondents. Judgment given on December 26, 1989.

COURT MARTIAL FOR BEATINGS

TSOFAN v. IDF ADVOCATE GENERAL

In the Supreme Court sitting as the High Court of Justice before Justice Moshe Bejski, Justice Dov Levin and Judge Ya'acov Kedmi, in the matter of *Jamal Tsofan, the Association for Civil Rights in Israel, and others*, Petitioners, versus *The Advocate-General of the IDF and Colonel Yehuda Meir and others*, Respondents (H.C. 425/89).

Military Law—Administrative Law—Unlawful Order by Officer to Assault Civilians—Refusal by Military Advocate—General to Prosecute before Special Court Martial—Intervention by Supreme Court—Military Justice Law, 1955, sections 68, 153, 281.

On June 19 and 21, 1988, some 20 youths of the villages of Beita and Hawara, in the West Bank, were rounded up by soldiers, taken outside the villages and severely beaten, on their limbs and other parts of their bodies, with clubs. During the beatings the youths were blindfolded, and their hands were bound. The legs of some of them were also bound and their mouths gagged. Thereafter, some of the youths required medical treatment and others were hospitalized.

According to a military police investigation, the above actions were carried out on the orders of Colonel Yehuda Meir.

The Military Advocate-General decided that Meir should be tried disciplinarily. He was accordingly tried by the Chief of the General Staff, and was convicted, under section 68 of the Military Justice Law of 1955, of the offence of exceeding his authority. He was sentenced to a severe reprimand, this being the maximum penalty which could be imposed upon him in disciplinary proceedings, as laid down in section 153 of the Law. At the same time, Meir was compelled, against his will, to terminate his active service in the army.

The Petitioners, some of whom were victims of the actions described, contended that the Advocate-General had exercised his discretion unlawfully in deciding that disciplinary proceedings were adequate in the above circumstances. They argued that Meir was guilty of unlawfully and intentionally causing grievous harm under section 329 of the Penal Law of 1977, which carried a possible sentence of 20 years' imprisonment. They therefore petitioned the High Court of Justice to order the Advocate-General to indict Meir before a Special Court Martial, on charges under that section.

The first judgment of the court was given by Justice Moshe Bejski. From the point of view of instituting criminal proceedings, he said, the Military Advocate-General was in a position very similar to that of the Attorney-General. The situations were not identical, for the former functioned within the army hierarchy. Moreover, he had to consider the promotion of high morale and discipline in the army, factors with which the Attorney-General was generally not concerned.

However, in deciding, under section 281 of the above Law, what type of criminal proceeding to institute in a particular case, he enjoyed the same independence, and his decisions in that regard were similarly subject to judicial review by the court. In the absence of precedents dealing directly with the tests to be applied by the court in reviewing such decisions, he added, the court would be guided by the tests applied to decisions of the Attorney-General.

Justice Bejski then examined several precedents of the Supreme Court reviewing decisions of the Attorney-General, including H.C. 650/82, and H.C. 223/88 (*The Jerusalem Post,* November 28, 1983, and November 22, 1989).

The tendency had been to widen the grounds upon which those decisions could be attacked, though this tendency, apparently, did not yet enjoy general acceptance. It was recognized, however, that such grounds were not limited to lack of good faith, dishonesty, or improper motives, but also included a material perversion of justice, extreme unreasonableness, unjust discrimination, or damage to the public interest.

The Advocate-General had justified his decision on three grounds, Justice Bejski said: the long period that had passed since the events described, when the intifada* had just begun, and it was decided to use force against those disturbing the peace; the lack of clarity as to how such force was to be employed; and the decision of the Chief of the General Staff that Meir terminate his active service in the IDF.

The first ground, said Justice Bejski, was unacceptable. An investigation had to be conducted, and it sometimes took years for a criminal matter to reach the court. A delay of some 15 months was certainly not too long.

As to the second ground, the court had to assume that the initial period of the intifada was particularly difficult for officers and men alike. However, could anyone speak of "lack of clarity" in relating to the events described? Acts of that kind appalled every civilized being, and no amount of uncertainty could excuse them.

This was compounded by the fact that the order had been given by a senior officer, who should have known that the moral quality of the IDF forbade such conduct. Indeed, one of the officers had protested, warning his men not to lose their humanity in carrying out the "order from above" and, in fact, the order was not carried out as severely as it might have been.

The third ground raised could also not be accepted, said Justice Bejski. He by no means underestimated the seriousness of Meir's being forced to end his army career, although he was awarded reasonable severance conditions, including a pension, and a suitable interim arrangement. His leaving the army, however, was no substitute for criminal proceedings against him.

Similar considerations applied to other professions, such as the law, or medicine, in which disciplinary proceedings were taken, which had no effect on criminal proceedings for the same misconduct.

---

* The uprising in the occupied territories.

The Petitioners had also contended that the Advocate-General had discriminated in favour of Meir, since other officers and men had been arraigned before special courts martial for much less serious offences. The court, said Justice Bejski, had received no responsible response from the Advocate-General to this charge.

In conclusion, Justice Bejski pointed out that the IDF, even in difficult times, had maintained the purity of its arms, and had taken the utmost care to fulfil the duties imposed on the State by international law. It had recognized the welfare of the population in the occupied territories, and the maintenance of order there, as basic values in the rule of law and the public interest.

In spite of the difficulties, an order such as that now discussed, which the Advocate-General regarded as manifestly illegal, was to be condemned, and the perpetrator indicted for the offence which his conduct established. Despite the considerations weighed by the Advocate-General, his decision constituted a material perversion of justice, justifying the interference of the court.

Justice Bejski proposed, therefore, that the petition be allowed.

Judge Kedmi concurred. The court, he said, did not take the place of the Advocate-General, and substitute its decision for his. Its task was limited to judging the legality of the decision. In doing so, it applied the objective test by examining the reasonableness of the decision, and the subjective test by examining whether the Advocate-General had acted in good faith. Moreover, the court adopted no stand as to the guilt or innocence of Col. Meir, or as to the punishment that should be imposed upon him.

It was abundantly clear, he continued, that Meir's conduct in giving the order aroused revulsion, and was to be stigmatized in the strongest terms. It was patently illegal, and blatantly contradicted the basic values of the people of Israel.

It had not been seriously argued, said Judge Kedmi, that the Advocate-General had acted in bad faith. Indeed, his report and recommendations negated such a conclusion. It remained, therefore, to examine his grounds for preferring disciplinary proceedings against Meir, and not indicting him before a Special Court Martial.

Judge Kedmi agreed with Justice Bejski that the period of time that had elapsed since the incidents in question was not a basis for complaint. He also agreed as to the argument of "lack of clarity" in the degree or nature of the force to be employed by the army. The extreme and inherent impropriety of the order was self-evident from every angle, and no "absence of clarity" as to the use of force in reaction to the violence of the intifada could obscure this fact.

The termination of Meir's army service tilted the balance in the Advocate-General's decision to be content with disciplinary proceedings. For that decision to be set aside, it was not sufficient to show that it was merely unreasonable. It had to be so materially unreasonable that no court could confirm it.

After serious doubts, said Judge Kedmi, he had regretfully reached the conclusion that the decision could not stand. It was clear that the termination of a senior field officer's service, with his whole career before him, was a very severe blow; and that was the step taken, at least formally, in the present case.

This step, however, lost a great deal of its force because of the circumstances. The termination was not sharp and immediate, so as to express the revulsion aroused by Meir's conduct. Moreover, it was effected on the basis of "understanding and consent," and was accompanied by arrangements as to leave, pension, and the promise of employment in a similar public institution. The reaction to Meir's conduct had to be punitive, so as to be an answer to the pain caused to the public by his behaviour.

It was true that Meir had also been tried disciplinarily, and had been severely reprimanded. Nevertheless, the decision of the Advocate-General to be satisfied with this sanction and the termination of Meir's army service — having regard particularly to how that termination was effected — and not to indict Meir before a Special Court Martial, was materially unreasonable. It could not, therefore, be confirmed.

Judge Kedmi emphasized that he did not purport to lay down any general rules. Each case had to be judged on its own circumstances.

Justice Levin agreed with his colleagues. In his view, the discretion of the Military Advocate-General in the present context was not less than that of the Attorney-General. The court too would only interfere in the most exceptional circumstances, where it was clear that there had been a serious error, or a material perversion of justice.

The Advocate-General had pondered a great deal before reaching his final decision. He had realized that the events described were so serious that some action had to be taken also against Col. Meir. Although that officer had not participated actively in what took place, he was deeply involved in the issue of manifestly illegal orders.

Justice Levin then examined the three grounds of the Advocate-General's decision, and concluded that none of them separately, nor all of them together, justified with any degree of reasonableness the failure to indict Meir before a Special Court Martial.

He agreed with his colleagues as to the element of the time that had elapsed since the events discussed. As to the lack of clarity in the use of force, he expressed his opinion that the more senior the officer, and the wider his powers, the heavier his duty to examine the legality and justification of orders issued.

He would have accepted the Advocate-General's third ground, Justice Levin continued, if the Chief of the General Staff had terminated Meir's active service in the army decisively and immediately. This, however, he did not do. The manner of the termination was such that it lost all its thrust.

For the above reasons, the petition was allowed, and the Advocate-General ordered to indict Colonel Meir before a Special Court Martial.

Yehoshua Shoffman appeared for the Petitioners, and Nili Arad, Director of the High Court Division in the State Attorney's Office, appeared for the Respondents.

Judgment given on December 24, 1989.

COALITION AGREEMENTS

SHALIT v. LIKUD AND OTHERS

In the Supreme Court sitting as a High Court of Justice before the President, Justice Meir Shamgar, Justice Aharon Barak, and Justice Eliezer Goldberg, in the matter of *Advocate Meshullam Shalit, Advocate Yitzhak Ben-Yisrael, and others*, Petitioners, versus *The Likud, Ma'arach and other Knesset Factions, the Attorney General, and others*, Respondents (H.C. 1601-1604, 1890/90).

Constitutional Law—Publication of Coalition Agreements between Knesset Factions—Intervention by Supreme Court—Basic Law: The Knesset, 1958, section 4—Basic Law: The Government, 1968, section 15—Knesset Elections Law (Consolidated Version), 1969, section 81(a)—Evidence Ordinance (New Version), 1971, sections 44, 45—Contracts (General Part) Law, 1973, section 39—Basic Law: Judicature, 1984.

Under section 15 of the Basic Law: the Government, of 1968: "When a government has been formed, it shall present itself to the Knesset, shall announce the basic lines of its policy, its composition, and the distribution of functions among the Ministers, and shall ask for an expression of confidence. The Government is constituted when the Knesset has expressed confidence in it, and the Ministers shall thereupon assume office."

The Petitioners applied to the High Court of Justice for an order directing the publication of the coalition agreements relating to the constitution of a government under the above section.

The first judgment of the court was delivered by Justice Meir Shamgar.

The replies of the different Respondents to the petitions, he said, had not been uniform. Some had recognized the obligation to publish the agreements, and had placed them before the court. The Attorney-General had submitted that the principle of publication should be accepted, but that it should take place when the government was presented to the Knesset.

Although the power of the court to intervene had not been challenged, it had also been argued that the question at issue should rather be decided by the Knesset itself in appropriate legislation.

Referring to section 4 of the Basic Law: the Knesset, of 1958, and section 81(a) of the Knesset Elections Law (Consolidated Version) of 1969, the President pointed out that political contracts, as reflected in coalition agreements between the various factions in the Knesset, were the result of the structure of Israel's regime and its system of proportional representation.

They were not necessarily governed by the general law of contracts. They were entered into by public officials charged by the electorate with the conduct of legislation and government. They existed for the promotion of the public welfare. They were not conceived for the protection of private and personal interests.

The democratic process demanded open clarification and free discussion of problems facing the State. The link between the public and its elected representatives did not cease after the elections. A democratic regime was built on the community being continuously and fully informed of what was taking place in public affairs. Such information could only be privileged from disclosure on exceptional grounds such as state security, or relations with foreign states, or the danger of damage to some vital public interest, within the meaning of sections 44 and 45 of the Evidence Ordinance (New Version) of 1971.

The purposes which a public agreement was designed to serve demanded the upholding of the public interest, and the observance of the rules of fairness and probity, in the activities contemplated by the agreement. It was on these factors that public confidence was based.

The public, in this context, included Knesset members themselves, who were required to vote on a motion of confidence under section 15 of the Basic Law: the Government, quoted above. The confidence of the public, however, could not be maintained on what was hidden from it. The necessity of publishing the agreements in question was a natural consequence of their avowed object — the protection of the public interest alone.

The question remained as to the court's function in the present context.

The court shared the opinion that the matter now raised should be regulated by legislation. Moreover, in the present legal-constitutional framework, any legislative solution was preferable to one which relied on the judicial interpretation of constitutional conceptions alone.

However, since the matter had been brought before the court, and in the absence of any legislation, it was proper that the court should exercise its powers under section 15 of the Basic Law: Judicature of 1984, and lay down the principles that should apply to the question before it.

The court was accordingly of opinion, the President concluded, that agreements between Knesset factions, between factions and Knesset members, and between members themselves, dealing with the functions of the legislature or of the executive, and entered into with a view to forming a government, should be published.

This applied equally to those who succeeded in forming a government, and those who failed to do so. The publication should take place no later than the presentation of the government under section 15 of the Basic Law: The Government, and in the Knesset itself. The technical details, however, could be laid down in the Knesset Constitution.

Justice Aharon Barak concurred. The political parties, he said, were the constitutional tool for crystallizing the political will of the people. Because of the electoral system, we had a multi-party regime, based on coalitions. Political agreements, therefore, were a vital factor in the political process.

It was only natural in this situation that the citizens, whose votes established the Knesset and the organs that governed the State, be kept aware of a political agreement, which frequently departed from, or added to, existing conceptions.

This was an essential feature of a democratic regime. It was only on the basis of full knowledge that the public could decide its stand, and engage in the free exchange of ideas between the electors and the elected.

It was also essential, Justice Barak added, that Knesset members themselves be kept informed of such agreements, for they were required to vote on the constitution of the new government. Indeed, the Attorney-General had informed the court that the agreements were placed before the Knesset before that vote took place.

A second basis for disclosing coalition agreements, said Justice Barak, was the public duty of the parties who made them. A Knesset faction was a constitutional entity, and a political party participating in the elections fulfilled a constitutional function. Factions and Knesset members performed a public duty under the law. In signing political agreements they were not acting for themselves, but as trustees for the public.

A private individual was entitled, subject to the demands of good faith as laid down in section 39 of the Contracts (General Part) Law, of 1973, to keep his information to himself. The information in the hands of a public official, however, was not his private property. It belonged to the public, and he was obliged to disclose it to the public. Fairness demanded that he act thus. A public official was obliged to disclose information, just as he was obliged to give the reasons for his decisions.

The third ground for disclosing the agreements in question was the right of the public, and the individual citizen, to know what was taking place in the public domain. As there was freedom of expression in a democratic regime, so there was the right to receive information on matters of public import.

As the court had often stressed, Justice Barak added, these rights were not absolute. It was sometimes necessary to strike a balance between them and competing factors as, for example, state security. In principle, however, there was a duty to disclose.

He agreed that coalition agreements should be disclosed, at the latest, before the vote of confidence under section 15 of the Basic Law: The Government.

Justice Barak then dealt with the place of the court in relation to the present petitions.

There was no formal difficulty, he said, in the court giving recognition to the duty of disclosure. Citing numerous precedents and legal texts, he pointed out that wide fields in the sphere of administrative law had been developed by judicial creation, by "judicial legislation." For example, in relation to tenders, the principles of natural justice, the rules where there were conflicting rights, and the principles of the exercise of administrative discretion.

Nevertheless, Justice Barak continued, there were areas in which the court's intervention, although possible, was undesirable.

This, in his view, was not such a case. The court's decision in the present instance was based upon well-known principles, as illustrated above, on which it had acted in many situations.

At the same time, it was desirable that the legislature deal with the subject of political agreements. The court could not lay down specific provisions. It could not impose a duty on a particular authority, such as the Knesset Speaker, or the State Comptroller, to examine the contents of an agreement. It could not create a "framework for political agreements," or lay down particulars as to the methods of publication.

Since, however, the legislature had not yet acted in this regard, it was left to the court to decide the matter on the strength of the basic principles of our system, and this it had done.

Justice Eliezer Goldberg agreed with his colleagues, and accepted the principles they had enunciated. Nevertheless, he was of opinion that the "natural" authority to deal with a constitutional question of primary importance, such as that now before the court, was the legislature, and not the judiciary. It was his view that even in the absence of norms in public law, it was not always for the court to develop them by judicial legislation, where the proper course was legislation by the Knesset.

The only reason for his agreement to the court's intervention in the present case, Justice Goldberg said, was the fact that if the question at issue remained unresolved until legislation was passed, the court would have failed to prevent the danger of damage to the fabric of our public life, with all its consequences.

For the above reasons, the petitions were allowed, and the Respondents ordered to publish the agreements referred to.

The first and second Petitioners appeared in person; Michael Corinaldi, Haim Cohen and Shmuel Moran appeared for the other Petitioners; Nili Arad, Director of the High Court Division of the State Attorney's Office, appeared for the Attorney-General; and Aran Palas, Hanan Meltzer, Oded Kariv and Eitan Haberman appeared for the other Respondents.

Judgment given on May 8, 1990.

Note: The following precedents cited in the judgments were reported in *The Jerusalem Post* on the dates indicated: H.C. 243/82, April 24, 1983, *supra* p. 5; E.A. 2/84, May 31, 1985; H.C. 372/84, October 22, 1984; H.C. 399/85, August 3, 1987, *supra* p. 47; H.C. 428/86, August 15, 1986; H.C. 680/88, January 20, 1989, *supra* p. 71.

OF THE A-G, THE BANKS, AND RESPONSIBILITY

GANOR v. ATTORNEY-GENERAL

In the Supreme Court sitting as a High Court of Justice before the President, Justice Meir Shamgar, Justice Aharon Barak, and Justice Shlomo Levin, in the matter of *Advocate Uri Ganor and others*, Petitioners, versus *The Attorney-General and others*, Respondents (H.C. 935, 940-943/89).

Administrative Law—"Public Interest"—Decision of Attorney-General Not To Prosecute Set Aside by Supreme Court—State Comptroller Law (Consolidated Version), 1958, section 14(b)—Commissions of Inquiry Law, 1968—Securities Law, 1968—Companies Ordinance (New Version), 1983—Accountants (Methods of Functioning) Regulations, 1973.

The Petitioners applied to the High Court of Justice to set aside the decision of the Attorney-General not to prosecute those allegedly responsible for manipulating bank shares, resulting in the stock exchange crisis of October 6, 1983.

The first judgment of the court was delivered by Justice Aharon Barak.

As a result of the crisis, he said, the State had undertaken to redeem the shares in question at their value prior to the closure of the stock exchange. The cost of this undertaking was $6.9 billion, and the question arose as to what had happened, and who was responsible.

Following a report by the State Comptroller, the Knesset State Control Committee decided, under section 14(b) of the State Comptroller Law (Consolidated Version) of 1958, to establish an Inquiry Commission, later known as the Bejski Commission, to investigate what had occurred. The Commission, acting under the Commissions of Inquiry Law of 1968, published its report on April 16, 1986. The allegations made, and the findings and recommendations of the Commission, were also investigated by the police. The Attorney-General found, however, that the police investigation added nothing to the Commission's report, which therefore remained the basis for his decision.

Justice Barak then reviewed the findings of the Commission. It had decided that the manipulation process revealed, *prima facie*, a number of criminal offences by the banks, and by those who assisted them. These were, in the main, contraventions of the Companies Ordinance (New Version) of 1983, the Securities Law of 1968, the Banking (Service to Customer) Law of 1981, the Accountants (Methods of Functioning) Regulations of 1973, and the crime of perjury.

After full consideration of the findings of the Commission and of the police, and of draft indictments prepared by the State Attorney's department, said Justice Barak, the Attorney-General had decided, on November 12, 1989, that a prosecution was not justified.

The Attorney-General had doubts as to whether there was sufficient evidence to support charges against the banks and bankers involved. Moreover, he was of the opinion that to prosecute them would not serve the public interest. The bankers, in his view, had already paid the price of their actions in accordance with the recommendations of the Commission. Moreover, a number of State authorities shared the blame for what had happened, and it would not be fair to single out the private sector for punishment. Furthermore, the purpose of criminal proceedings was to identify the wrongdoers, reveal improper practices, punish, and prevent further crimes. All this had already been achieved by the Commission.

The Attorney-General had also taken into account the long period that had elapsed since the Commission had submitted its report. He was of the opinion that it would not be right to turn the clock back, and impose on the public the expense, weariness and strain which reopening the whole matter would involve.

In addition, the Attorney-General had decided to refer the allegations against the accountants to their professional association for its further investigation and recommendation.

After holding, on the basis of Supreme Court precedents, that the Petitioners had locus standi to approach the court, Justice Barak turned to the elements to be considered by the Attorney-General in weighing the "public interest" involved.

These elements were the seriousness of the offence, the personal circumstances of the suspect, and other factors, such as possible damage to State security, or the pressures on the prosecution or on the courts, which would justify a decision not to prosecute. There were sometimes conflicting interests. The prosecution had to fix its priorities and, like every administrative authority, had to weigh only relevant considerations, in good faith, without capriciousness and unjust discrimination, fairly and reasonably.

He was satisfied, Justice Barak continued, that the Attorney-General had weighed relevant considerations exclusively in reaching his decision. Moreover, although there was a feeling that this was a case where, perhaps, serious offenders were freed from blame while many others, guilty of petty crimes, were prosecuted and punished, there was insufficient evidence relating to similar situations to establish that there had been unjust discrimination.

On the other hand, however, the Attorney-General's decision that there was no "public interest" in instituting the prosecutions demanded by the Petitioners, was inherently unreasonable.

There was an uneven balance between the various factors involved. The circumstances relating to the alleged offences, particularly those concerning securities, were serious. The criminal activities of the banks and bankers were conducted in secrecy over a long period. Thousands of citizens lost their money, and the enormous sum the Treasury was obliged to pay was a heavy burden. The public interest in punishing those responsible, and deterring the banks, and other financial institutions, from similar behaviour, was of the greatest weight.

If the "earthquake," and the share manipulation which followed, did not justify prosecution, when would the prosecution of banks and bankers guilty, *prima facie*, of offences relating to securities, ever be justified? The various factors taken into account by the Attorney-General in deciding as he did could not be balanced against the other considerations mentioned above.

His opinion in this regard, Justice Barak continued, was strengthened by the fact that the prosecution of the offenders was consistent with the recommendations of a Commission acting under statutory authority. Its recommendations did not bind the Attorney-General, but they were certainly of great weight. The Commission was objective, fair and serious, and the public expected that its recommendations would be accepted.

The Attorney-General had acted lawfully in referring the allegations against the accountants to their association. On the other hand, he had acted wrongly in deciding not to prosecute before considering the association's recommendations. It was his duty to weigh what would be brought before him in accordance with the accepted principles, and then decide what course to follow.

Justice Barak then dealt with the power of the court to interfere in the Attorney-General's discretion as to whether or not to institute a prosecution. Citing numerous Supreme Court precedents [see end of article], he pointed out that the court would not substitute its discretion for that of the Attorney-General. Moreover, a mere error of the Attorney-General was not sufficient to warrant interference. The decision had to be unlawful. Where his decision was attacked on the ground of unreasonableness, it had to be real and extreme.

That was the situation in the present case, and the intervention of the court was accordingly justified.

Justice Barak proposed, therefore, that the Attorney-General's decision not to prosecute on the ground of "public interest" be set aside. The matter would be returned to him to weigh, in the case of the banks and bankers, whether there was sufficient proof, *prima facie*, to sustain a conviction. He was to do the same in the case of the accountants, after the Accountants' Council had completed its investigation.

Justice Meir Shamgar concurred.

As a general rule, he said, the Attorney-General should prosecute where there was *prima facie* proof of an offence. The exception to the rule existed where a prosecution would not be in the public interest. In making his decision, the Attorney-General had to take into account that all were equal before the law, and that the State was concerned in the elimination and deterrence of crime, and in the protection of its victims.

The court, he said, would not interfere in the decision of a statutory authority only because it took a decision which the court, in its place, would not have taken. Where, however, its deviation from the path of reasonableness was inherent and real, there was no alternative but to intervene.

Justice Shlomo Levin agreed with his colleagues.

For the above reasons, the petition was allowed.

Uri Ganor, Haim Hadash, Michael Corinaldi, Giora Ardinset and Yonatan Ben-Natan appeared for the Petitioners, and Nili Arad, Director of the High Court Division of the State Attorney's Office, Dr. Mishael Cheshin, Zvi Agmon, and Meshulam Shalit appeared for the Respondents.

Judgment given on May 19, 1990.

Supreme Court precedents cited in the judgments were reported in *The Jerusalem Post* as follows: H.C. 428/86, August 15, 1986; H.C. 680/88, January 20, 1989, *supra* p. 71; H.C. 223/88, November 22, 1989, *supra* p. 116.

DEMOLITION HALTED

NASMAAN v. IDF COMMANDER IN GAZA STRIP

In the Supreme Court sitting as a High Court of Justice before the Deputy-President, Justice Menahem Elon, Justice Theodore Orr, and Judge Ya'acov Kedmi, in the matter of *Shuki Nasmaan and Halil Haladi*, Petitioners, versus *The IDF Commander in the Gaza Strip*, Respondent (H.C. 802/89).

Administrative Law—Demolition of House—Order Based on Incorrect Facts Set Aside—Defence (Emergency) Regulations, 1945, Regulation 119.

The Respondent, acting under Regulation 119 of the Defence (Emergency) Regulations of 1945, which have remained part of the local law in the Gaza Strip since their promulgation in the time of the British Mandate, directed the expropriation, sealing off and demolition of parts of the house of the first Petitioner and the house of his neighbour, and the expropriation and sealing off of part of the house of the second Petitioner. (The text of Regulation 119 appeared in *The Jerusalem Post* on August 9, 1989, *supra* p. 99.)

The Respondent's directions relating to the houses of the Petitioners themselves were dealt with in a previous judgment of the court on November 21, 1989, and the judgments now reported dealt with his direction regarding part of the house of the first Petitioner's neighbour. The direction in question was given by the Respondent on the basis of acts alleged to have been committed by one Abd Abayed, who lived in the house.

The first judgment of the court was delivered by Judge Ya'acov Kedmi.

In addition to her general contentions in the case, he said, counsel for the Petitioners had argued that errors in one of the Respondent's grounds for his direction with regard to the neighbour's house justified its being set aside.

The Respondent had stated, in the ground in question, that "Abayed had cooperated, in the framework of his activities in a committee of Helem [a movement of Palestinian nationalistic committees] in assaulting persons suspected of collaboration [with the authorities] and dealing in drugs. This he had done while disguised. He had also taken part in setting fire to the Income Tax office in Gaza. In his examination, he had admitted committing the above acts."

Counsel had pointed out that there was no admission by Abayed in his statement of assaulting suspected collaborators nor of setting fire to the Income Tax office in Gaza, and it was on these errors that she relied.

He could not accept counsel's argument, said Judge Kedmi. Abayed had admitted in his statement that he had joined a group of Helem in his neighbourhood, and that on the instructions of his commander, the first Petitioner, "we began to act against collaborators and drug dealers."

He had also admitted that, in the framework of Helem, he had taken part in beating the drug dealers Halim Dalu and Jamal Diab, and also in beating a man who had taken it upon himself to act against a suspected collaborator, instead of acting through the People's Committee.

He had also admitted that he had heard from his companions in the group that they had thrown a loaded pipe on the house of a suspected collaborator, and that, like his companions, he had committed the acts in which he participated with his face covered.

It was true, said Judge Kedmi, that setting fire to the Income Tax office was not mentioned by Abayed in his statement. It had been mentioned, however, by the first Petitioner, who said in his statement that Abayed had taken part in that act. In his opinion, this error of the Respondent had no significance, since the burning of the Income Tax office was only an addition to the other grounds on which he had relied. The drafting of the Respondent's grounds showed clearly that this was so. He had relied, in the main, on Abayed's acts as detailed above.

Having regard to the facts detailed by the court in its earlier judgment relating to the houses of the Petitioners themselves, the grounds relied upon by the Respondent, without the burning of the Income Tax office, were sufficient to justify his direction. The error of the Respondent was merely technical, and not substantive. There was no basis, therefore, for setting his direction aside.

Judge Kedmi proposed, therefore, that the petition, insofar as it related to the neighbour's house, be dismissed.

Justice Theodore Orr dissented from his colleague.

The Respondent, he said, had relied on three facts: that Abayed had himself attacked collaborators; that he had taken part in setting fire to the Income Tax office; and that he had admitted to these allegations.

These three facts were incorrect. A careful reading of Abayed's statement did not support his admission of the allegations that he had attacked collaborators. In regard to the arson relating to the Income Tax office, it had to be remembered that those responsible for that offence had been prosecuted, and that Abayed was not among those charged. It followed that not only did Abayed not admit his guilt in that regard, but the military prosecutor apparently did not consider the evidence sufficient to prove his participation.

He did not agree with his colleague, Justice Orr continued, that the Income Tax office allegation was only a supplementary consideration of the Respondent in reaching his decision. Moreover, it was the duty of the court to review the Respondent's decision to issue the directive in question, by inquiring whether he had acted lawfully. It was not for the court to place itself in the Respondent's shoes, and ask itself what it would have done in the same circumstances.

Once it was shown that the Respondent had relied on incorrect facts, the proper course was to return the matter to him for reconsideration on the basis of the correct facts. It was impossible to know what he would have decided if incorrect facts had not been placed before him.

In conclusion, Justice Orr stressed that this case was concerned with the destruction and sealing off of a building occupied by other persons, who would suffer as a result, although they themselves had done no wrong. The court had held that it would not interfere in the decision of the Military Commander under Regulation 119 above, where he had acted reasonably. However, in view of the harsh results of the Military Commander's decision, each case had to be examined with the utmost care, to ensure that he had acted lawfully, relying on the relevant facts alone.

Justice Orr proposed, therefore, that the petition be allowed, and the case returned to the Respondent for reconsideration.

Justice Menahem Elon agreed with Justice Orr.

Petitioner's counsel had argued, he said, that a direction under Regulation 119 should only be given where the person affected had admitted the facts alleged against him. He did not agree with this contention. Moreover, he did not find it necessary to discuss the weight of the evidence required to justify such a direction.

In the present case, Justice Elon continued, the Respondent had given his direction on the basis of facts which were incorrect. He agreed that the proper course in such circumstances was to return the matter to the Respondent for his reconsideration on the basis of the correct facts.

For the above reasons, and by majority decision, the petition was allowed, and the Respondent's direction in regard to the house of the first Petitioner's neighbour was set aside. The matter was returned to the Respondent for reconsideration.

The Respondent was ordered to pay the first Petitioner's costs in the sum of NIS 2,000, with interest and linkage according to law.

Lea Tzemel appeared for the Petitioners, and Senior Assistant State Attorney Yochi Gnessin for the Respondent.

Judgment given on May 6, 1990.

A BELLY DANCER AND KASHRUT

RASKIN v. JERUSALEM RELIGIOUS COUNCIL

In the Supreme Court sitting as a High Court of Justice before Justice Gavriel Bach, Justice Theodore Orr, and Judge Shaul Aloni, in the matter of *Ilana Raskin*, Petitioner, versus *The Jerusalem Religious Council, Rabbi Yitzhak Kolitz and Rabbi Shalom Mashash*, Respondents (H.C. 465/89).

Administrative Law—Kashrut Certificate—Effect of Kashrut of "Immodest" Dancing at Hotel—Jewish Law—Refusal of Certificate Set Aside—Jewish Religious Services Law, 1971—Kashrut (Prohibition of Deceit) Law, 1983, section 2.

The Petitioner earns her living as an oriental, or belly, dancer at functions in various places, including entertainment halls and hotels in Jerusalem. Towards the end of 1988 there was a fall-off in the number of invitations she received. When she inquired, it emerged that the fall-off was due to a warning issued to hotel-and hall-owners that they were liable to lose their kashrut certificates if they permitted "immodest" performances in their premises.

Having failed in her attempts to obtain the cancellation of the warning, the Petitioner applied to the High Court of Justice for a declaration that it was unlawful.

The first judgment of the court was delivered by Justice Theodore Orr.

Kashrut certificates in Jerusalem, he said, were issued by the second and third Respondents as "local rabbis," as defined in section 2(a) (2) of the Kashrut (Prohibition of Deceit) Law of 1983; and their directives were enforced by the Religious Council under the Jewish Religious Services Law of 1971.

The legal provision at the heart of the present dispute, he continued, was in section 11 of the 1983 Law, under which: "In issuing a kashrut certificate, the rabbi shall have regard to the kashrut laws only." The Petitioner contended that the term "kashrut" referred to the kashrut of the food alone, while the Respondents argued that that expression also embraced kashrut in the halachic sense: the fitness of the place, and what happened there, according to Halacha.

Kashrut certificates, said Justice Orr, were issued by the first and second Respondents by virtue of their powers under a secular Law. They were in the same position, therefore, as any other administrative authority exercising statutory powers. They were obliged to act strictly within those powers. If they exceeded their authority and, in exercising their discretion, relied on irrelevant factors beyond what the Law permitted, the court was entitled to intervene, and set their decision aside.

It was true that the issue of the certificates was placed by the 1983 Law in the hands of a religious body. That Law was to be interpreted, however, so as to give effect to the intention of the legislature. The question was, therefore, in which sense the term "kashrut" was used in section 11 of the statute.

It sometimes happened that the legislature used the same expression in different Laws, bearing a different meaning in each one. A clear example was the use of the term "Jew," which bore a secular connotation in the Law of Return, and a religious connotation in the Rabbinical Courts Jurisdiction (Marriage and Divorce) Law of 1953. The same question arose in the case of the Messianic Jews (H.C. 265/87, *The Jerusalem Post*, January 3, 1990, *supra* p. 126.)

The first test of the legislative intent was the language of the 1983 Law itself. Its purpose, as its name declared, was the prohibition of deceit in regard to kashrut, not the imposition of kashrut. It related to "eating houses" where "the sale or serving of commodities to the public for consumption on the spot is carried on," and to those parts of a hotel where food is prepared or served.

Section 3 of the Law prohibited the holder of a kashrut certificate from selling or serving commodities not kosher according to the law of the Tora. Moreover, the Regulations of 1988 framed under the Law in question clearly applied to the kashrut of the food alone, and not to the kashrut of the place.

Justice Orr went on to examine the legislative history of the 1983 Law, citing, *inter alia*, the speech of Dr. Yosef Burg, then minister for religious affairs, in presenting the proposed Law to the Knesset. The minister had made it clear that the intention of the Law was to ensure the kashrut of food "and not relate to other matters." The history of the Law, said Justice Orr, therefore supported his conclusion that its sole purpose was to prevent deceit in regard to the kashrut of food, and nothing more.

Justice Orr then dealt with a number of the Respondents' arguments in support of their attitude. Their counsel had conceded that "preservation of modesty" was not a valid condition for the issue of a kashrut certificate, but he could not explain why, if that were so, the Petitioner's dances were a valid reason for refusal.

The court had asked to be referred to a halachic ruling which justified the Respondents' attitude, but no such reference had been forthcoming. Moreover, although the Law in question applied to the whole country, counsel was unable to cite another instance outside Jerusalem in which a certificate had been refused because of dances such as those of the Petitioner.

Other arguments of the Respondents, such as the false impression which a kashrut certificate would create as to the general conditions of the place in question, were also to be rejected, said Justice Orr. It was also argued that the kashrut overseer could not perform his duties adequately, since Halacha forbade him to be present in the hall when the Petitioner performed. The overseer, however, was also not present at the swimming pool at a hotel, but that did not affect his activities.

Justice Orr also dealt with other examples before the court of conditions imposed by the Respondents, such as a ban on missionary activity in a hotel, or a ban on women carrying the Tora scroll, or a ban on a party on New Year's Eve.

Having regard to the purpose of the Law in question, Justice Orr concluded, it was clear that the Respondents, in refusing a kashrut certificate on the basis of the Petitioner's dances, had exceeded their powers. They had relied on invalid grounds that had no relevance to the kashrut of food, which was the sole factor they were entitled to consider.

Justice Orr proposed, therefore, that the petition be allowed.

Justice Gavriel Bach concurred.

The Respondents had to distinguish, he said, between factors that related directly to the kashrut of food, and those that did not do so, although dealt with in Halacha.

One example cited by counsel related to desecration of the Sabbath. If, in a particular place, food was prepared in desecration of the Sabbath, the

Respondents would be entitled to take this factor into account in considering the issue of a certificate. They would not be entitled to take into account, however, the fact that the guests reached the place by travelling on the Sabbath, or that music was played there contrary to Halacha.

All the more were the Respondents precluded from taking into account factors completely unconnected with the kashrut of the food, such as that those responsible for the catering belonged to a particular stream in Judaism, or that there would be some ceremony of which the Respondents did not approve.

The Respondents would do well to revise their attitude, Justice Bach continued, not only because of the legal position, but because wide sections of the population saw and enjoyed dances of the kind performed by the Petitioner. Times changed, and what was once regarded as immodest was no longer so regarded by the majority of the public. Another factor was that many people who organized family celebrations, and who invited the Petitioner, or others, to perform the same type of dances, were themselves concerned that the food served should be kosher.

Justice Bach then cited a responsum of the late Rabbi Moses Feinstein, of the U. S., one of the great halachic authorities of our time. He had ruled that a kashrut certificate, and kashrut supervision, could be accorded to the restaurant of a Jewish sports club if the food served was kosher, provided that there would be no cooking on the Sabbath, and that guests would be permitted to drink milk and eat milk ice-cream after a meat meal if they so desired. Rabbi Feinstein had stated in his responsum that the certificate related only to the kashrut of the food, and not to the people who sold it.

Justice Bach also cited a similar responsum of Rabbi Ovadia Yosef, who expressed his agreement with Rabbi Feinstein. He had also stressed that the certificate related to the food alone, and that the kashrut overseer could not protest the freedom and liberty in our land, "which had no connection with the actual certification of the Rabbinate relating to the food."

If the above-mentioned eminent rabbis had ruled as they did in regard to a factor which was certainly associated with the food itself, said Justice Bach, it was surely desirable to follow the same path in matters which were quite unconnected with the kashrut of the food, and its preparation.

In conclusion, Justice Bach mentioned that his concurrence with Justice Orr was based on the interpretation of the relevant Law, and that his other comments were *obiter dicta*, and only supplementary.

Judge Shaul Aloni agreed with his colleagues.

For the above reasons, the petition was allowed, and the Respondents were ordered to pay the Petitioner's costs in the sum of NIS 5,000.

Netta Goldman appeared for the Petitioner, and David Kirschenbaum and Michael Doron for the Respondents.

Judgment given on May 27, 1990.

THE KNESSET AND THE COURTS

LE'OR MOVEMENT v. KNESSET SPEAKER

In the Supreme Court sitting as a High Court of Justice before the Deputy-President, Justice Menahem Elon, Justice Aharon Barak, and Justice Ya'acov Maltz, in the matter of *The Le'or Movement and others*, Petitioners, versus *The Speaker of the Knesset and others*, Respondents (H.C. 142, 172/89).

Constitutional Law—Law Passed by Knesset in Contravention of Basic Law Invalidated by Court—Basic Law: The Knesset, 1958, sections 4, 46—Political Parties (Financing) Law, 1973.

Under section 4 of the Basic Law: The Knesset, of 1958, "The Knesset shall be elected by general, national, direct, equal, secret and proportional elections, in accordance with the Knesset Elections Law; this section shall not be varied save by a majority of the members of the Knesset." Under section 46 of the Law, added by a 1959 amendment, "The majority required by this Law for a variation of section 4, 44, or 45, shall be required for decisions of the Knesset plenary at every stage of law-making, except a debate on a motion for the Knesset agenda. In this section, variation means both an express and an implicit variation."

Under the Knesset Constitution, a government Bill is presented to the House, and debated by the Knesset in three readings. In the case of a private member's Bill, however, there is a preliminary procedure, under which the House decides whether or not to refer the Bill to committee. If it does so, the committee will either prepare the Bill for its first reading, or propose that the plenum remove it from the agenda. If the first course is followed, only then does the usual procedure of three readings commence.

The elections to the 12th Knesset took place on November 1, 1988, and the parties' election expenses were borne by the State in accordance with a key laid down by the Knesset Finance Committee, as provided for in the Political Parties (Financing) Law of 1973. On November 17, 1988, the Finance Committee decided to increase the "financing unit" on which the key was based, and laid down, in addition, that this decision was to apply retroactively to the expenses of the elections to the 12th Knesset.

The Petitioners applied to the High Court of Justice to set aside the Finance Committee's decision as illegal. However, before the petition was heard, a private member's Bill was presented to the Knesset to confirm the committee's decision. At the preliminary hearing, the plenum decided, by a simple majority, to refer the Bill to the Finance Committee.

That committee returned the Bill to the plenum for its first reading. The Bill passed its first reading, and was then again referred, in the ordinary way, to the Finance Committee, by a majority of 64. The Finance Committee returned the Bill to the plenum for its second and third readings. It was passed, in each case, by a majority of 68, and became a Law.

The Petitioners then again applied to the High Court to declare the Law illegal. They argued, first, that the provision increasing the "financing unit" of the parties' expenses retroactively constituted a variation of the principle of equality enshrined in section 4 of the Basic Law. Section 46 of that Law required that the special majority laid down in section 4 was to apply "at every stage of law-making," which included the preliminary debate in the case of a private member's Bill. Since, in the present case, the Bill had been referred to the Finance Committee, at that stage, by only a simple majority of the members present, the decision of referral was illegal and the Law, therefore, was invalid.

The Petitioners also argued that the decision of the Finance Committee sanctioning the retroactive operation of the increased unit was unlawful, on the basis of unjust discrimination, and it followed that the decision of the plenum confirming the Finance Committee's decision was also unlawful. They also contended that the Law was illegal in deviating from "objective considerations of the public welfare or the welfare of the State, or the recognized legitimate interests common to all."

The first judgment of the court was delivered by Justice Aharon Barak.

The decision of the Finance Committee of November 11, 1988, he said, was unlawful. The decision to apply the increased expenses retroactively changed the relative rights of the parties at the time of the elections, and created inequality. Had the competing parties known then of the committee's decision, they might have acted differently. Those who acted within the law would lose, and those who acted against the law would gain.

The Finance Committee, like any other public administrative authority, was obliged to act without discrimination, and strictly within its statutory powers. The Political Parties (Financing) Law did not empower the committee to take decisions of this kind.

Moreover, the committee's action offended against the principle of equality in section 4 of the Basic Law, and its decision was "a stage of law-making" within the meaning of section 46 of that Law. Its decision, therefore, required a majority of the members of the Knesset. Since it was passed by only a simple majority of those present, it was unlawful for that reason too.

It was not correct, Justice Barak continued, that the decision of the plenum confirming the unlawful decision of the Finance Committee was, for that reason, also unlawful. The plenum was a sovereign body, and it was entitled to pass legislation which created discrimination if it saw fit. The question arose, however, as to the validity of "ordinary" legislation, such as the amendment to the Parties Financing Law under discussion, if it conflicted with a Basic Law whose provisions were "fortified" by requiring, for their variation, a special majority. Relying on several authorities, including English, American and South African, he held that the Basic Law took precedence.

It now remained to decide, Justice Barak said, whether the necessary majority of Knesset members had confirmed the Parties Financing Law "at every stage of law-making," as required by section 46 of the Basic Law. The required majority had passed the Financing Law at each of the three readings; but the decision at the preliminary debate to refer the Law to the Finance Committee had been passed by a simple majority alone.

The preliminary debate was also a "stage of law-making," said Justice Barak, but the question was whether it was covered by the exception mentioned in section 46, namely, "a debate on a motion for the Knesset agenda."

A Law was to be interpreted so as to express the intention of the legislature. The first test was the language of the Law itself. It was well established, however, that the court was also entitled to examine other reliable sources to ascertain that intention, including the legislative history of the enactment, and the parliamentary debates in which it was considered.

After an exhaustive review of the history of section 46, Justice Barak concluded that the preliminary debate on a private member's Bill had always been regarded as a debate on a motion for the agenda. That had always been the legislative intention, and the court should interpret the section accordingly. The Law now attacked had been passed by the Knesset as required by the Basic Law, and its validity, therefore, was not impugned.

Finally, Justice Barak referred to the argument that the court should invalidate the Law in question as deviating from the accepted standards relating to the welfare of the State. The court had held consistently that Laws of the Knesset are not subject to judicial review as to the legality of their content, but may possibly be reviewed if passed in a manner contrary to special provisions in a Basic Law, as in the present instance. As a famous English judge had said, "The proceedings here are judicial, not autocratic, which they would be if we could make Laws instead of administering them."

Justice Barak proposed, therefore, that the petition be dismissed.

Dealing with the power of the court to intervene in the acts of the legislature on the basis of the content of a Law, Justice Menahem Elon, delivering the second judgment, quoted English and Talmudic sources. It was a fundamental feature of our democratic system, recognizing the distinction between the three branches of government — the legislature, the executive and the judiciary — that the court does not interfere in the acts of the lawmaker.

The main exception to the above rule, the Deputy-President said, was where a Basic Law laid down special provisions as to the enacting of a statute. In that case, the legislature itself enjoined the court to uphold those special provisions, thus, in a sense, upholding its own sovereignty.

Justice Elon agreed with Justice Barak that the Law attacked in this case conflicted with the element of equality contained in section 4 of the Basic Law. He also agreed that, for this reason, the decision of the Knesset's Finance Committee was unacceptable, although he expressed some reservations as to the power of the court to intervene in decisions of Knesset committees. He was also of the opinion that the preliminary debate in the case of a private member's Bill was "a stage of law-making" within the meaning of section 46 of the Basic Law. He differed from his colleague, however, as to whether that debate was one "on a motion for the Knesset agenda," as stated in section 46.

The Deputy-President agreed that, while relying in the main on the language of a statutory provision, the court was entitled to examine the relevant legislative history and parliamentary proceedings in order to ascertain the intention of the legislature. In the present case, however,

Justice Barak had given full consideration to what was said before the Law was passed, but had paid insufficient attention to what was said after its enactment.

Justice Elon then examined in great detail the history of the Law, relevant parliamentary proceedings both before and after its enactment, and relevant provisions of the Knesset Constitution.

His conclusion was that Justice Barak's finding that the preliminary debate in question was "a debate on a motion for the Knesset agenda," was unjustified. In his view, this finding was clearly inconsistent with the language of the section. If the legislature had also wished to make the preliminary debate referred to an exception to the requirement of section 46, it could have said so. This it did not do, and it was inconceivable that the court would interpret the section in such a way as to add something that was not there.

The Law now attacked constituted a serious infringement of the principle of equality in elections. Any deviation from that principle had to be examined with the greatest care, and any statutory provision supporting such an infringement had to be passed by the legislature in strict accordance with the procedure laid down. This procedure demanded a majority of Knesset members for referring the Bill to committee, and that majority had not been obtained.

The conclusion was, therefore, said Justice Elon, that as the decision at the stage of the preliminary debate to refer the Bill to the Finance Committee was passed by a simple majority only, its enactment was contrary to the provisions of section 4 of the Basic Law: The Knesset. The Law was accordingly invalid.

Justice Elon proposed, therefore, that the petition be allowed.

Justice Ya'acov Maltz concurred with Justice Elon. He relied, in the main, on the wording of the exception "a debate on a motion for the Knesset agenda." This wording, he said, did not include the preliminary debate on a private member's Bill. Had the legislature intended to make an exception of such a debate, it should have said so in clear terms. If it made a mistake in not saying so, it should amend section 46 accordingly.

As Justice Elon had said, any deviation from the principle of equality in elections should be passed by a majority of Knesset members, and not merely by a simple majority of those present. A hasty decision on a matter of such importance should be avoided. That also applied to the preliminary debate on a private member's Bill.

For the above reasons, and by majority decision, the petition was allowed.

Dr. Michael Corinaldi appeared for some of the Petitioners, Ze'ev Treinin appeared for some of the Respondents, and Nili Arad, Director of the High Court Division of the State Attorney's Office, appeared for the Speaker of the Knesset.

The judgment was given on July 1, 1990.

EMERGENCY POWERS AND THE LEGISLATURE

AVRAHAM PORAZ v. ISRAEL GOVERNMENT

In the Supreme Court sitting as a High Court of Justice before Justice Shlomo Levin, Justice Gavriel Bach and Judge Mordechai Ben Yair, in the matter of *Avraham Poraz MK*, Petitioner, versus *The Government of Israel and others*, Respondents (H.C. 2994/90).

Constitutional Law—Misuse by Minister of Emergency Powers—Issue of Emergency Regulations While Bill Pending before Knesset—Intervention by Supreme Court—Law and Administration Ordinance, 1948, section 9.

On July 2, 1990, Emergency Regulations (Plans for the Erection of Dwellings), issued by the Minister of Building and Housing, were published in the Government Gazette. The regulations were authorized by the government despite the opposition of the Minister of the Interior, under section 9(a) of the Law and Administration Ordinance of 1948.

The regulations contained various provisions for simplifying, accelerating, or eliminating some of the processes of confirming building plans and obtaining permits for the erection of a maximum of 3,000 dwellings. They also contained directives for exempting imported housing units from compliance with the required standards; and they authorized the minister to order local authorities and the Israel Electric Corporation to connect dwellings to the necessary services.

At the time the above regulations were issued, a government bill called the Planning and Building Procedures (Interim Provisions) Bill — 1990, was pending before the Knesset. This bill also contained provisions for the speedy solution of the housing problem of new olim, young couples, and the homeless. On June 26, the chairman of the Knesset Interior Committee informed the housing minister that the Ministerial Legislation Committee was considering the bill, and that the steps for its being passed would be speeded up so as to give him the necessary powers as soon as possible. He was also invited, before deciding on the regulations, to meet the committee and the interior minister. Nevertheless, the regulations were issued.

The bill passed its first reading on July 2, and on July 9, during a Knesset debate on the bill, the Petitioner asked the housing minister why emergency regulations were necessary if the interior minister said they were not. The former replied that the regulations were designed as a model test in the struggle against bureaucracy, and for shortening procedures. He knew that some people were afraid of emergency regulations. These regulations, however, which would be valid for only three months (under section 9(c) of the above Ordinance), and which applied to only a small number of housing units, should give no cause for concern. On July 11, the bill passed its second and third readings and became a Law. The Petitioner then moved the High Court of Justice to declare the regulations invalid.

The judgment of the court was delivered by Justice Shlomo Levin. Counsel for the government, he said, had explained that the purpose of the regulations was to find quick solutions to the current housing shortage, and to test the feasibility of erecting prefabricated units in Israel. The 3,000 units were a pilot project and, if it succeeded, more units would be erected. The building sites would be prepared and the foundations laid within the 3-month period, and the units would be supplied by December 15, 1990.

The Petitioner, Justice Levin continued, had attacked the regulations on a number of legal grounds. His counsel had contended, *inter alia*, that the housing minister had relied on irrelevant considerations in issuing the regulations. The material before the court, said Justice Levin, did not support this argument. The minutes of the meeting of the government at which the matter at issue had been considered had not been handed to the court, and the remarks of the minister in the Knesset did not show that he had taken irrelevant matters into account.

Petitioner's counsel had also argued, Justice Levin continued, that the housing minister had erred in using emergency regulations to achieve a purpose which could, and should, have been achieved by legislation of the Knesset.

Justice Levin then cited Supreme Court precedents as to the issue of emergency regulations under the Law and Administration Ordinance (H.C. 372/84 — *The Jerusalem Post* of October 22, 1984), and under the Commodities and Services (Control) Law of 1957. Three prerequisites had to be satisfied: there had to be a specific lawful purpose — described in the latter Law as an "essential activity"; the minister had to act within his powers under the Law; and the minister had to give proper legal consideration to the relationship between the desired objective and the use of emergency powers. It was abundantly clear that the first condition was satisfied. In present circumstances, with thousands of immigrants reaching Israel and with the whole country geared to absorb them, it was imperative to employ unconventional means to remove bureaucratic obstacles and secure the necessary resources to achieve the objective quickly and efficiently. The court had no doubt that the minister genuinely believed that emergency regulations were the proper means to be employed in this context.

It was also clear, said Justice Levin, that the minister was empowered under the ordinance to issue emergency regulations in the existing circumstances. These particular regulations, however, contained far-reaching provisions, including the suspension of Laws of the Knesset, disregarding plans submitted under the town-planning Laws, and exemptions from licences, permits, and authorizations.

Any mistake in applying these provisions could cause endless damage. The need for fast action was perhaps inevitable. If, however, it was possible, at the same time, for the legislature itself to act on the same issue, it was proper for the executive authority to desist from exercising emergency powers. Petitioner's counsel had argued, therefore, that the third prerequisite mentioned above had not been fulfilled; the minister had not weighed the possibility that the same purpose could be achieved by ordinary legislation or, if he had weighed this possibility, he had disregarded it.

Counsel's last contention, said Justice Levin, was correct. Citing legal authorities, he pointed out that the conception that emergency regulations should be made only where there was no possibility of action by the legislature, had already been expressed in a proclamation issued five days before the Law and Administration Ordinance was enacted. Moreover, the Attorney-General, in a 1985 directive, had asked ministers to apply this principle and, where it was possible, to consider presenting the text of the proposed regulations in a bill to the Knesset. The legislature could then decide, urgently, whether to enact a Law in the language of the regulations, or in different language, or to invalidate the regulations after a specified period.

In the present case, the housing minister knew, before issuing the regulations, that the Knesset intended to enact a Law on the same subject, and such a Law was in fact passed after the necessary procedures had been accelerated. What prevented him from asking the legislature to include his proposals in the Law? If the Knesset had agreed, the regulations would have become superfluous. If the Knesset had disagreed, its decision would mean that it was against the regulations, in which case, too, they could not have been issued. The court had witnessed a kind of race between the minister and the Knesset — who would arrive first. The minister's disregard of the principle discussed above was a material flaw in the issue of the regulations, which justified their being set aside.

The conclusion of the court would, in the ordinary course, involve invalidating the regulations from the date of their issue, Justice Levin continued. However, the laying down of roads and the preparation of building sites, authorized by the regulations, had already begun, and the judgment of the court would presumably involve changes. It was also possible that the Knesset would validate, by legislation, all or some of the steps already taken.

The court would order, therefore, that its decision would only become operative three weeks after its having been given.

Ra'anan Har Ze'ev appeared for the Petitioner, and Nili Arad, Director of the High Court Division of the State Attorney's Office, appeared for the Government.

The judgment was given on July 17, 1990.

NO ABSOLUTE RIGHT TO DEMONSTRATE

KACH MOVEMENT v. MINISTER OF POLICE

In the Supreme Court sitting as the High Court of Justice before Justice Gavriel Bach, Justice Theodore Orr, and Judge Mordechai Ben-Yair, in the matter of *The Kach Movement*, Petitioner, versus *The Minister of Police and others*, Respondents (H.C. 2936/90).

Administrative Law—Right to Demonstrate—Police Refusal of Permit Upheld

The Petitioner applied to the police for permission to hold public meetings on July 3, 1990, in the afternoon and evening, in the Jerusalem suburbs of East Talpiot (Armon Hanatziv) and Neve Ya'acov. The subject for discussion at the meetings was described in the applications as a "referendum," and the purpose of the meetings was said to be "informative."

On July 1, the Southern District commander of the police informed the Petitioner of the refusal of each of its applications on the following grounds: "The police have placed reinforcements in the district in which you wish to hold your meeting, in order to restore quiet and security in the area. In view of the recent occurrences in this area, we feel there is a real risk that a public meeting at the time and place requested will endanger public order and the security of the population. I have decided, therefore, to refuse the permit sought. At the same time, I confirm the grant of a permit for a public meeting at the hour requested, in the center of the city, at a place agreed upon in advance with the police."

The Petitioner was not satisfied with the reply, and applied to the High Court of Justice to order the police to grant the permission requested.

The judgment of the court was delivered by Justice Gavriel Bach. The Petitioner's spokesman, he said, had informed the court that despite the general definition in the applications to the police of the subjects and purposes of the meetings, the Petitioner's object was to explain its own policies, in those two very suburbs, against the background of the violent incidents which had recently happened there, in which Jewish residents had been injured.

The court was of the opinion, said Justice Bach, that there was no unreasonableness or other basic flaw in the decision of the police to justify its intervention in this case. The police had to realize, on the one hand, that it was sometimes not sufficient to grant a permit to demonstrate at any place it might indicate. The exact location for a demonstration, selected by Applicants, was frequently of great importance to them for achieving their aims, and the police should respect their wishes wherever this was possible.

On the other hand, there could be a particularly grave fear that the demonstration, at the place requested, would include violent clashes which the police would be unable to control by the use of reasonable force. In such circumstances, there was no basis for the court to interfere in the exercise by the police of their discretion, directed to prevent a serious disturbance of the public peace (see H.C. 606/87, *The Jerusalem Post* of November 19, 1987 — and also H.C. 153/83, *The Jerusalem Post* of August 19, 1984).

To avoid misunderstandings, Justice Bach continued, the present judgment of the court should not be interpreted as blanket authority to "close" certain areas of Jerusalem to gatherings of the Petitioner or any other body. It all depended on the circumstances of each case. In the present instance, the Petitioner had chosen the two suburbs mentioned a short time after serious clashes between Arabs and Jews. The meetings were planned to take place in close proximity to Arab villages, the residents of which were said to be responsible for these occurrences.

The aim of the police was, on the one hand, to calm these areas by increasing their presence there and, on the other hand, to prevent gatherings which would inflame the passions of the local populace. The court could find no fault with this decision.

For the above reasons, the petition was dismissed.

Noam Federman, spokesman of the Kach Movement, appeared for the Petitioner, and Advocate Nili Arad, Director of the High Court Division of the State Attorney's Office, for the police.

Judgment given on July 3, 1990.

WORKING WOMEN AND DISCRIMINATION

NEVO v. NATIONAL LABOR COURT AND OTHERS

In the Supreme Court sitting as a High Court of Justice, before Justice Gavriel Bach, Justice Shoshana Netanyahu and Judge Hanoch Ariel, in the matter of *Dr. Naomi Nevo*, Petitioner, versus *The National Labor Court, the Jewish Agency, and others*, Respondents (H.C. 104/87).

Labor Law—Retiring Age of Women—Unjust Discrimination—Intervention by Supreme Court in Judgment of National Labor Court—Equal Retiring Age for Men and Women Workers Law, 1987.

The Petitioner was employed by the Jewish Agency from July 1, 1962, as a senior sociologist, and on August 1, 1983, she was made responsible for sociology in the Agency's Settlement Department.

The working conditions of Agency employees are regulated by collective agreements containing provisions as to retirement and pensions effective since August 1, 1953. Under those provisions, the age for retirement on pension is 65 years for men, and 60 years for women. The Petitioner was informed, therefore, that she was obliged to retire on February 1, 1985, on completing her 60th year.

The Petitioner applied to the District Labor Court in Tel Aviv to declare the different ages of retirement for men and women unlawful on the basis of unjust discrimination. Her application was refused and she appealed to the National Labor Court. The appeal was dismissed and she petitioned the Supreme Court to intervene.

The judgment of the Supreme Court was delivered by Justice Bach. Citing Supreme Court precedents, including *Yosifof*'s case (Cr.A. 112/50 — Selected Supreme Court Judgments (English), Vol. 1, p.174), he pointed out that not all discrimination was unlawful. As a general principle, all persons were equal before the law. If, however, there were real and substantial differences between them which were relevant to the purpose to be achieved, discrimination would be permissible.

The fixing of a compulsory retirement age was designed to enable an employee to be relieved, in his later years, of his daily tasks, and to enable the employer to refresh his work force by new and younger employees. It had been argued that the earlier enforced retirement of women was a benefit which lightened the burden on a wife and mother, and that women welcomed the opportunity to retire at an earlier age. These arguments, said Justice Bach, were unconvincing.

There was no support for the view that it was necessary to lighten a woman's burden at the age of 60. On the contrary, women enjoyed a longer life expectancy than men, which seemed to point in the opposite direction. Not only did the earlier retirement confer no benefit on women, but it carried with it a number of disadvantages.

Retirement often created frustration and serious personal emotional problems, particularly now when people live longer and enjoy better health in their later years. Earlier retirement for women also involved economic loss, for a woman was not only forced to forfeit five years' salary, but also lost five years' seniority in the computation of her pension. Women in a profession, such as the Petitioner, only entered the labor force after long academic studies, and thus required a longer period to reach their full potential.

Moreover, their reaching higher grades was often delayed by their duties as wives and mothers. Their progress in their employment could also be hindered by an employer's inclination to prefer the advancement of an employee who was not faced with enforced early retirement.

It was difficult to find any logical basis for the discrimination now discussed, Justice Bach continued, particularly when it applied to women of the age of 60. One could understand some distinction between the sexes with younger women, bringing up young children, in regard to work hours, leave and the performance of particularly hard physical tasks.

Most women of 60, however, had established their own independent lives. It was understandable to afford them the option of early retirement. To force them to retire early, under modern conditions, just because they were women, was unjust and unreasonable discrimination, which was quite unacceptable.

Justice Bach then referred to the Equal Retiring Age for Men and Women Workers Law, enacted by the Knesset on March 17, 1987. This Law abolished compulsory early retirement at a particular age, but left women the option of early retirement where such had been provided for in a collective agreement.

This statute was enacted after the Petitioner's appeal to the National Labor Court had been heard; and since it contained no provision giving it retroactive force, it could have no effect on the Petitioner's rights. The Law, however, and the explanatory notes to the draft Law, made it clear that the legislature itself regarded the discrimination now in issue, as unlawful.

Justice Bach also cited judgments of the Court of Justice of the European Communities, which had reached the same conclusion.

The Jewish Agency's counsel had argued that the purpose of the provision in question in the collective agreement had been to improve the position of women employees, and not to worsen it. He was prepared to assume, said Justice Bach, that the Agency had had no intention of harming its women employees. It was clear, however, he said, on the basis of Supreme Court and English precedents, that the test to be applied was objective, and not subjective. The motives of the Agency, therefore, were irrelevant.

The National Labor Court, Justice Bach continued, had inferred from existing labor legislation prior to the Equal Retiring Age Law of 1987, that the Knesset had implicitly recognized the legality of different retiring ages for men and women in collective agreements.

After reviewing existing statutes relating to the age of retirement and to benefits to be received after retirement, Justice Bach held that the above inference was unjustified. Quoting Supreme Court precedents, including the *Shakdiel* case (H.C. 153/87 — *The Jerusalem Post* of June 6, 1988; Selected Supreme Court Judgments [English] Vol. 8, p. 186)), he emphasized the general rule that statutes must always be interpreted so as to preserve basic rights, including the right of equality, and not restrict them. There was nothing in previous legislation, nor in the Equal Retiring Age Law, to justify the discrimination now complained of.

Justice Bach then reiterated the rule that the Supreme Court would not interfere with decisions of the National Labor Court save where there had been a substantive error of law, or where justice demanded its intervention. In the present case there had been a substantive error of law, and justice demanded the court's intervention since the Petitioner had been deprived of her basic rights of equality and freedom of occupation.

For the above reasons, Justice Bach proposed that the petition be allowed, and the parties ordered to enter into negotiations to afford the Petitioner her rights in terms of the court's judgment. If no solution was reached within a reasonable time, the Petitioner could renew her application to the District Labor Court.

Justice Netanyahu concurred, and expressed her regret that in Israel, in our times, it was not clear and self-understood that forcing a woman to retire earlier than a man was unjust discrimination.

Women had always played their full part and had shared equally with men in every field of activity since the early pioneering days of the State. Their contribution had not fallen short, despite the extra burdens of home and motherhood. The main discrimination was not the woman employee's financial loss, but being deprived of the opportunity to fulfill herself just at that time in her life when it was most feasible.

Judge Ariel agreed with his colleagues. He had already expressed the opinion, in previous judgments, that the Supreme Court should intervene in decisions of the National Labor Court only where this was imperative for doing justice, and where a principle influencing the general law was laid down. This was such a case.

For the above reasons, the petition was allowed in the terms proposed by Justice Bach.

Avigdor Feldman and Professor Frances Raday appeared for the Petitioner, and Haim Bar-Sadeh for the Jewish Agency.

Judgment given on October 22, 1990.

AN END TO SUFFERING

EYAL v. VILENSKY AND OTHERS

In the District Court of Tel Aviv, before Judge Uri Goren, in the matter of *Binyamin Eyal*, Plaintiff, versus *Dr. Nahman Vilensky and others*, Defendants (O.S. 1141/90).

Administrative Law—Authority of Court Permitting Doctors to Detach Terminally-Ill Patient from Life-Support System—Declaratory Order.

The Plaintiff, a man of 50, suffers from a terminal disease known as amyotropic lateral sclerosis. The disease induces a progressive paralysis of certain muscles of the body and, in its final stages, the patient is unable to swallow, speak or cough, or control his breathing mechanism. The progress of the disease is irreversible and, in the words of one specialist, the patient's life becomes "a hell on earth."

The Plaintiff applied to the court for an order declaring that he was entitled to prevent the use of a life-support system in his body, which would prolong his life artificially when his medical condition deteriorated.

Judge Goren pointed out first, in his judgment, that although the Plaintiff was hospitalized in a private, and not a government, hospital, the matter at issue was of great public importance. He had therefore invited the Attorney-General to appear as representing the public interest.

Since the Plaintiff's disease was incurable, Judge Goren continued, his hospitalization was aimed solely at supervision and easing the burden of his last days. He received full supportive treatment under medical care, and was better off, from that point of view, than he would be in his own home.

Sooner or later, the stage would be reached at which the Plaintiff would be unable, independently, to supply the necessary oxygen to the tissues in his body. This development was unavoidable, as the Plaintiff himself, his doctors and his family, well knew. When the above stage arrived, the Plaintiff would die of suffocation unless his breathing were induced mechanically by a life-support system introduced surgically into his body.

The Plaintiff had requested his doctors not to take the step described to prolong his life and it was quite clear that he had done so with full knowledge and appreciation of what was involved. The doctors, Judge Goren said, were therefore in a dilemma: on the one hand, they understood the Plaintiff and respected his wishes; on the other hand, they were not certain that the law permitted them to accede to his request.

It had been suggested that the Plaintiff should be taken home; the problem facing the doctors would then be solved, and the Plaintiff's wishes would be fulfilled. However, the Plaintiff's family, who were deeply devoted to him, had correctly objected to this course. Professor Shlomo Shibolet, a specialist in internal diseases and rehabilitation, had testified that such a step would be cruel, both to the Plaintiff and to his family.

Judge Oren pointed out that, according to the evidence before him, medical ethics created no difficulty in the present case. Professor Shibolet had stated that his oath did not oblige him to take surgical means to prolong life and, in this case, cause the patient untold suffering for no purpose. In such circumstances, he would prescribe drugs to dull the patient's pain.

The medical world, Judge Goren said, did not expect the legal profession to decide what treatment was proper in a particular case. However, the court was asked to lay down criteria as to what course the doctor should follow in the dilemma now discussed, while the final decision was that of the doctor, and not of the court.

Judge Goren then cited an article by Professor Amos Shapiro describing the wide range of circumstances in which the present problem could arise, and the number of persons or bodies concerned in its solution — the patient himself, if he was able to express his wishes; his family; the doctors; the competent medical authority on questions of medical ethics and the court.

The judge agreed with the author, who had not suggested answers to the numerous questions raised, that it was necessary to devise a logical process for examining and considering the facts of each particular case and taking a rational decision. The present case was one in which the court could initiate that process by laying down some criteria, which could later be extended.

There was no legislation, and there appeared to be no Israeli precedent, dealing directly with the matter now at issue, Judge Goren continued. However, the Attorney-General had submitted that the doctors were entitled to respect the Plaintiff's wishes, provided he was fully conscious when the fateful decision had to be made, and that the decision had to be taken at the commencement of the process of death.

The court inferred from this submission that the State would not regard the course suggested as a criminal offense. Moreover, if the court accepted this result, some defense would be available to the doctors or institution involved against possible claims for damages.

In the present case, Judge Goren added, the Plaintiff's family had initiated the proceedings and had made it clear that they released the doctors
and the hospital from all responsibility.

There could be no question of extending the solution proposed by the
Attorney-General, Judge Goren continued. The provisions of the Penal
Law, and the principle of the sanctity of life, severely limited the court's
powers in this field. On the other hand, he said, citing Supreme Court
precedents, the sanctity-of-life principle was limited to cases where the
doctors acted to save life or help a patient. Where their action would bring
the patient no advantage whatever, this principle could not apply.

Judge Oren then referred shortly to Jewish law relating to the issue
before the court, citing an article by Dr. Avraham Steinberg on "Mercy
Killing in the Light of Halacha". A distinction was drawn, he said, between
a positive act to shorten life and the taking of no action to continue life by
artificial means. A positive act was forbidden, but there was a conflict of
opinion as to the omission to take steps to preserve life. He would content
himself with saying that the prevention of suffering in a man's last mo-
ments was known to Jewish law and was accepted by some authorities.

Consequently, said Judge Goren, he was prepared to accept the submission of the Attorney-General, with the two conditions proposed, but with
the addition of a further condition now laid down by the court. It was
imperative, he said, that the decision in question, involving as it did medical
knowledge, and moral, religious and ethical values, be taken only by a
senior doctor, at least of the grade of a hospital superintendent or department
head, who was equipped to give proper consideration to all the elements
involved.

In conclusion, Judge Goren pointed out that the court's decision had
been given in urgency, to solve the immediate problem of the Plaintiff and
his family. He anticipated that the Supreme Court would, in due course,
lay down clearer and wider directives governing the matters which had
been raised.

For the above reasons, the claim was allowed, and a declaration issued
that the superintendent of the hospital, or one of its senior doctors, was
entitled to include, among his other considerations, the Plaintiff's wish not
to be attached to a life-support system when his condition deteriorated and
his breathing mechanism was impaired.

Yitzhak Hashan and Shirra Dunevich appeared for the Plaintiff, Yitzhak
Meron for the Defendants, and Rahel Zakkai, Senior Assistant District
Attorney, Tel Aviv, for the Attorney-General.

Judgment given on October 25, 1990.

DEMOLITION — BUT NOT AS PUNISHMENT

A.C.R.I. v. IDF COMMANDER OF SOUTHERN DISTRICT

In the Supreme Court sitting as a High Court of Justice before the Deputy-President, Justice Menahem Elon, Justice Shoshana Netanyahu and Justice Ya'acov Maltz, in the matter between *The Association for Civil Rights in Israel*, Petitioner, versus *The IDF Commander of the Southern District*, Respondent (H.C. 4112/90).

Administrative Law—Demolition of Houses by Army not Punishment—"Imperative Military Requirements"—Refusal of Court to Intervene—Defence Emergency Regulations, 1945, Regulation 119.

On September 20, 1990, an army reservist, Amnon Pomerantz, was brutally murdered by a frenzied mob at the entrance to the el-Bureij refugee camp in the Gaza district. On September 24, the Petitioner was told that some buildings in the vicinity of the crime would be demolished by the army later that day, and that the occupiers had received insufficient notice to enable them to submit their arguments, and approach the court.

This summary action, the Petitioner argued, was unlawful, and conflicted with the decision of the Court in H.C. 358/88 (see *The Jerusalem Post* of August 9, 1989, *supra* p. 98). The Petitioner averred that it was not yet clear whether the occupiers of the buildings in question were in any way connected with the murder. It was also explained to the Court that, since the camp was under curfew, the occupiers themselves had been unable to present the petition. The Petitioner moved the Court to set the demolition order aside and to issue an interim injunction restraining the army from acting until a final decision was given.

The petition and application for an injunction were filed in the evening of September 24, and an interim injunction was then issued. After hearing the full arguments of the parties on the application on the following day, the Court decided that an injunction was unjustified. It therefore set aside its order of the previous evening, stating that its reasons would be handed down at a later date.

The reasons for the court's decision were delivered in due course by Justice Elon. The Respondent, he said, had filed an affidavit and had also appeared and explained his grounds for issuing the order complained of. Since December 1987 the whole area had been subject to a wave of terrorist incidents and one of the points affected was the road at the entrance to the el-Bureij camp. This point, as other roads in the area, was the scene of the throwing of stones and petrol bombs and the erection of obstacles which impeded the flow of traffic, and endangered the lives of both military personnel and civilians.

There was the added feature that a number of narrow alleys converged on the road in question, affording a safe escape route to rioters, thus preventing their capture. Moreover, these alleys led to a nearby mosque, into which the soldiers could not enter. He added that the army had sealed off these alleys from time to time, but the local inhabitants had reopened them.

In view of the large number of incidents at this point, and the last serious occurrence in which Amnon Pomerantz had lost his life, the Respondent had decided, after consultation with the Chief of the General Staff and the Military Advocate General, that the most effective way of controlling that particular area was to widen the road at the entrance to the camp. This would enable the army to exercise much better supervision, and prevent the type of incidents described. The Respondent had demonstrated with the aid of maps what he intended to authorize.

The Respondent had emphasized that his action was dictated by security considerations alone; it was in no sense intended to punish people who had been in no way connected with the recent murder. Indeed, two houses of camp residents who were suspected of being involved in the murder had been sealed off and, after the proper procedure had been followed, would be demolished under the powers given him in Regulation 119 of the Defense (Emergency) Regulations of 1945 (see *supra* p. 99).

In the present instance, not only was no punishment intended, but the occupiers concerned would be properly compensated and, where necessary, satisfactory alternative arrangements would be made for them. Prior notice had been given to the occupiers, but the matter was of extreme urgency in view of the particular circumstances he had described.

Petitioner's counsel, Justice Elon continued, had not disputed the facts averred by the Respondent. He had submitted, however, that the requirement of giving such notice to the occupiers as would enable them to appeal to the proper authorities and, if necessary, to approach the court, still applied, as laid down in H.C. 358/88, above. The State Attorney, on the other hand, had argued that where, as the court itself had said in H.C. 358/88, "military operational circumstances" made it imperative for the army to act urgently, it was entitled to do so, even if persons whose rights would be affected had not been given an adequate opportunity to present their case.

Citing Supreme Court precedents and Jewish law, Justice Elon then stressed the cardinal importance of a man's right to be heard before action affecting him is taken. Where, however, there were competing basic rights, the court was obliged, as was pointed out in the leading case of *Kol Ha-Am* (Selected Judgments of the Supreme Court [English], Vol. 1, p. 90), to strike a balance, and give precedence to that right which was more pressing in the particular circumstances.

In the present matter, the military commander had to act according to local law, and also international law, as contained in Articles 43 and 23 of The Hague Convention of 1907, and Article 53 of the Fourth Hague Convention of 1949. However, as stated by the scholar J. S. Pictet, "The prohibition of the destruction of property situated in occupied territory is subject to an important reservation: it does not apply in cases 'where such destruction is rendered absolutely necessary by military operations.' The occupying forces may therefore undertake the total or partial destruction of certain private or public property in the occupied territory when imperative military requirements so demand."

In the instant case, the Respondent had given the problem before him the most careful consideration and had also consulted the most senior officers before taking his decision. It was his task to maintain order and security in the area under his command; and the action now complained of was, in his view, an urgent military necessity. In these circumstances, there was no basis for issuing the interim injunction sought.

Justice Elon stated, in conclusion, that Petitioner's counsel had informed the court that in view of its decision, he would withdraw the petition and approach the court later, if necessary.

Yehoshua Schoffman and Neta Goldman appeared for the Petitioner, and the State Attorney, Dorit Beinish, for the Respondent.

The reasons were handed down on October 31, 1990.

UNDERSTAND FIRST — THEN SIGN

LIPPERT v. TEFAHOT-ISRAEL MORTGAGE BANK

In the District Court of Jerusalem sitting as a Court of Civil Appeals before the Deputy-President Judge Ya'acov Bazak, Judge Tzevi Tal and Judge Shalom Brenner, in the matter of *Allan Lippert*, Appellant, versus *Tefahot-Israel Mortgage Bank Ltd.*, Respondent (C.A. 31/90).

Commercial Law—Signatory as Surety "Customer" of Bank—Surety Misled by Bank not Liable—Standard Contracts Law, 1964—Guarantee Law, 1967—Banking Licensing Law, 1981—Banking (Service to Customer) Law, 1981, sections 1, 3, 4, 17.

The Appellant, at the relevant time a new immigrant from France, signed as surety for a loan of 500,800,000 old shekels advanced by the Respondent bank to Rudy Atlan and Roger Nakash, known as the firm of "Nakash Brothers". Atlan and Nakash met the Appellant, who worked at that time as a waiter, by chance, and they persuaded him, as a fellow Frenchman, to guarantee the loan. According to the relevant documents, the loan was made for the purchase of apartments.

"Nakash Brothers" did not buy apartments, but pocketed the money and absconded. Indeed, Nakash was subsequently extradited to France on a charge of murder. Before even two months after the grant of the loan, the Bank sued the Appellant in the Jerusalem Magistrates Court on his suretyship. The claim succeeded, and the Appellant appealed to the District Court.

In giving judgment the court referred, first, to the Appellant's argument that the deed of suretyship which he had signed was, in fact, "not his deed" — an argument known, in legal terminology, as *"non est factum"*.

The Appellant stated in evidence that he thought he was signing a guarantee for rent payable by new immigrants, in the same way as a guarantee for the payment of his own rent as a new immigrant had been signed at the bank of the Jewish Agency. Only later did he discover that he had signed a guarantee in a commercial bank for the purchase of apartments. In France, so he testified, only a person who at least owned a house, would be accepted as a guarantor for so large an amount, and not a new immigrant who had nothing, and earned his living as a waiter. He was certain, therefore, that his guarantee was for rent, as he said.

The magistrate had correctly rejected this argument, the court continued. As he had held, a man who knowingly signed a deed of suretyship was bound by his signature, even if it transpired that the document contained conditions different from those he thought it contained. There was, therefore, no ground for interfering with this finding.

Appellant's counsel had also argued, the court said, that the Appellant was not liable to the bank, since the relevant provisions of The Banking (Service to Customer) Law of 1981 had not been complied with.

The expression "service" is defined in section 1 of the Law as "any service performed by a banking corporation within the scope of its activity as defined in Chapter 3 of the Banking Licensing Law of 1981". Under section 17 of the Service to Customer Law, "The provisions of this Law shall apply notwithstanding any waiver or agreement to the contrary".

The Appellant identified himself in the bank by his immigration certificate and, as the magistrate had pointed out, he could not then read or write Hebrew, and could only say a few words. He was clearly unable to read and understand the loan agreement, and the long and complicated deed of suretyship printed in small letters.

Appellant's counsel argued, therefore, that the bank had been obliged to explain to the Appellant, in simple terms which he could understand, the meaning of what he was signing. This, the bank agreed, was not done. Counsel contended, therefore, that the Appellant was misled in breach of section 3 of the Service to Customer Law, and that his ignorance of the language and his inexperience were exploited in breach of section 4 of that Law.

The magistrate held that a surety was not a "customer" of the bank within the meaning of the above sections and, further, that there had been no exploitation or misleading on the part of the bank.

The court did not agree that a surety was not a "customer" in the present context. The Supreme Court had held that a surety was a "customer" of the bank for the purposes of the Guarantee Law of 1967, and the Standard Contracts Law of 1964, and there was no reason why that should not apply equally to the Banking (Service to Customer) Law. The willingness of the bank to extend credit on the basis of the suretyship was a service to the surety. It was difficult to conceive that the Banking Law protected the "direct" client, and not the "indirect" client, who was often more vulnerable than the "direct" client.

The court was of the opinion, moreover, that the Appellant had been misled by the omission of the bank — albeit not intentional — to explain to him the full nature of his obligation. It referred in this respect to a directive of the Examiner of Banks, urging them to ensure that new immigrants were fully informed of what transpired.

The bank, the court said, was a commercial enterprise operating for profit. It protected itself by standard contracts entirely in its own favor. In its dealings with a surety, all the benefit accrued to the bank, while the surety incurred all the risk of loss. The lot of a surety was vividly described in the Book of Proverbs: *"Give not sleep to thine eyes, nor slumber to thine eyelids"*.

It was the bank's duty to explain to the Appellant, at least, that although it was a mortgage bank, and although the loan was given to purchase apartments, he would have to repay the loan even if no apartments were purchased, and no mortgages were registered. The bank's omission, therefore, was misleading, and the bank was in breach of section 3 above.

The bank, the court continued, had also exploited the Appellant's ignorance of Hebrew "to bring about a transaction on unreasonable conditions".

The conditions may have been reasonable for the bank, but it was utterly unreasonable for a person in the Appellant's situation to guarantee a housing loan in a large sum of money, while he ran the risk that the main security — the property to be mortgaged — might not even exist. And that was in fact what happened. There had also been a breach, therefore, of section 4 of the Service to Customer Law.

The above Law did not provide that a transaction brought about in breach of its terms was void. On the other hand, it did provide, in section 15, that a person who suffered damage as a result of a breach of the Law could claim compensation under The Civil Wrongs Ordinance.

Perhaps, therefore, the proper course would be to dismiss the appeal and leave the Appellant to sue the bank for damages, while ordering a stay of execution of the Magistrates Court judgment against the Appellant until the indebtedness of each party to the other was known. The court had decided, however, to save the parties what would probably be prolonged and expensive litigation, and to declare that the Appellant was not liable on the suretyship which he had signed.

The bank was ordered to pay the Appellant's costs and counsel's fees, in both courts, in the sum of NIS 6,000, linked to the Consumer Price Index.

Oded Ben-Ami appeared for the Appellant, and Shlomo Ben-Shoham for the bank.

Judgment given on December 11, 1990.

DEFENSE KITS AND DISCRIMINATION

MORCOS v. MINISTER OF DEFENSE

In the Supreme Court sitting as a High Court of Justice before Justices Aharon Barak, Shoshana Netanyahu and Theodore Orr, in the matter of *Milady Morcos*, Petitioner, versus *The Minister of Defense and others*, Respondents (H.C. 168/91).

Administrative Law—Unjust Discrimination—Equal Distribution of Gas Masks to All Residents of Occupied Territories—Intervention by Supreme Court— Hague Convention of 1907, Article 43.

During recent months, the army authorities began distributing defensive kits to residents of Israel to meet Iraqi gas or chemical attacks against the civilian population. The distribution was first carried out in urban areas, on the basis of their being the most exposed to attack.

On January 13, 1991, the distribution was extended to the residents of rural localities, including towns and villages in the area of Judea, Samaria, and the Gaza Strip; but the Arab residents of that area were excluded.

On that day, therefore, the Petitioner, a resident of Bethlehem, moved the High Court of Justice to order the distribution of the kit to all the inhabitants of the area in question.

The petition was brought before the duty judge, who directed that it be heard before a full panel on the following day.

On January 14, the court summoned the Attorney-General to appear, and after hearing his representative it granted an interim order, and directed the Respondents to file their reply within five hours.

The judgment of the court was delivered by Justice Barak.

The Respondents' reply, he said, had been furnished by Brigadier Freddie Zach, the deputy coordinator of activities in Judea, Samaria and the Gaza Strip. He had explained that those areas were not regarded as exposed to Iraqi attack, and that there was no need, therefore, to distribute defense kits to their inhabitants. At the same time, he had given particulars of a number of other measures that had been introduced to protect the inhabitants in case of need.

Wide publicity had been given, both in leaflets and in the media, including Arabic television, to the instructions to the population on how to seal their homes, and protect themselves in other ways. More than 1,000 medical personnel — doctors, nurses, and ambulance crews — had received instruction on how to act in an emergency. The necessary equipment had been provided, and the hospitals in the cities had been properly organized.

In addition to the measures described above, said Justice Barak, a contingency plan had been prepared to provide defense kits for the residents of Judea and Samaria who were likely to be endangered by reason of their proximity to large communities of Israelis, such as those in the belt surrounding Jerusalem, and those close to the "Green Line", such as Kfar Sava and Netanya.

There were already 173,000 kits available, which would be distributed if a real emergency arose; and another 100,000 kits had been ordered. The difficulty was, however, that there was a shortage of kits for infants and children, and not all Israeli children had yet received kits.

The Minister of Defense had decided, therefore, that no kits at all should be distributed for the time being in the areas described above, so as to avoid a situation in which adults had the kit, while children did not.

Brigadier Zach had explained that the Israeli residents of Judea, Samaria and the Gaza Strip, although situated in an area not regarded as a danger zone, had received defense kits. The reason was partly their close links with the State of Israel in regard to many aspects of day-to-day living, such as study, and family and work connections. It was therefore anticipated that these inhabitants would continue to reach Israel in the course of their daily lives also in periods of emergency.

Respondents' counsel had emphasized that Judea, Samaria and the Gaza Strip were under "belligerent occupation", and were covered, therefore, by the annexes to the Hague Convention of 1907.

Under Article 43 of that Convention, the occupying power was obliged to protect the security of the population "as far as possible". He submitted, therefore, that in light of the degree of danger anticipated, the authorities had discharged this obligation, having regard to the shortage of defense kits.

Counsel had also argued that the question of the distribution of kits — and, indeed, the whole subject of civil defense — involved security, military and political considerations, which fell solely within the province of the defense authorities. These matters, he contended, were non-justiciable. Moreover, any intervention by the court would have no practical effect, in view of the current shortage of defense kits.

It was the duty of the occupying power in a belligerent occupation, Justice Barak continued, to protect the security and welfare of the civilian population, which in the present context meant both Jews and Arabs.

The Respondents had admitted that defense kits should be distributed to inhabitants of Judea and Samaria close to Jewish-populated districts, but had withheld that distribution because of the shortage of kits for children. This consideration was unreasonable. The fact that not all the children would be protected was no ground for depriving the adult population of the protection to which they were entitled.

The above ruling would have been sufficient for disposing of this petition, said Justice Barak, were it not for the fact that Israeli residents of Judea and Samaria and the Gaza Strip had received kits — which, in itself, was a wise decision — while the Arab residents had not received them. The military commander was not entitled to discriminate between different classes of the population.

It has been said that "when the cannons roar, the muse is silent". But roaring cannons did not release the military commander from his duty to observe the law.

The strength of a community to withstand its enemies was the realization that it was fighting to preserve values worthy of defense. One of those values was the rule of law, and the duty of the commander to act without discrimination did not cease because security tensions increased

Since there were not sufficient kits — although it seemed that there had been ample time to procure them — the court could not order their distribution now. It would, however, order them to be distributed as soon as they were received, and it would order that every effort be made to secure the necessary quantity as soon as possible.

The argument of non-justiciability was entirely without substance, Justice Barak concluded. A contention of unjust discrimination was always justiciable.

No expert knowledge was needed to know that the Israeli population was more exposed to danger than the population of the administered territories, or that inhabitants close to Israeli areas were more exposed than those far away from them. Also, it required no expert knowledge to know that all are equal before the law.

For the above reasons, the petition was allowed.

The Respondents were ordered to distribute immediately the 173,000 defense kits currently available to adults living in the belt around Jerusalem, and in areas close to the Green Line; to make every effort to procure the necessary kits for the children involved, and to distribute them as soon as they were received; and to make every effort to procure kits for all the inhabitants of Judea, Samaria and the Gaza Strip, and distribute them immediately they were received.

Linda Breyer appeared for the Petitioner, and Senior Assistant State Attorney Malchiel Blass for the Respondents.

Judgment given on January 14, 1991.

CONDOLENCE VISITS DURING WORK

NATIONAL INSURANCE INSTITUTE v. RAHAMIM

In the National Labor Court before the President, Judge Menahem Goldberg, the Deputy-President, Judge Stephen Adler, Judge Yitzhak Eliasoff, Workers' representative Yisrael Behr, and Employers' representative Yehudit Huebner, in the matter of *The National Insurance Institute*, Appellant, versus *Tikva and Na'ama Rahamim* (representing the late David Rahamim), Respondents (Shin Vav/0-119).

Labor Law—"Work Accident"—Accident to Employee During Condolence Visit in Working Hours—National Insurance Law (Consolidated Versions), 1968, section 35.

The deceased, David Rahamim, was the director of a division of the Israel Defense Forces archives in the Ministry of Defense. On March 24, 1986, together with four other workers in his unit, he paid a condolence visit, during working hours, to the director of the photographic laboratory of the archives. He fell on the steps of the house he was visiting, suffered a leg injury, and was taken to hospital.

There was no control of employees' attendance at the archives, and the deceased, as a divisional director, did not require permission to leave the premises. He was under no obligation to visit his colleague, and he had received no instruction to do so, as a senior worker, in the name of his unit. He paid the visit purely out of feelings of personal regard towards a fellow worker.

There were no official instructions as to condolence visits to colleagues, but it was not disputed that it was customary to pay such visits during working hours, and that there had been no objection to this practice.

The deceased applied to the District Labor Court of Tel Aviv for recognition of his fall as a "work accident", as defined in Section 35 of the National Insurance Law (Consolidated Version) of 1968 — namely, "an accident which occurred in the course and in consequence of his work with or on behalf of his employer . . .".

The application was allowed, and the Respondent institute appealed to the National Labor Court.

The judgment of the National Court was delivered by Judge Adler. Appellant's counsel had stressed, he said, that the deceased was not obliged to make the visit, and she had argued that there was no connection between the visit and the deceased's employment.

Respondents' counsel had submitted that a condolence visit by a director of the archives was particularly important. She had also sought to distinguish between such a visit and a visit, for example, to a medical clinic, or to a celebration during working hours, since the employee had no personal interest in a condolence visit.

Judge Adler then referred to the principles laid down by the court to determine whether an accident occurred "in the course and in consequence of" a worker's employment. The worker need not actually be engaged in his work. It was sufficient if what he was doing was consistent with, and incidental, to his employment. The continuation of the employment was not necessarily interrupted by the worker doing something not specifically imposed upon him by his employment and, as a general rule, an accident during normal working hours was to be regarded as a work accident.

The question always was the causal connection between the accident and the employment. It was a question of degree, depending on the circumstances of each particular case. Where the causal connection was too remote, the accident would not be regarded as a work accident within the meaning of Section 35 of the Insurance Institute Law.

The condolence visit in question was not part of the deceased's official duties. He was not instructed to pay condolence calls, and there was no evidence that his employer expected him to do so. He did not use official transport for the visit. The fellow-worker who had died was not employed in the deceased's unit, was not his superior in the archives, and was also not subject to his supervision. The work relationship between them, therefore, did not require the deceased to make the visit.

The deceased had not been obliged to make condolence visits during working hours. It was possible that a worker would be obliged to attend a circumcision ceremony, or a funeral, at a particular time during working hours. A condolence visit, however, or a visit to a patient in a hospital, could be made at some other time. The bereaved colleague would not be offended if the visit were made out of working hours. On the contrary, he would be more appreciative of his fellow-worker giving up part of his free time for that purpose.

It had indeed been proved that it was customary for employees to pay condolence visits during working hours, and that even where the directors of the concern affected had objected to this practice, they had done nothing to stop it.

The fact, however, that an employer tolerated certain activities during working hours did not mean that they were covered by Section 35 of the above Law. The court had heard that it was customary, in certain sectors of the public service, for employees to leave their offices during working hours to attend to their own affairs, but that did not turn an occurrence during their private activities into a work accident.

Respondents' counsel had argued, the Deputy-President continued, that the deceased's action had indirectly benefited his employer since it had contributed to a feeling of solidarity and belonging among the workers in the archives. The deceased's employer, however, was not interested in losing the work hours during the condolence visit. It was true that employers were concerned with fostering good human relations between their employees, but not all the activities of employees which improved human relations were protected under the "umbrella" of work accident insurance.

Private parties of employees, dinners at restaurants, attending dances and wedding receptions, and weekend sports activities of employees, all promoted good relations. The precedents of the court showed, however, that not all such activities created the necessary basis for an accident which occurred to be a "work accident" under Section 35 of the above Law.

For the above reasons the appeal was allowed, and the decision recognizing the deceased's accident as a "work accident" was set aside, with no order as to costs.

Ruth Horen appeared for the Appellant, and Lonnie Goldstein for the Respondents.

Judgment given on November 29, 1990.

FAIR APPOINTMENTS

CROWN v. STATE SERVICE COMMISSIONER

In the Supreme Court sitting as a High Court of Justice before the Deputy-President, Justice Menahem Elon, and Justices Moshe Bejski and Eliezer Goldberg, in the matter of *Dr. Ya'acov Crown (Keren)*, Petitioner, versus *The State Service Commissioner and others*, Respondents (H.C. 703/87).

Administrative Law—Advertised Post in State Service Already Filled by Temporary Employee—"Equality of Access"—State Service Appointments Law, 1959, section 19—State Service Regulations, Regulations 18, 132.

The Civil Service Commissioner published a call for candidates for the post of a doctor to undergo specialized study in the women's and maternity department in the Sheba Medical Center at Tel Hashomer. The call for job-Applicants was governed by Section 19 of the State Service (Appointments) Law of 1959, under which, subject to certain exceptions, a vacancy must be publicly announced "when the post has fallen vacant or is likely to fall vacant". Under Section 24 of the Law, candidates must undergo examinations, and "the most qualified candidate shall be appointed".

The Petitioner obtained his degree at the University of Rome, and received his license to practise in Israel in 1982. Thereafter, he applied a number of times for a post enabling him to specialize in gynecology, and appeared before examining boards established by rules published in 1961 under Section 25 of the above law. In each case, however, he failed to obtain a post, and in 1987 he submitted his candidature for the above-mentioned post at Tel Hashomer. His application was again rejected, and he petitioned the High Court of Justice to intervene.

The judgment of the court was delivered by Justice Elon. The Petitioner's main argument, he said, was that the candidate who was accepted by the examiners, Dr. David Bider, already occupied, as a temporary employee, the very post for the filling of which the examination was conducted. The result was, the Petitioner submitted, that the examiners had decided, a priori, to endorse Dr. Bider's candidature.

The Petitioner also argued that there had been irregularities in the proceedings of the examinations board, and that he was, in fact, the most qualified candidate for the post in question.

The Deputy-President then dealt in some detail with the Petitioner's specific allegations against the examiners, and found them to be without foundation. The chairman of the examining board had filed an affidavit describing how the examiners had considered the material before them, and how they had reached their conclusions. The Court was satisfied that they had not been influenced by the fact that Dr. Bider was already temporarily filling the post, and that their decision that he was the best qualified candidate was genuine.

However, the court was obliged, Justice Elon continued, to deal with the fact that the post advertised, and considered by the examiners, was already filled by a temporary employee. The Petitioner had alleged that this was the case on all the other occasions in which he had submitted his candidature and had been examined, and was the position generally in regard to vacancies in the State medical service.

This feature raised the question whether the principle of equality of access, which was fundamental where there was competition for a particular post, had been observed.

At the request of the Court, Justice Elon said, the Respondents had placed additional material before the court in regard to the feature mentioned above, and had also explained the steps that were now being taken to ensure that the inequality complained of — namely, that of a temporary employee competing for the post which he himself held — would be eliminated.

The Court welcomed these steps, which would fulfill the requirement of Section 19 of the above Law that a vacancy be announced "when the post has fallen vacant or is likely to fall vacant". Moreover, Section 18.132 of the Civil Service Regulations specifically provided that only in exceptional circumstances should a post be filled temporarily. The Court stressed, however, that it was satisfied that in this case the principle of equality of access had not been breached.

The Court also commented on the fact that Dr. Bider, who was recommended by the examiners, had been confirmed in the post in question before the petition had been lodged. He had also stated in his affidavit that he would complete his six years specialized study in July 1989, and he had stressed the damage that would be caused to him (being in no way responsible for the Petitioner's grievances), were the petition to be allowed.

In the result, the petition was dismissed. Since, however, it was the action of the Petitioner that led to the necessary steps being taken to remedy the inequality in the examinations process to which he had drawn attention, the Civil Service Commissioner and the examinations board were ordered to pay his costs in the sum of NIS 3,000.

Shimon Shover appeared for the Petitioner, and Osnat Mandel, Senior Assistant State Attorney, for the State.

Judgment given on March 14, 1991.

DEFAMATION AND THE PRESS

YAIR KLEIN v. BEN-YISHAI AND YEDIOT AHARONOT

In the District Court of Jerusalem, before Judge Dalia Dorner, in the matter of *Yair Klein and four others*, Plaintiffs, versus *Ron Ben-Yishai and Yediot Aharonot, Ltd.*, Defendants (C.C. 893/89).

Torts—Defamation in Newspaper—Defences of Truth, Public Interest, and Good Faith—Defamation Law, 1965, sections 1, 3, 14, 15, 16.

The Plaintiff Klein served in the Israel Defense Forces for many years as an instructor and commander; and at the time of his release was a deputy brigade commander with the rank of lieutenant-colonel. After his release, he founded a company known as Hod Hahanit, Ltd., for furnishing instructional and training services to military organizations in fighting terror, and for exporting arms.

In 1987, Klein entered into a contract with an organization in Colombia called "The Cattle-Breeders Association", and thereafter provided that association with three courses in fighting terror, and also supplied it with military equipment for this purpose.

Following the publication of reports that Klein, his company and other Israelis had been involved in assisting the Colombian drug cartel, the newspaper *Yediot Aharonot* instructed its reporter Ron Ben-Yishai to investigate the matter and prepare articles accordingly. Pursuant to his inquiries, the paper published two articles by Ben-Yishai stating that, according to the Colombian security authorities, Klein and his associates had given instruction to a body serving the drug cartel; that they knew of the connection between that body and the cartel; and that they had received a fee of

$800,000, which they had transferred to Israel through a network of haredim (strictly-observant Jews).

On the basis of these articles, Klein and four of his associates sued Ben-Yishai and the newspaper for damages for defamation. The Defendants pleaded truth and good faith, adding that Klein's four associates had not even been mentioned in the articles. They also counter-claimed for damages for the alleged defamation of Ben-Yishai by the Plaintiffs at an interview-evening published in a local paper *Netanya News*.

In giving judgment, Judge Dorner pointed out that the defamatory nature of the above articles within the meaning of Section 1 of the Defamation Law of 1965, was not in dispute: they could lower him in the estimation of others, or expose him to hatred, contempt, or ridicule; or bring him into disrepute because of his acts, conduct, or qualities; or injure him in his business, vocation, or profession.

At the same time, the Defendants argued that the statement about the transfer of the money to Israel was not defamatory, and in any case was only an incidental detail which could not injure the Plaintiffs.

It was for the Plaintiffs to prove, Judge Dorner continued, that they were defamed, and they could do this, under Section 3 of the above Law, on the basis of extrinsic circumstances. The names of Klein's four co-Plaintiffs had not been mentioned in the articles, and the extrinsic circumstances were not sufficient to prove that the articles referred to them. Their claim, therefore, was to be dismissed.

Judge Dorner then turned to consider the Defendants' plea of truth under Section 14 of the Defamation Law, namely, "that the matter published was true and the publication was in the public interest, provided the publication did not exceed what was necessary from the point of view of that interest". The section adds that "this defense shall not be denied by reason only that the truth of an incidental detail which is not actually injurious has not been proved".

Public interest had been proved, Judge Dorner continued, and the factual dispute as to the connection between "The Cattle-Breeders Association" and the drug cartel and Klein's knowledge of that connection, was narrow indeed. This being a civil, as distinct from a criminal, case, the Defendants were not required to show more than a balance of probabilities in their favor.

On the other hand, the Supreme Court had held that where a man was defending his good name, the weight of evidence required of the Defendant increased with the seriousness of the defamation. At the same time, the court could rely on circumstantial evidence, supporting direct evidence by common sense and experience of life.

Judge Dorner then examined the evidence in detail, taking into account, *inter alia*, statements of Klein himself, including those made in the course of a criminal trial against him arising out of the same circumstances, payments made to him, the nature of the instruction and training and type of equipment he supplied, and his contacts with Israeli and Colombian personnel in regard to his operations.

Her conclusion was that the connection of the "Association" with the drug cartel had been established, and that the fact that Klein knew of that connection or, in the earlier stages, had at least turned a blind eye to it, had also been proved. The truth of the transfer of $800,000 to Israel through an Orthodox network had not been proved, but that was "an incidental detail" within the meaning of Section 14 of the Law, quoted above.

The Supreme Court had held in the leading case of *Kol Ha'am* (Selected Supreme Court Judgments [English], Vol. 1, P. 90), Judge Dorner continued, that freedom of expression (which also covered freedom of the press) was a "supreme value" in a democratic society.

It was not absolute, but relative, since other competing values such as a man's right to his good name were also to be recognized. The Defamation Law laid down the points of balance between these values, one of which was the defense of good faith defined in Section 15 of the Law. As the Supreme Court had held, this defense also covered, in certain circumstances, untrue publications. However, the defenses of truth and good faith were not mutually exclusive, and could be raised together.

Section 15 of the Law enumerated a number of circumstances in which a publication, made in good faith, was protected, and Section 16(a) of the Law provided that, subject to certain exceptions set forth in Section 16(b), where a Defendant proved that he made the publication in such circumstances, and did not exceed what was reasonable, his good faith was to be presumed.

The view had been expressed that the press, by virtue of its importance in a democratic society, should be accorded a special status; and that it should be entitled to the defense of good faith wherever it published something in the circumstances set forth in Section 15, without any exceptions. The Supreme Court, however, had not accepted this view.

The question to be decided in the present case, therefore, Judge Dorner continued, was whether the articles had been published in good faith in the circumstances set forth in Section 15(2) of the Law, which were appropriate in this instance, namely, that "the relations between the Defendants [Ben-Yishai and the newspaper] and the person to whom the publication was addressed [the public], imposed on the Defendants a legal, moral, or social duty to make the publication".

Judge Dorner then held that the publication of the articles assumed great importance in view of the nature of the information published, particularly against the background of publications in 1988 in the Colombian press, which had damaged Israel considerably. She was satisfied, therefore, that the relationship between the newspaper and its reporter, on the one hand, and the public, on the other hand, imposed upon the former the moral and social duty to make the publication.

The good faith of the Defendants had been proved, both subjectively and objectively, Judge Dorner held. Ben-Yishai had traveled to Colombia, had interviewed numerous people — Colombians, Israelis, and others — to verify his facts, and every care had been taken to check the material before publication. The Defendants, therefore, had established the defense provided by Section 15 of the law.

The counter-claim, said Judge Dorner, was based upon the statements that Ben-Yishai was "the trumpet of others" and "a hireling of the Americans, had received money from them, and was simply the servant of his masters". It was true that calling someone "a hireling of the Americans" was not in itself defamatory, but the words, spoken in their context, accused Ben-Yishai of serious journalistic dishonesty.

They were therefore defamatory in terms of the Law. There was no basis, however, for attributing responsibility to the other four Plaintiffs. It would be sufficient in the circumstances, Judge Dorner said, to order Klein to publish a retraction of his words in the *Netanya News* and in the paper *Hadashot*.

In the result, the claim and the counterclaim against Defendants Nos. 2-5, were dismissed. The counterclaim against Klein was allowed, and he was ordered to publish the retraction mentioned above.

Yigal Shapiro appeared for the Plaintiffs, and Mibi Moser for the Defendants.

Judgment given on March 25, 1991.

NON-INTERVENTION IN SECURITY ISSUES

FEDERMAN AND HANEGBI v. MINISTER OF DEFENCE

In the Supreme Court sitting as a High Court of Justice before the President, Justice Meir Shamgar and Justices Eliezer Goldberg and Ya'acov Maltz, in the matter between *Noam Federman and Tzahi Hanegbi*, Petitioners, versus *The Minister of Defence and others*, Respondents (H.C. 1414, 1422/91).

Administrative Law—Order by Minister of Defence to Release Over 1,000 Political Prisoners—Refusal of Court to Intervene.

The Petitioners moved the High Court of Justice to set aside the Respondents' decision to release more than 1,000 convicts and detainees (residents of Judea, Samaria and the Gaza Strip) at present imprisoned following incidents connected with the intifada.

The Petitioners had complained, said the Court in its judgment, both as to the timing and as to the scope of the releases authorized. They had expressed their fear that the grounds for the decision were not objective, and that all the relevant factors had not been considered.

Counsel for the State, the Court continued, had replied that the decision in question was of a military-security nature, and had been made by the competent authorities within the powers conferred upon them by law. She had explained that the decision was based upon objective grounds alone, which had been weighed in accordance with defined criteria.

Counsel had also explained that the files of those to be released had been examined, and that only those prisoners who had been accused of comparatively light offenses which had not caused any physical or emotional damage, and who were not suspected of terrorist activity, were to be freed.

She had added that every prisoner released would have completed at least two-thirds of his sentence or detention, or that only a month or two months of that period would still remain to be served.

The Court said that the petition raised the questions whether the order had been given by the competent authorities, and whether the Court would examine the considerations relied upon by those authorities in a matter of this kind.

As to the first question, the Court was satisfied that the order had been given by the authorities empowered to do so by law and, indeed, the

Petitioners had conceded this fact after the explanations furnished by counsel for the State.

As to the second question, the Court continued, the matter in dispute was clearly one of policy relating to a military issue. Referring to the Supreme Court precedent of *Neiman* (E.A. 2, 3/84, *The Jerusalem Post* of May 31, 1985), the Court reiterated that it was not enough for a Petitioner who was dissatisfied with a particular policy, or who had doubts as to its efficacy, or who thought he had a better solution, to move the Court to intervene.

The Court did not sit as a general policy review board, but as a judicial tribunal to determine whether the facts brought before it disclosed, *prima facie*, a legal flaw which would justify its interference. No such flaw was revealed in the present case.

Citing further Supreme Court precedents, including that of *Barak* (H.C. 228/84, *The Jerusalem Post* of July 4, 1984), the Court held that the matter now considered was one for the government which was empowered, within the sphere of its responsibility, to take a decision after weighing all the relevant considerations of policy and security in accordance with the legal principles applicable.

In conclusion, the Court said that its decision was not to be understood as indicating that it regarded with equanimity the scope of the facts brought before it by the State. At the same time, no legal ground for its intervention had been shown.

For the above reasons, the petitions were dismissed.

Federman appeared in person, Elazar Mor appeared for Hanegbi, and Nili Arad, Director of the High Court Division of the State Attorney's Office, for the State.

Judgment given on April 10, 1991.

INSCRIBING A SOLDIERS' TOMBSTONE

GINNOSAR v. MINISTER OF DEFENSE

In the Supreme Court sitting as a High Court of Justice before Justices Shlomo Levin, Gavriel Bach and Theodore Orr, in the matter of *Yossi Ginnosar*, Petitioner, versus *The Minister of Defense and others*, Respondents (H.C. 1438/91).

Military Law—Administrative Law—Refusal to Permit Engraving of Gregorian Date of Death on Soldier's Tombstone Set Aside—Military Cemeteries Law, 1950, sections 2, 5, 12, 13.

Shahar Ginnosar, the Petitioner's son, was killed while serving in the Gaza Strip on March 11, 1991. The Petitioner requested the military authorities to permit the engraving on his son's tombstone of the Gregorian calendar date of his death, in addition to the universally-prevailing Hebrew date of death; and also of the fact that he had fallen in the Gaza Strip. The Petitioner's first request was refused, and he moved the High Court of Justice to intervene.

The Court, in its judgment, referred at the outset to the relevant provisions in the Military Cemeteries Law of 1950. Section 5 of the Law requires a tombstone to be erected, at the expense of the State, on every military grave, the shape and dimensions of the stone being prescribed by a competent officer.

Under Sections 12 and 13 of the Law, the minister of defense is required to appoint a public advisory board, and is empowered to make the necessary regulations. Under Section 2 of regulations published in 1956, the board is required to advise the minister, *inter alia*, in laying down "the shape of tombstones, and the text and type of the writing thereon".

There were conflicts of opinion in the advisory board, the Court continued, in regard to the need for the uniformity of tombstones, the significance of the Hebrew date, and the possibility that acceding to the Petitioner's request would lead to applications by other bereaved parents to add to the text on existing stones.

The board finally decided, by a majority, to recommend the rejection of the Petitioner's request, and another similar request presented to it; and the minister accepted the recommendation on the sole ground that the uniformity of the shape of tombstones and the writing thereon was to be preserved.

There was no doubt, said the Court, that the uniformity of tombstones was a relevant consideration which the minister was entitled to consider, and that any addition to the standard text would disturb that uniformity. At the same time, each application by parents had to be considered on its own merits. The principle of uniformity was not always observed. Indeed, in this very instance, the addition of the fact that the Petitioner's son had fallen in Gaza was permitted; and the Petitioner had cited other cases in which additions to the standard text had been allowed.

The minister was obliged to weigh the sentiments of bereaved parents, who wished some personal or other detail to be written on the stone, as against other factors such as uniformity; and, if he failed to attach to those sentiments the weight they deserved, the Court would tend to intervene. The Court had already invalidated a condition in a contract issued by a Hevra Kadisha (burial society), precluding the engraving of the accepted general date of death on tombstones in a civilian cemetery.

In the circumstances of the present case, the Court then held, the desire for uniformity could not stand against the wishes of the fallen soldier's family. As Petitioner's counsel had correctly pointed out, most of life's affairs were conducted on the basis of the generally accepted date, which appeared, in addition to the Hebrew date, in identity cards and in birth and death certificates, and which was also a governing factor in commercial matters.

The date on which the Petitioner's son fell was a vital detail connected with his military service. Moreover, the Petitioner did not request the general date in place of the Hebrew date, but only in addition thereto.

Counsel for the State had argued, the Court added, that the fact that only two applications for the addition of the general date on tombstones had been made, showed that this request was exceptional. The absence of other similar applications, however, the Court said (if such was the case) only showed that other families had reconciled themselves to the army's ruling, but did not show that that ruling had accorded with their wishes.

For the above reasons, the petition was allowed, and the refusal of the minister to accede to the Petitioner's wishes was set aside.

Amnon Zichroni appeared for the Petitioner, and Nili Arad, Director of the High Court Division in the State Attorney's office, for the State.

Judgment given on April 11, 1991.

CONSPIRACY TO PAY UNAUTHORIZED ALLOWANCE

MIZRAHI v. ISRAEL PORTS AND RAILWAYS AUTHORITY

In the National Labor Court before the Deputy-President, Judge Stephen Adler and Judges Yitzhak Eliasoff and Amiram Rabinowitz, Workers' Representative Yisrael Ziv and Employers' Representative Ari Tivon, in the matter of *Yehoshua Mizrahi and others*, Appellants, versus *The Israel Ports and Railways Authority*, Respondent (Shin Vav/3-92).

Labor Law—Unlawful Payments to Port Servants Set Aside—Ports and Harbors Authority Law, 1961, sections 18(b), 29(b).

The Appellants, employees of the Respondent, who had been engaged in operational duties at Ashdod Port, were transferred, at various times during the years 1966-1971, to act as instructors. As compensation for loss of income caused by the transfer, the Respondent paid the Appellants an agreed premium of 30 percent and, in addition, a global allowance for 30 (and later for 52.5) hours overtime a month, which they received even if, for any reason, they were absent from work.

The Appellants also received a further increment, known as "the one-hour addition" for every day of actual work in the port; this had been promised to them by their immediate superior. The Respondent State Authority which, so it contended, had learned of this increment only in 1977, refused to sanction its continued payment, and the Appellants applied to the District Labor Court in Beersheba to reverse this decision.

The application failed, and the Appellants appealed to the National Labor Court.

The first judgment of the National Labor Court was delivered by Judge Adler. The facts found by the District Labor Court, he said, established that the additional increment had been promised to the Appellants without their being required to work during the extra hour mentioned. It was true that they were required to report as having worked during the extra hour, but these reports were fictitious.

The payment was based on a conspiracy between the instructors and subordinate officials of Ashdod Port, who had acted beyond their powers. The conspiracy was aimed at misleading the Ports Authority, with the object of giving the instructors an additional income beyond the official limits, and without the knowledge of the workers in Haifa Port.

There was ample foundation for the District Court's finding, the Deputy President continued, that the directorate of the Ports Authority did not know the true nature of the increment in question. It had been paid for some 10 years, until 1977, and the Authority, having been mislead by the instructors' reports, believed that the payment was made for actual work done.

The true nature of the payment came to light only when the Haifa Port workers demanded the same increment, and the Authority then stopped the payment.

Citing Labor Court precedents based upon rulings of the Supreme Court, Judge Adler held that the obligation of a statutory authority to perform its promises depended upon the fulfillment of four conditions:

That the maker of the promise acted within his powers; that he intended it to have legal force; that the Authority was able to keep the promise; and that there was no legal justification for altering or repudiating it. Only the third condition, he said, was fulfilled in the present case.

The facts showed, the judge continued, that the maker of the promise was the instruction assistant in the port. There was no evidence that the personnel department or the port manager knew of it. There was no written confirmation and no contract. Neither the instruction assistant, nor his "unofficial" superior (who did know about it), was empowered to bind the Ports Authority. It was clear, therefore, that the first condition had not been fulfilled.

Neither the instruction assistant, nor the others who knew of his promise, intended that the arrangement should have legal force, Judge Adler held. The increment was intended to give instructors a payment to which they were not entitled under the conditions applicable to port workers. Under Section 18(b) of the Ports and Harbors Authority Law of 1961, the conditions of employment and remuneration of the Authority's employees "shall be fixed by agreement between the Authority and the organization representing the greatest number of the Authority's employees".

Legal rights relating to employment conditions were laid down in open legal contracts, he pointed out, and not in agreements intended to deceive the State Authority concerned.

As to the fourth element, the court had held repeatedly that the interests of the State demanded the maintenance of high standards in the public service. The arrangement now considered, under which workers reported overtime for work they did not do — and their reports were confirmed by their superior knowing they were false — was improper, and offended against the accepted norms of public administration.

It was for the Court to support the action of a State Authority which refused to honor an arrangement of this kind.

Judge Adler then considered the argument of Appellants' counsel that the arrangement in question was valid under the Law of Contracts, and after citing Supreme Court and Labor Court precedents, found counsel's contention untenable.

The judge proposed, therefore, that the appeal be dismissed.

Judge Rabinowitz concurred. Referring to Section 18(b) of the Ports and Railways Authority Law, cited above, he stressed that the object of the legislation was that working conditions of employees of the ports were to be laid down by the central authority and not by local officials. While Section 29(b) of the Law did empower the Authority to delegate its powers to subordinate officials, including port managers, there was no evidence of such delegation in the present case.

The question arose, said Judge Rabinowitz, whether the making of the payment in question over a period of almost 10 years did not create a custom which should now be honored. The fact was, however, that the Authority believed that the payment was made in return for additional work actually performed, and not as an extra payment for ordinary work. The custom, therefore, was based on an error induced by an unauthorized act, and should not be continued.

The other members of the court agreed.

For the above reasons, the appeal was dismissed.

Menahem Avner appeared for the Appellants, and Nohum Feinberg for the Ports Authority.

Judgment given on January 31, 1991.

ANNULLING A BRAZILIAN 'ADOPTION'

GONSALES AND VASCONSALES v. TURGEMAN AND THE ATTORNEY-GENERAL

In the Supreme Court sitting as a High Court of Justice before the Deputy-President, Justice Menahem Elon, Justice Moshe Bejski and Judge Hanoch Ariel, in the matter of *Rosilda Gonsales and Bruna Vasconsales*, Petitioners, versus *Simha and Ya'acov Turgeman and the Attorney-General*, Respondents. (H.C. 243/88).

*Personal Status—Habeas Corpus—Petition by Brazilian Parents for Return of
    Child Adopted by Israelis—Adoption of Children Law, 1981—Basic Law:
    Judicature, 1984, section 15(d)(1).*

During the years 1983-1984 the Respondents made efforts, through the
Ministry of Labor and Social Affairs, to adopt a child. They were finally
informed, in December '84, that in view of the long waiting list and for
reasons of age their application could not be granted. They then heard of
the possibility of adopting a child from Brazil and, after meeting some
couples who had adopted Brazilian children, they consulted an Israeli
advocate who, they understood, could arrange such an adoption.

The advocate, informing the Respondents that a Brazilian adoption was
perfectly legal, required them to furnish various documents, including
medical certificates and certificates from their employers, a report on their
financial standing and a report of a social welfare officer. The Respondents
complied and were told by the advocate that he had translated all the
documents into Portuguese and had forwarded them to Brazil.

He also referred the Respondents to one Herlet Hilo, on whose instructions they traveled to Brazil on September 3, 1986. The Respondents had
no knowledge of either Portuguese or English, and relied entirely on what
they were told.

The second Petitioner, Bruna, the daughter of the first Petitioner and one
Luis Vasconsales, was born in Brazil on June 12, 1986. On October 13, 1986,
she was abducted from her parents' home. Despite desperate efforts by her
parents, who had even secured an interview with the Brazilian minister of
justice, she was not traced.

The Respondents, on reaching Brazil, met three other Israeli couples
who had traveled there for the purpose of adopting children. They were
instructed by the advocate, by telephone, to wait at a certain hotel, and after
some delay they were told by one Mirabel to travel to Paraguay. They did
so, and after some delay the child Bruna was handed into their custody,
together with what purported to be her birth certificate and an adoption
certificate in their favor.

They then returned to Israel with Bruna. The advocate translated the
documents into Hebrew to enable the necessary formal steps to be taken.
Bruna, who was born into the Catholic faith, was converted to Judaism and
was duly registered as the Respondents' adopted daughter in the Interior
Ministry's records.

In the meantime, a British television team was preparing a feature program on the adoption of Brazilian children. It reached Mirabel's office in Paraguay and discovered in Bruna's file a handwritten note containing the Respondents' names and address. In this way, Bruna's whereabouts were discovered; and the Petitioners thereupon moved the Supreme Court, sitting as a High Court of Justice, to issue a writ of habeas corpus, directing the Respondents to restore Bruna to the custody of her natural parents.

The first judgment was delivered by Justice Elon, who said the parties had submitted to a "tissues test", as a result of which Bruna's paternity, as the daughter of the first Petitioner and Luis Vasconsales, had been almost conclusively established. It had also not been necessary, he continued, to consider the legal validity of a Brazilian adoption order, since it was clear that no such order relating to Bruna had ever been made.

Bruna's original birth certificate had been handed to the court, and the particulars there recorded were quite different from those appearing in the birth and adoption certificates handed to the Respondents by Mirabel.

Moreover, the woman who had abducted Bruna had been convicted, and it was also inconceivable that any adoption in Brazil, without the parents' consent, would be lawful without an order of court. It was for the Respondents to produce such an order, and they had not done so.

Petitioners' counsel, said Justice Elon, had attacked the Respondents' good faith, but there was no basis whatsoever for such an allegation. They had been guided by an advocate and had been required to produce documents. There was no reason to believe that they had any suspicion that there was some irregularity in what was done.

The Deputy-President then pointed out that under Section 15 (d)(1) of the Basic Law: Judicature, of 1984, the court was empowered "to make orders for the release of persons unlawfully detained or imprisoned". Citing Supreme Court precedents, including the case of *Amado* (Selected Supreme Court Judgments [English], Vol. 1, p. 299), he emphasized that such orders were usually of a temporary nature, since it was the District Court which heard witnesses and investigated facts in detail.

The Supreme Court, sitting as a High Court of Justice, acted, in this context, to restore the status quo. The usual cases involving children were those in which one spouse had removed a child from the other's custody in breach of an order of court, and the Supreme Court had acted to restore the former situation, leaving it to the District Court to make a final decision, having regard to the best interests of the child.

The critical question in the present context, in which the natural parents of a child sought to recover custody from persons who had no legal right of custody whatsoever, was to what extent, if at all, the best interests of the child were to be considered.

Justice Elon then reviewed extensively the relevant statutory provisions and Supreme Court precedents relating to the custody of children, establishing the principle that the right of natural parents to the custody of their children is paramount. The consideration of the welfare of the child could become relevant only where the grant of custody to the natural parents would result in real and substantial damage to the child. Justice Elon also found support for this view in the Adoption of Children Law of 1981.

Justice Elon considered in detail the opinions of experts as to the effect on Bruna of her return to her parents. It was true that the Respondents had given her a warm and loving home, but the evidence did not show that real and substantial damage would be caused to her by her return to her parents.

He also dealt with the argument that she had been converted to Judaism, and should not be returned to a Catholic environment. In this regard, Justice Elon cited the Prophet Micah (4, 5): "*For let all the peoples walk each one in the name of its God*", and held that there was no reason why she should not be brought up in the religion of her parents.

In any event, he held that her conversion was of no effect, since it had been carried out without the consent of her parents or legal guardians. He also referred in this context to the sometimes desperate efforts made by Jewish survivors of the Holocaust to restore children saved by non-Jews to their people and their faith.

In conclusion, Justice Elon held that, in this case, where the child had been abducted by a criminal act from her parents, the consideration of the child's welfare could be taken into account by the court — the upper guardian of all minors — only if the damage she would suffer would be exceptionally severe and irreversible. Since this had not been proved, the order sought should be made.

Justice Elon paid tribute to the Respondents, who had shown patience and understanding and had accepted the ruling of the court in a noble and generous spirit.

Justice Bejski concurred. He differed from Justice Elon in regard to the analogy of cases involving adoption; but he agreed that in the circumstances of this case the child should be restored to her parents.

Judge Ariel also concurred. He added that, had there been any evidence of real and serious damage to the child, it would have been proper to refer the case to the District Court for consideration. In the circumstances, however, that course was unnecessary.

For the above reasons, the petition was allowed, and an order made for the return of the child Bruna to her parents.

Shimon Shover and Eli Cohen appeared for the Petitioners, and Gershon Schneider appeared for the Respondents.

Reasoned judgment handed down on March 28, 1991.

ADOPTION PROBLEMS

A. B. v. ATTORNEY-GENERAL

In the Supreme Court sitting as a Court of Civil Appeals before the Deputy-President, Justice Menahem Elon, and Justices Shoshana Netanyahu and Ya'acov Maltz, in the matter of *A. and B.*, Appellants, versus *The Attorney-General*, Respondent (C.A. 3236/90).

Personal Status—Adoption—Child not to be Handed to New Parents before Final Order—Youth (Care and Supervision) Law, 1960, section 12—Adoption of Children Law, 1981, sections 12, 13—Capacity and Guardianship Law, 1962.

The proceedings before the court related to the fifth child of the Appellants, born on February 20, 1988. On March 30, 1988, she was handed over temporarily to foster parents by order of a magistrate under Section 12 of the Youth (Care and Supervision) Law of 1960, since her parents were unable to receive her.

On April 17, 1988, the Attorney-General applied to the District Court of Tel Aviv to declare her adoptable under Section 13(7) of the Adoption of Children Law of 1981, on the ground, as there provided, that her parents, due to their conduct or situation, were not capable of taking proper care of her.

At the same time, the court was asked to make an order under Section 12(c) of the Adoption Law which provides that "where it appears to a welfare officer that the case suffers no delay and circumstances so require,

he may, even without the consent of the parents or the declaration of the
child as adoptable . . . hand him over to a person who has agreed to receive
him into his house with a view to adopting him. An act under this section
shall require the approval of the court . . .".

The District Court made an order under this section on April 26, 1988,
and the child was handed over to the proposed adoptive parents on May
4 of that year.

The Appellants' third and fourth children, a boy and a girl, were born
respectively on July 2, 1978, and June 29, 1980. With the Appellants'
consent, they were both handed into the care of foster parents, who were
later appointed additional guardians of the children with full powers. The
foster parentage had proved very successful, and the children had maintained contact with their natural parents and family.

The foster parents were also prepared to accept the youngest child into
their care, thus enabling her to grow up with her elder sister.

The District Court pronounced judgment in regard to the child's adoption on August 8, 1989. It rejected the proposal that she be handed into the
care of her parents, and also refused to allow her to join her sister in the
foster parents' home. It decided to declare her adoptable, and ruled that
her best interests demanded that she be adopted by the proposed adoptive
parents, in whose home she had already been living since May 4, 1988. Her
parents then appealed to the Supreme Court.

The judgment of the Supreme Court was delivered by Justice Elon.
Appellants' counsel, he said, had not challenged the District Court's decision in regard to the mother's unsuitability to bring up the child (for health
reasons), but argued that that factor should not affect the court's judgment
in regard to the father. His main contention, however, was that the District
Court had failed to give full consideration to the possibility of placing the
child with the foster parents who were already bringing up her elder sister.

This course would ensure that the child would remain with her own
natural family, and was clearly preferable to her adoption by strangers.

Justice Elon found no fault with the District Court's decision relating to
the undesirability of the father's rearing the child. He held, however, that
that court had erred in its approach to the possibility of her being placed
with the foster parents of her sister. The District Court had proceeded on
the basis of a supposed general assumption, supported, as it held, by
experts and Supreme Court precedents, that in the case of a child of tender
years, adoption was preferable to foster parentage.

There was no such general rule, the Deputy President continued, and this error had inhibited the District Court from giving the proposal of foster parentage any real serious consideration. Justice Elon then emphasized the nature of the judge's role as the "father" of all minors. The famous dictum of our sages that "the judge has no more than what his eyes see, his ears hear, and his heart understands" was in no field more apt than in the highly delicate and awesome task of deciding the whole future of a child.

There were no general rules. Once the court had decided that a child was adoptable under Section 13 of the Adoption Law, the only question at issue was the best interests of the child, and this depended on the circumstances of each particular case.

In this instance, said Justice Elon, he would have been inclined to rule that the child should be placed in the home of her sister's foster parents, with all the clear advantages which that course would afford. On the other hand, the child had now lived with her adoptive parents for some considerable time. She was handed into their care on May 4, 1988. The District Court had given judgment on August 8, 1989, about five months of this delay having been caused by the tardy submission of the Respondent's written summations.

Moreover, contrary to the usual practice of expediting the hearing of cases of this kind, the hearing of the appeal began only on November 7, 1990. It was imperative that steps be taken to avoid delays of this kind.

The placing of the child in the home of her proposed adoptive parents, under Section 12(c) of the Adoption Law, was a misapplication of that section, and a serious mistake, Justice Elon continued. As the section itself prescribed in clear language, it was only to be invoked where "the case suffers no delay and circumstances so require".

There appears to have been no reason at all to place the child in her proposed adopted home at the very outset of the adoption proceedings, and thus create facts which introduced grave complications which should never have arisen. There were sufficient possibilities under the Youth (Care and Supervision) Law of 1960, and the Capacity and Guardianship Law of 1962, to place a child elsewhere. Section 12(c) of the Adoption Law should only be applied in exceptional circumstances, in which the contact between the child and its family should be maintained, subject to proper measures to preserve secrecy as to the identity of the propo d adoptive parents.

In all the circumstances, the court had decided to r ceive further expert evidence as to the best interests of the child. It had been advised, by a psychiatrist it had itself appointed, that the adoption order should stand. The child had had no contact whatsoever with its natural family. She had been successfully absorbed into the home and family of her adoptive parents, and was progressing well.

Although her sister's foster parents were also eminently suitable to bring her up, and although she would then be in contact with her own family, the trauma which would be caused by changing her whole environment at this stage would cause her serious and irreversible damage.

In view of all the circumstances, said Justice Elon, and after much anxious consideration, the court had decided to dismiss the appeal, and confirm the adoption order of the District Court.

Uriah Bar appeared for the Appellants, and Eilata Ziskind, Senior Assistant State Attorney, for the Attorney-General.

Judgment given on June 3, 1991.

RESTRAINING FREEDOM OF OCCUPATION

GISLER v. COHEN

In the National Labor Court, before the President, Judge Menahem Goldberg, the Deputy-President, Judge Stephen Adler, Judge Yitzhak Eliasof, Workers' Representative Esther Herlitz and Employers' Representative Arye Eban, in the matter of *Tsur Gisler Ltd., Avraham Tsur, and Ya'acov Gisler*, Appellants, versus *Mordechai Cohen and others*, Respondents (Dalet-Bet-Ayin-Nun-Aleph/3-148).

Labor Law—Freedom of Occupation—Restraint of Trade—Contracts (Remedies for Breach of Contract) Law, 1970, section 3—Agency Law, 1965, sections 6, 7—Contracts (General Part) Law, 1973, section 39.

Tsur and Gisler conducted a business consisting mainly of marketing holiday camping equipment. They decided later to operate the business through a company, and the first Appellant was founded for this purpose. The company was registered in June 1990, and was used for the operation of the business from the beginning of January 1991.

Cohen, the first Respondent, was employed by Tsur and Gisler at the beginning of 1990, and was responsible for the marketing and sale of various imported products. In his employment contract, signed by him and Gisler, he undertook, *inter alia*, not to deal with, or render any services to, any other business manufacturing or marketing products similar to those of the Appellants.

This undertaking was to endure during the period of his employment, and for three years thereafter.

Cohen left the Appellants' business in October 1990 and some two months later entered the employ of the other Respondents, who conducted a similar business. The Appellants then brought an action against Cohen and the other Respondents in the District Labor Court of Tel Aviv, and also applied for a temporary order restraining Cohen from having any contact whatsoever with the Appellants' customers, or engaging in any way in developing or marketing similar products, until judgment was given on their claim.

The District Court refused the application, and the Appellants appealed to the National Labor Court.

The judgment of the National Court was delivered by Judge Goldberg. The District Court, he said, had held that there was no basis for any claim by the Appellant company against Cohen and his present employers. Section 3 of the Contracts (Remedies for Breach of Contract) Law of 1970, entitled the "injured party" to a contract — which had been broken — to claim that the contract be enforced.

In the present case, however, the District Court had held that the Appellant company was not a party at all to the contract with Cohen. Cohen had left his employment with Tsur and Gisler before the company started operating the business, and there was nothing to show that Gisler had signed the employment contract with Cohen as representing the company, or that the company had taken any steps to adopt that contract.

Appellants' counsel had argued, on the other hand, that under Sections 6 and 7 of the Agency Law of 1965, a person or corporation could ratify a contract entered into on their behalf by someone unauthorized to do so, and that the Appellant company had ratified the contract in the present case.

The Appellants' contention was correct, the President ruled. Citing several precedents and legal texts, he pointed out that the mere fact that Tsur and Gisler had contemplated the formation of a company to conduct their business, was sufficient to enable that company, when registered, to ratify the contract previously made.

Moreover, the company's ratification of the contract need not be specific, but could be implied from the circumstances. It had even been suggested, in this regard, that the fact that the company had instituted a claim to enforce the contract was in itself sufficient to show its ratification. The Appellant company, therefore, was entitled to lodge its claim, and apply for the temporary injunction.

The same result would be reached, Judge Goldberg continued, by applying the doctrine of good faith, imported into the Israeli law of contracts by Section 39 of the Contracts (General Part) Law of 1973. The matter at issue was not to be judged by formal and technical considerations, such as whether the Appellant company had been registered or not when Cohen's employment contract was signed. It was clear that Gisler's and Cohen's intention was to protect the business against unfair competition on Cohen's part; whether that business was the firm of Tsur and Gisler, or assumed the form of a company which they established, was of no significance.

The Respondents had attacked the reasonableness of the provisions in the contract restricting Cohen's freedom of occupation, Judge Goldberg continued. The precedents showed that this aspect had been tested under three heads: the nature of the restriction, the period during which it operated and the area of the restriction.

A restriction on usual, day-to-day, activities was unreasonable, while a restriction on specific business activities would be recognized. The restriction in the present case, he held, fell into the latter category. Moreover, a period of two or three years, and the imposition of the restriction over the comparatively small area of the State of Israel, could not be reasonably assailed.

The Respondents had argued, Judge Goldberg said, that an appeal court will not readily interfere in the discretion of a lower court in regard to the grant or refusal of temporary relief. That was generally correct. In the present case, however, Cohen's continuing activity on behalf of a business dealing in the same products as those of the Appellants, would, *prima facie*, cause damage to the latter. It was true that the District Court had set early dates for the hearing of the main action, but this fact did not justify refusing the temporary injunction.

Respondents' counsel had also pointed to the damage which would be caused to Cohen himself by the injunction sought. It was true, of course, that Cohen would suffer damage. On the other hand, a man who signed a contract must be prepared to honor his bond. It was quite unacceptable that he should be allowed to honor only those provisions in the contract which suited him, and disregard those which he later found to be inconvenient.

Finally, Judge Goldberg said that the court had no intention, in this appeal, of restricting the District Court in dealing with the main claim. It was concerned with the question of temporary relief alone, and with the facts as they appeared, *prima facie*, at this stage of the litigation.

For the above reasons, the appeal was allowed, and the temporary injunction granted, subject to the furnishing of security by the three Appellants, and a third party, in the sum of NIS 30,000 for the payment of any damage suffered by Cohen, should the main claim be dismissed. Moreover, Cohen was ordered to pay the Appellants' costs in the sum of NIS 2,000, together with VAT.

Ehud Schneider appeared for the Appellants, and Avraham Goldberg for the Respondents.

Judgment given on May 2, 1991.

RABBINICAL REJECTION OF CONVERSION IS OVERRULED

RAVIV v. REHOVOT RABBINICAL COURT AND MINISTER OF INTERIOR

In the Supreme Court sitting as a High Court of Justice before the President, Justice Meir Shamgar, and Justices Aharon Barak and Gavriel Bach, in the matter of *Lirit Sylvie Raviv*, a minor, Petitioner, versus *The District Rabbinical Court of Rehovot and the Minister of Interior*, Respondents (H.C. 3023/90).

Personal Status—Conversion—Jurisdiction of Rabbinical Courts—Palestine Order-in-Council, 1922, Articles 40, 51—Rabbinical Courts Jurisdiction (Marriage and Divorce) Law, 1953—Arbitration Law, 1968, section 3—Law of Return, 1950, section 4B—Population Registry Law, 1965, section 3A(b).

The Petitioner, who was born on September 28, 1985, underwent an Orthodox conversion to Judaism on December 29 of that year. She was later adopted by a Jewish couple who had been married both in an Orthodox

Jewish ceremony and by a civil marriage officer in the U.S. They are now both citizens and residents of Israel.

In May 1987, the Petitioner's father furnished the Ministry of the Interior with the necessary particulars for the Petitioner's registration, including her conversion certificate. He was referred to the Rabbinical Court, the secretary of which endorsed on the certificate a notification that "this certificate may be accepted". The Petitioner's father then again approached the Interior Ministry, which again referred him to the Rabbinical Court to obtain its certificate confirming the conversion.

The Petitioners' parents then applied formally to the Rabbinical Court to make the order required. In giving judgment, the court stated, *inter alia*, that "In the proceedings before us, it emerged that the Applicants do not observe the religious commandments and it follows, of course, that they will educate the child so as not to observe the commandments which a Jew is enjoined to observe". The court also cited Jewish law sources supporting the conclusion that the legality of the conversion was in doubt.

The application, therefore, was refused, the court adding that, when the child grew up, she would be required to undergo immersion again, if she undertook to observe the commandments according to Jewish law.

The Petitioners' parents lodged an appeal to the Supreme Rabbinical Court of Appeals, and the Petitioner, in her own right, acting through her parents as her guardians, petitioned the Supreme Court to set aside the judgment of the District Rabbinical Court.

The judgment of the Supreme Court was delivered by Justice Barak. It had at one time been the policy of the Ministry of the Interior, he said, not to register a convert as a Jew without the confirmation of the Ministry for Religious Affairs. Following a Supreme Court decision in another case, however, that policy had been changed, and the Petitioner had accordingly been registered as a Jewess on the basis of the information furnished by her parents and the certificate of her conversion outside Israel.

There was, therefore, no longer any need to consider granting an order against the Minister of the Interior.

Justice Barak then considered whether a question as to the validity of a conversion fell within the jurisdiction of a Rabbinical Court. Citing Supreme Court precedents, he pointed out that Article 51 of the Palestine Order in Council of 1922, as amended, conferred jurisdiction on Religious Courts, concurrent with that of the civil courts, in matters of personal status, namely, "suits regarding marriage or divorce, alimony, maintenance, guardianship, legitimation, inhibition from dealing with property of persons who are legally incompetent, and the administration of property of absent persons". Conversion was not included.

Moreover, the Rabbinical Courts Jurisdiction (Marriage and Divorce) Law of 1953 granted those courts exclusive jurisdiction in matters of marriage and divorce alone, and also jurisdiction, by consent of the parties, only in matters of personal status. The result was that matters of conversion fell within the residual jurisdiction of the District Courts which were empowered, under Section 18 of the Courts Law of 1957, following Article 40 of the Order in Council, to deal with any matter "not within the exclusive jurisdiction of another court or tribunal".

It had been argued, Justice Barak continued, that even if the existing statutory provisions did not confer jurisdiction upon the Rabbinical Courts, it had been conferred in this case by the consent of the parties to regard the court as an arbitrator, or as a tribunal exercising religious jurisdiction. The functioning of the Rabbinical Court as an arbitrator, so it was said, could be based either upon the Arbitration Law of 1968 (and it appeared that that court did in fact so function), or on the basis of long-established custom.

Both of these conceptions, however, were fraught with difficulty. How was it possible for a court of law established by the State to act as an arbitrator in matters beyond its jurisdiction? Was it at all conceivable that a Magistrates' Court, for example, could deal as an arbitrator with a monetary claim which fell beyond its jurisdiction? Moreover, Section 3 of the Arbitration Law invalidated a submission to arbitration in a matter which could not legally be the subject of an agreement between the parties.

Was it possible, he asked, that the validity of a conversion could be the subject of such agreement? In the present case, however, the court was not required to answer these questions for the reason that the Petitioner's parents did not approach the Rabbinical Court as an arbitrator. They did not "consent" to approach that court at all. They were referred to that court by the Interior Ministry as the competent court to pronounce on the validity of the conversion.

The questions posed above would perhaps, one day, demand an answer, but they were not pertinent to the present dispute. It was perhaps possible, Justice Barak continued, to regard the Rabbinical Courts as competent tribunals to rule on questions of Jewish law, apart from their functions as laid down in the Laws of the State. Thus it was accepted, for example, that they effected conversions, since the Halacha demanded that this act be performed by a Beit Din (a religious court), and it followed, so some scholars had suggested, that they were also competent to rule on the validity of conversions which had already taken place outside Israel.

On the other hand, some writers had also indicated the difficulties which could be caused by this kind of double jurisdiction of Rabbinical Courts which functioned within the official framework of the State. The decisions of an unofficial Beit Din were not — and did not even purport to be — legally binding, and there was no danger of the public, or the State authorities, being misled into thinking that they were. Decisions of the official Rabbinical Courts, however, were subject to review by the Supreme Court, and they were not entitled to exceed the jurisdiction conferred upon them by law. The present case was an example of the confusion referred to above, said Justice Barak. Both the Interior Ministry and the Petitioner's parents had been misled into believing that the Rabbinical Court was the proper official forum to determine the validity of the conversion. It was on that basis that the parents approached that court. There was no question of their having consented to accept that court's ruling.

The judgment invalidating the conversion, therefore, was given in excess of jurisdiction, and was of no legal effect whatsoever. Since the Rabbinical Court judgment was invalid for lack of jurisdiction, said Justice Barak, there was no need to deal with the other arguments of Petitioner's counsel.

He found it necessary, however, to make two comments. Firstly, there was no basis, *prima facie*, for the Rabbinical Court to enquire into matters which succeeded the conversion, even if, under the Halacha, subsequent events could affect its validity. The court was asked to give its ruling regarding a conversion which had already been effected at a given time and place, by a given Beit Din.

The ruling was required for purposes of registration, and section 4B of the Law of Return of 1950, dealing with converts and, in its footsteps, Section 3A(b) of the Population Registry Law, dealt *prima facie* with a formal specific act of conversion which had already taken place. To say otherwise would mean that all the conversions were "conditional", and all the converted Jews were "conditional Jews", all depending on future events.

This conception negated the very purpose of the Law of Return.

Secondly, said Justice Barak, the examination of the facts by the Rabbinical Court, recorded in four lines, was as short as could be. The record stated: "The Applicants: We adopted a daughter in the U.S., and she was converted there. She was three months old when she was converted. The child's name is Sylvie, ID 011731114, born on 13 Tishri, Tasham (28.9.85). Doesn't attend synagogue every Sabbath. Travels occasionally on the Sabbath. Lights electricity on the Sabbath. Presents a conversion certificate".

Was it possible, on the basis of evidence such as this, to destroy the world of a child and her parents, and to cast doubt on her being a Jewess?

Justice Barak then quoted the following extract from a precedent in which he had dealt with a decision of the Rabbinical Court of Haifa, "I cannot but express my deep sense of shock at the approach of the District Rabbinical Court which, on the basis of a few replies to questions which it had itself initiated ["I eat treif (unclean food), do not go to the mikveh (ritual bath) and do not observe the Sabbath"], was prepared to rule 'not to recognize her conversion and her joining the family of Israel, since her being received, and her accepting the necessary obligations, were based on deceit. Her conversion, therefore, and her marriage to her husband, are declared void.'

"It follows 'that she has no rights' in her husband's property".

"Can a factual finding be reached in this way, and is this the way to decide a person's fate? This is a case dealing with the liberty of a human being in the fullest sense possible. Is this the path chosen by the Haifa District Rabbinical Court?" And, in conclusion, Justice Barak repeated his question: Can a person's fate be decided in this manner?

For the above reasons, the petition was allowed, and the decision of the Rabbinical Court set aside.

Yosef Ben-Menashe appeared for the Petitioner and Shaul Gordon for the Minister of the Interior.

Judgment given on July 8, 1991.

THE KFAR HANASSI POWER STATION

MOVEMENT FOR QUALITY OF GOVERNMENT v. NATIONAL PLANNING BOARD

In the Supreme Court, sitting as a High Court of Justice, before Justices Aharon Barak, Shoshana Netanyahu and Theodore Orr, in the matter of *The Movement for the Quality of Government in Israel and its Directors*, Petitioners, versus *The National Board for Planning and Building, and others*, Respondents (H.C. 2324/91).

*Administrative Law—Allegation that Confimation of Town Planning Scheme
Based on Inadequate Grounds—Refusal of Court to Interfere—Planning and
Building Law, 1965.*

Some years ago, Kibbutz Kfar Hanassi decided to promote a scheme for
the erection of a hydro-electric plant and the establishment of an active
tourist site, based on the natural environment of the mountainous gorge of
the River Jordan flowing towards Lake Kinneret. Under the scheme, about
a third of the river's flow would be diverted at a certain point into an
artificial lake. By exploiting the varying height of the terrain, the flow of
these waters would operate turbines and thus produce electricity. The
waters would then rejoin the Jordan River in its natural course.

On December 6, 1990, the planning scheme embracing the above project
was published for approval under the Planning and Building Law of 1965.
The Petitioners then moved the Supreme Court, sitting as a High Court of
Justice, to set aside the legal steps taken to confirm the scheme and the
permit granted to the kibbutz to erect the projected power station.

The judgment of the court was delivered by Justice Orr, who described
at the outset the steps taken to advance the project before the formal
procedures prescribed in the above Law were followed. Agreement had
been reached in 1985 with the Nature Reserves Authority and the National
Water Commissioner. Guidelines for the preparation of a paper on the
influence of the project on the environment had been given by the Interior
Ministry, and the necessary confirmations for the erection of the plant had
been secured after consultations between the Ministry of Energy and Infra-
structure and the Israel Electric Corporation.

Justice Orr then dealt in some detail with the discussion of the scheme
by numerous bodies until its publication for approval in December 1990.
He pointed out that the District Planning Commission had considered
objections, including those of the Ministry for the Environment, and the
Nature Protection Society. It had decided that the project would not
damage the natural surroundings, and that its controlled development
would improve the area immeasurably for the benefit of hikers and
holidaymakers. It was of opinion that all the reservations about damage
to the quality of the surroundings had been adequately met. It had decided,
therefore, to confirm the scheme.

The Petitioners, Justice Orr continued, had raised a number of technical
legal arguments against the acceptance of the scheme. Their main contentions, however, were that not all the relevant facts had been placed before

the authorities concerned, and that the latter had not given adequate consideration to the facts that were before them. They also contended that the decision to approve the scheme was unreasonable, stressing in this regard the special character of the River Jordan from the historical, emotional and national aspects, and the possible danger to the river and its natural surroundings.

Justice Orr then examined — and dismissed — the technical arguments of Petitioners' counsel. He added that the Respondents, for their part, had argued that the Petitioners had no legal standing to present the petition, and also that they had delayed unduly in approaching the court. He found it unnecessary, however, to consider these contentions, since the court had in any event decided to dismiss the petition on its merits.

There was no substance in the argument, said Justice Orr, that the facts before the different authorities were incomplete, or that their consideration of the scheme had been inadequate. In fact, almost all the planning authorities in the State had been party, in one way or another, to the discussions on the scheme and the decisions reached.

The time devoted to considering the project, the number of bodies involved, the documents and information before the National Planning Board and the Planning Commissions and the conditions in the scheme itself and the solutions it contained — all these factors showed that all the relevant information had been placed before the authorities, and that it had been adequately considered.

Referring to the argument of reasonableness, Justice Orr pointed out that, as in many other matters of public dispute, there were many different opinions, sometimes poles apart. Every opinion was supported on some grounds or other; and the question was whether the court should intervene in a decision of the planning authorities, which had preferred one approach over others and had decided to confirm the scheme.

Judges sat amongst their people, and it sometimes happened that they were inclined to differ from decisions of the administration. Where there were a number of options, it was possible that the court itself would have decided otherwise. That, however, was a test which it was not permitted to apply.

Citing Supreme Court precedents, Justice Orr held that the sole question was whether the decision reviewed was one which a reasonable administrative authority could reach. If the decision was one of many which a reasonable authority could make, the court would not interfere. It was the duty of the court to review administrative decisions on the basis of reasonableness, and it was for the court to decide the limits of what was reasonable.

However, the court was not entitled to substitute its discretion for that of the authority designated by law to make the decision in question. It was also to be borne in mind that the court would hesitate to interfere in a decision which was based, as in the present case, on the opinion of experts in the particular field affected.

Applying the above test, it could not be said that the scheme in question exceeded what was reasonable, and there was no ground, therefore, for the court to intervene. Justice Orr pointed out, however, that the scheme itself contained provisions for proper supervision of its implementation, and of the plant and the tourist site to be established. It was not to be forgotten that there was only one River Jordan, with all the importance attaching to it from so many aspects. The court assumed, therefore, that the necessary supervision would be adequate and continuous.

For the above reasons, the petition was dismissed.

Advocate Har Zahav appeared for the Petitioners; Uzi Fogelman, Senior Assistant State Attorney, for the State; and Advocates Rosenbloom, Meltzer, and Reshef for the other Respondents.

Judgment given on June 23, 1991.

TELLING A WORKER TO STAY HOME

HISTADRUT v. TAHAL

In the National Labor Court, before the President, Judge Menahem Goldberg, the Deputy-President, Judge Stephen Adler, Judge Yitzhak Eliasof, Employees' Representative Dov Frankel and Employers' Representative Avraham Cohen, in the matter of *The Histadrut (General Labor Federation), The National Workers' Committee of Tahal and Abraham Kostika and 30 others*, Appellants, versus *Tahal and another*, Respondents (Nun Aleph/4-21).

Labor Law—Validity of Employer's Order to Worker to Stay Home—Collective Labor Agreements.

Tahal, the Israel Water Planning Company, encountered financial difficulties, and on August 26, 1990, it cancelled the collective agreement relating to the employment of its workers.

On December 6, 1990, it instructed Abraham Kostika and 30 other workers not to appear at work, advising them at the same time that they would continue to receive their wages. Neither the collective agreement nor any other contract obliged Tahal actually to provide work for its employees. The basis for Tahal's decision was its inability to provide work and the saving of operational services such as electricity, water and private telephone calls.

The Appellants moved the District Labor Court of Tel Aviv to order the Respondents, *inter alia*, to return the workers affected to regular employment. The application was dismissed, and the Appellants appealed to the National Labor Court.

The judgment of the National Court was delivered by Judge Adler, who dealt first with Tahal's obligations within the framework of its individual relationship with its workers, as distinct from the requirements of the collective work agreement. Since Tahal was under no express obligation to provide work for its employees, he said, the question was whether that relationship embraced an implied term obliging it to do so.

Citing Israeli precedents, he pointed out that labor contracts had been held to contain implied terms in regard, *inter alia*, to the employee's obligation to do his work, the parties' duty of good faith, the duty to give adequate notice of dismissal or resignation and the employee's duty not to act against his employer's interests.

No clear decision had been given, however, on the question now at issue.

The Deputy-President then quoted legal texts stating the law in Britain, Germany and Japan, and he also referred to the court's own precedents bearing, albeit indirectly, on the instant problem. Having regard to the Foundations of Law Statute of 1980, introducing "the principles of freedom, justice, equity and peace of Israel's heritage" to fill a lacuna in the law, he also examined in some detail the approach of Jewish Law to the question now raised.

As a general rule, Judge Adler concluded, an employer was not obliged to provide work for his employees, although some exceptions had been recognized.

In the light of the authorities cited, Judge Adler held that the following factors, *inter alia*, should be weighed by the court in deciding whether the employer's failure to provide work for the employee constituted a breach of his obligations and, if so, whether the court would order the employer to provide such work:

—Whether the work carried rights additional to the worker's wages, such as a portion of the profits; whether stopping the work would affect the employee's professional status and ability to secure other employment, such as in the case of an actor; or whether, on the other hand, he would prefer to remain at home while receiving his full salary; whether depriving the employee of work would injure his dignity;

— Also, whether the major part of the worker's wages were received on the basis of the actual work he performed, as in the case of a sales agent who was paid a premium on sales; whether the employer acted in good faith; whether the employer acted in agreement with the worker's representative organization; whether the employer's decision stemmed from the opposition of the employee's fellow-workers to his presence at work; and whether the employee was ordered to stay away from work for a limited period, or permanently.

In the present case it was clear beyond any doubt, on the basis of undisputed evidence, that Tahal was unable to provide work for Kostika and his 30 fellow-workers. As a general rule, a worker was not entitled to sit at his place of work when there was no work to be done. In these circumstances, Tahal was not obliged to supply these workers with an office and telephone, while being prepared to pay their full wages.

There was no evidence that Tahal would not be prepared to return the workers if and when work became available, or that it had acted in bad faith; and Tahal could not be expected to employ these workers at the expense of other workers and the company itself.

For these reasons, the Appellants' claim, within the framework of the individual relations between Tahal and the workers, was correctly dismissed.

Judge Adler then turned to the obligations of Tahal within the framework of the collective work agreement. The fact was, he said, that the collective agreement of August 1989 (which, in any case, contained no provision obliging Tahal to keep the employees at work) had been cancelled before the workers had been instructed not to come.

The question arose, however, whether there was any other basis for the Appellants' claim. Another collective agreement between Tahal and the Histadrut, relating to the former's financial rehabilitation, precluded Tahal from dismissing more workers before April 1991. It was necessary to consider whether there had been a breach of that agreement, and whether, in the circumstances, Tahal was obliged to negotiate with the Histadrut in good faith before issuing the instruction in question.

There had been no breach of the other collective agreement, Judge Adler held. Moreover, there was a conflict of opinion among the authorities concerning the employer's obligation to negotiate in good faith in the circumstances of this case. There was, however, no necessity to decide this point, for it was plain that Tahal had taken the action complained of in good faith, to save expenses and support the company's recovery plan; and it had provided the Histadrut with full and accurate particulars of its policy, and the reasons for it.

Moreover, the Appellants had not asked the court to order Tahal to negotiate with the Histadrut. The Appellants' claim, therefore, could not be based on the collective agreements, or on circumstances connected with them.

For the above reasons, the appeal was dismissed, with no order as to costs.

Yosef Katz appeared for the Appellants and Yoram Fay for the Respondents.

Judgment given on April 11, 1991.

WIRE-TAP VERSUS PRIVACY

STATE OF ISRAEL v. ILUZ

In the Supreme Court sitting as a Court of Criminal Appeals before the President, Justice Meir Shamgar, and Justices Dov Levin and Ya'acov Maltz, in the matter of *The State of Israel*, Appellant, versus *Asher Iluz and others*, Respondents (Cr. A. 2286/91).

Evidence—Telephone Conversation Monitored by Police—Judge's Permit Defective—Evidence Inadmissible—Defendant's Acquittal Confirmed—Secret Monitoring Law, 1979, sections 6, 13(a)—Courts Law (Consolidated Version), 1984, section 42—Courts Regulations (Procedure Relating to Secret Monitoring), 1985.

The Respondents were tried in the District Court of Tel Aviv for trafficking in drugs. The prosecution relied, inter alia, on telephone conversations which had been secretly monitored by the police under the Secret Monitoring Law of 1979. Under Section 6 of that Law, the President of a District Court or, in his absence, a Deputy-President, may, on the application of a police officer of the rank of *Nitzav-Mishne* (Chief Superintendant), or higher, empowered by the Inspector-General of Police, issue an order permitting secret monitoring to prevent offenses or detect offenders. Under Section 42 of the Courts Law (Consolidated Version) of 1984, the President may also delegate this power to a Deputy-President of the Court.

The Respondents contended that the necessary order had not been proved, and that evidence of the conversations was therefore inadmissible under Section 13(a) of the Law, which provides that "nothing recorded by way of secret monitoring in contravention of this Law shall be admissible as evidence in court".

The District Court accepted this argument, and therefore acquitted some of the Respondents completely, acquitting others of some of the charges against them. The State then appealed to the Supreme Court.

The judgment of the Supreme Court was delivered by Justice Shamgar, who examined the relevant provisions of the above Law, and also the Courts Regulations (Procedure Relating to Secret Monitoring), of 1985, dealing with the application for a judicial order under Section 6 of the Law. In this regard, he referred particularly to the form set out in the schedule to the regulations, embodying in one document the application for the order of the President or Deputy-President of the court, the record of the hearing before him, and also the order made by him on the application.

The first part of the above form, the President continued, contained the particulars of the person whose conversations were to be monitored, the grounds for the application, the place and method of monitoring, and the period for which the permit was requested. The second part of the form, headed "For Use by the Court", contained the name of the police officer appearing (whose rank, as laid down in Section 6(b) of the Law, was to be not lower than Sgan-Nitzav [Superintendent]), the fact that he had been properly warned to tell the truth, and his declaration that the facts alleged in the first part of the form were true.

The form then provided for the signature of this second part by the President or Deputy-President, making it clear that the warning and declaration were to be made before him, and confirmed by him. The third part of the form was headed "Decision" and contained a space for the judge's signature.

The above form, Justice Shamgar continued, accorded with the spirit of the Law. The wealth of detail, and the declaration demanded, expressed the legislative intention of protecting the individual against the invasion of his privacy, on the one hand, and on the other hand, enabling the intervention of the authorities to protect the security of the State, or to prevent offenses or detect offenders. To achieve this intention, Section 2(a) of the Law made unlawful monitoring a criminal offense; and under Section 13(a), nothing recorded in secret monitoring could be used in evidence.

In the present case, said Justice Shamgar, the signature of the Deputy President of the District Court who heard the application for the monitoring permit, appeared only at the end of the second part of the form. In fact, it appeared that the form then in use by the police contained only the first two parts, while the last part was not placed before the judge at all.

The State argued, however, that the one signature which did appear was to be regarded as confirming both the giving of the declaration by the police officer, and the granting of the permit.

The questions arising in the present context, the President continued, were whether it was obligatory to give the permit requested in writing and, if so, whether that obligation was substantive, or only required for purposes of evidence; and what were the meaning and effect of the form, signed as it was, in the present case.

After comparing the relevant sections of the above Law with other statutory provisions, Justice Shamgar held that the permit in question had to be in writing. It was clear that the police application had to be in writing; moreover, the section did not deal with a permit issued by an administrative authority, but by a senior judicial officer, who was required to grant the permit, in an order of court, on the basis of the application and declaration appearing in the same form, as laid down in the schedule to the regulations. The legislative intention that the permit was to be written was, therefore, quite clear.

Whether the necessity of writing was substantive or only probative, Justice Shamgar continued, depended on the intention of the legislature. Was writing required "*ad solemnitatem*", to prevent the legal act in question being performed in haste or light-headedly, or was the intention merely "*ad probationem*", to protect the parties concerned against the weak memory of witnesses, or the danger of perjured evidence. There were three main features in the present case, he held, which showed that the requirement of writing was substantive.

Justice Shamgar referred first, in this context, to the legislative history of the Secret Monitoring Law. It was clear from the explanatory notes accompanying the bill presented to the Knesset that the proposed Law was regarded with the utmost seriousness. Secondly, the officer presenting the application to the court, being specifically empowered to do so by the Inspector-General of Police, and the officer appearing before the court, were both required to be of senior rank. Moreover, only the President or Deputy-President of the court were empowered to grant the permit, and a refusal of the permit was subject to appeal to the Supreme Court.

Thirdly, Justice Shamgar continued, the making of unauthorized monitoring a criminal offense, and making the evidence thereby obtained inadmissible in court, constituted a glaring departure from the accepted rules of evidence in Israel. Citing Supreme Court precedents, including the case of *Vaknin* (H.C. 249/82 and F.H.9/83 — *The Jerusalem Post* of June 27, 1983, and November 23, 1988), he pointed out that Israel, like the UK, had never accepted the "Fruits of the Poisoned Tree" rule recognized in American jurisprudence, excluding evidence unlawfully or improperly obtained.

One statutory exception to the Israeli practice was found in Section 32 of the Protection of Privacy Law of 1981, which excluded evidence obtained in contravention of that Law unless the court decided otherwise. The Secret Monitoring Law, however, went even further, for no discretion was given to the court to admit the evidence.

Justice Shamgar held, therefore, that the requirement of a written order permitting the monitoring was substantive. The Law in question sanctioned an invasion of the right of privacy to which every person was entitled. Its provisions, therefore, were no mere formality, but had to be strictly observed.

It followed, in the present case, that no written order by the Deputy President of the District Court had been proved. There was nothing to show that his signature on the second part of the form was intended to indicate his acceptance of the application, and his granting the permit sought. Citing precedents, including the case of *Shnir* (Cr A. 869/81 — *The Jerusalem Post* of February 25, 1985), Justice Shamgar noted that if a written order had been given, but had been lost or mislaid, it could perhaps be proved by secondary evidence. In the present case, however, the Deputy President concerned had no recollection of the application, and it would clearly be improper for the officer who appeared before him, and was an interested party, to testify as to the implications of the signature on the second part of the form.

The result was, said Justice Shamgar, that no proof had been submitted of the grant of a permit as required by the Law, and the acquittal of the Respondents, therefore, was correct. It was to be hoped, he added, that errors of this kind relating to the form in question, would not recur.

For the above reasons, the appeal was dismissed.

Nava Ben-Or, Senior Assistant State Attorney, appeared for the State, and Moshe Tram, Zion Amir, Ya'acov Hovav and Moshe Sherman appeared for the Respondents.

Judgment given on July 31, 1991.

DETENTION DURING TRIAL

STATE OF ISRAEL v. VISHNITZKY AND SHALOM

In the Supreme Court, before the Deputy-President, Justice Menahem Elon, in the matter of *The State of Israel*, Applicant, versus *Erez Vishnitzky and Yosef Shalom*, Respondents; and *The State of Israel*, Applicant, versus *Erez Vishnitzky*, Respondent. (Miscellaneous Applications [C] 3267, 3691/91).

Criminal Procedure—Detention During Trial—Gravity of Offence in Itself Usually Insufficient—Importation, Possession, and Trafficking in Drugs—Complete House Arrest—Criminal Procedure Law (Consolidated Version), 1982, sections 53, 54.

On April 26, 1990, the Respondent Vishnitzky was charged in the District Court of Haifa with importing into Israel, and possessing for purposes of trafficking in drugs, 29.686 kilograms of heroin and 650.85 grams of opium. The Respondent Shalom was charged with possessing 1.967 kilograms of heroin, being part of the above consignment, and of attempting to possess the lot.

Both Respondents were also charged with breaking in. According to the indictment, the whole consignment was imported into Israel by Vishnitzky. While the drugs were still in the container, however, the police removed them, substituted other material in similar parcels, and left only 1.967

kilograms of heroin. The Respondents broke into the container and, after removing the parcels, were arrested.

Under Section 53 of the Criminal Procedure Law (Consolidated Version) of 1982, where an accused person is under arrest, and his trial in the court of first instance is not terminated by judgment within one year of the indictment being filed, he shall be released. Under Section 54 of the Law, a Justice of the Supreme Court may, nevertheless, order the extension of the arrest, or a re-arrest, for a period not exceeding three months, and he may do so again from time to time.

The Respondents had been detained since their arrest, and their trial was nowhere near its conclusion. By consent of the parties, the Supreme Court had already extended the Respondents' detention for an additional three months, and the State now applied for an order directing their detention for a further such period.

Counsel for the State, the Deputy-President said in his judgment, had relied on the unusual seriousness of the Respondents' alleged crimes, stressing the enormous quantity of heroin which the case involved. It was unthinkable, he argued, that people who trafficked in drugs on that scale should be allowed to wander about freely in the marketplace.

Respondents' counsel, on the other hand, had submitted that the court should not deny their clients' freedom for what could be a very lengthy period of unknown duration by repeated extensions of their detention. Only six out of some 45 prosecution witnesses had so far been heard, and there was no knowing what the future held in this regard.

Justice Elon then cited Supreme Court precedents, including Application 3838/90 (*The Jerusalem Post* of December 12, 1990), in which the principles to be applied in applications of this nature were laid down. The considerations ordinarily applicable in regard to detention of a suspect before and during his trial were no longer valid after a year had elapsed.

The legislature had decided that, after a year, a suspect, still presumed to be innocent, "shall be released". It had emphasized, in the clearest possible terms, the importance of preserving the individual's right to liberty; and it was only in the most exceptional circumstances, therefore, that that right was to be curtailed.

It was true, said Justice Elon, that the gravity of the alleged offense, and the law's delays in the courts, were not, as a rule, in themselves sufficient ground for detaining suspects, or accused persons whose trial had already commenced, beyond a year. There were, however, other ways of ensuring the suspect's appearing at his trial, and avoiding interference with the witnesses or the proceedings, such as laying down appropriate conditions for bail, or other conditions for the suspect's release.

Moreover, if the suspect's or accused's freedom had to be curtailed, he should not necessarily be held in a prison or detention center but could be confined to his home, subject to proper conditions being prescribed.

In all the circumstances, Justice Elon ordered that Vishnitzky, in addition to providing bail and the suretyship of a third party, be confined to his home, subject to seeing his counsel in her office, and reporting daily to the police. Justice Elon imposed similar, but less stringent, conditions for the release from detention of the Respondent Shalom.

After the above decision, which was given on the basis of the documents before the court, the State requested the court to amend its order regarding Vishnitzky by directing him to be confined to his home absolutely, and Vishnitzky's counsel requested to be heard in order to persuade the court to modify the conditions of bail, and permit her client to leave his home for purposes other than to consult with her and report to the police.

She stated, *inter alia*, that her client required dental treatment, and that the frequent visits of the police to his home disturbed his parents. She requested that he be permitted to stroll outside his home, as prisoners are allowed their daily exercise, and that he be enabled to make small purchases, such as cigarettes.

After considering all the circumstances, however, and ruling that in this particular case the extreme gravity of the Respondent's alleged offense was in itself a factor the court should take into account, Justice Elon accepted the arguments of the State, and ordered that Vishnitzky be confined to his home completely.

He also ordered that any change of circumstances regarding the Respondent's being confined to his home (as distinct from his detention in a prison or detention center), which the parties may wish to bring before the court, need not be brought before the Supreme Court, but were to be considered by the District Court which was trying his case.

Justice Elon noted that with the increasing sophistication of criminal activity in certain fields, such as drug trafficking, and the increasing burden on the courts, the problem which arose in the above applications was bound to become more and more acute. The time had arrived, therefore, to lay down general procedures governing "house arrest" as an alternative, in proper circumstances, to detention in a prison or detention center.

Yehoshua Resnik, Senior Assistant State Attorney, appeared for the State, Pnina Dvorin for Vishnitzky, and Dror Makrin for Shalom.

Judgments given on August 7 and August 18, 1991.

REPAYING A CO-OP'S DEBTS

PRI HA'EMEK COOPERATIVE v. SDE YA'ACOV

In the Supreme Court, sitting as a Court of Civil Appeals, before the Deputy-President, Justice Menahem Elon and Justices Aharon Barak and Eliyahu Matza, in the matter of *The Pri Ha'Emek Agricultural Cooperative Society and another*, Appellants, versus *The Sde Ya'acov Workers' Settlement, and others*, Respondents. (C.A. 524,528/88).

Commercial Law—Cooperative Societies—Liability of Member for Society's Debts— Cooperative Societies Ordinance, 1933, section 65—Cooperative Society (General Provisions) Regulations, 1976, regulation 2A.

On September 18, 1987, a general meeting of Pri Ha'Emek, a central cooperative society comprising kibbutzim and moshavim, decided by a majority representing kibbutzim against a minority representing moshavim, to impose the debts of the cooperative on its members.

The extent of each member's liability was left to an arbitrator, who made his award on December 1, 1987. At the instance of the moshavim, the District Court of Nazareth declared the decision of the general meeting and the arbitrator's award unlawful, and the Appellants appealed to the Supreme Court.

The judgment of the Supreme Court was delivered by Justice Barak, who noted at the outset that the Attorney-General, regarding the matter as one of public importance, had also appeared in the appeal. The Appellants, he said, had relied on Regulation 2A(a) of the Cooperative Society (General Provisions) Regulations of 1976, issued by the minister of labor, under which a cooperative society was empowered, by the decision of a general meeting, to impose upon its members the covering of the society's deficits, and the payment of its expenses and debts.

The Respondents, however, had supported the ruling of the District Court that the above regulation was unlawful since the minister, in issuing it, had exceeded his powers under the enabling statute, the Cooperative Societies Ordinance of 1933. He would first consider the question at issue, said Justice Barak, within the context of private law, dealing with the relationship between the cooperative and its members and, if necessary, would then examine, within the context of public law, the powers of the minister under the Ordinance referred to.

The Attorney-General had submitted that a clear distinction was to be drawn between the relationship of the cooperative as an independent legal entity with third parties, and its relationship with its members. The cooperative expressed the ideology of cooperation and equality between its members. In the latter context, therefore, he argued, the members were to be regarded as principals, and the cooperative as their agent.

It followed, so he contended, that the debts of the cooperative were the debts of its members, who could be made liable for their payment.

A cooperative society, said Justice Barak, was juristically a person, distinct from its members. Citing numerous precedents and legal texts, and comparing societies with limited liability companies and partnerships, he stressed that the debts incurred by the society were its own debts, and not the debts of its members.

He also noted that it was not the profits from its capital investment that were a society's main concern, but improving the members' lot by mutual and cooperative effort. As with companies, there were circumstances in which "the veil could be lifted" where, for example, the corporate nature of the society had been abused. As a general rule, however, the corporate character of the society was to be honored.

The rules of a society constituted a contract between it and its members, and a general meeting was not empowered to change that contract and, as the District Court had expressed it, "put its hand in a member's pocket" to pay its own debts.

Justice Barak then turned to consider the validity of Regulation 2A(a) above. It was true, he said, that the minister of labor was enabled, under Section 65 of the above Ordinance, to make regulations, *inter alia*, "for the powers to be exercised" by a society's general meeting.

However, after enunciating the general principles applicable, and citing numerous authorities, including the cases of *Sheib* (H.C. 144/50, Selected Supreme Court Judgments [English], Vol. 1, p. 1]; *Barzilai* (H.C. 428/86, *The Jerusalem Post* of 15 and 18 August, 1986, and Selected Judgments [*Supra*], Vol. 6, p. 1); and *Medinvest* (H.C. 256/88, *The Jerusalem Post* of January 17, 1990, *supra* p. 130), he emphasized that the rule of law demanded a balance between individual rights and those of the community.

This balance, in turn, justified the rule that basic provisions must be laid down by the legislature itself, while subsidiary legislation should be permitted to deal solely with the means and procedures for giving effect to the intentions of the legislature.

After a critical examination of the provisions and implications of the above Ordinance, including its legislative history, and emphasizing the recognition of private property as one of the basic rights of the individual, Justice Barak agreed with the District Court that the regulation in question went too far: the powers of the minister did not extend to permitting a general meeting of a cooperative to impose its obligations on its members without their consent.

If the legislature had intended that a society, through its own institutions, be empowered to take so drastic a step as to interfere with the individual's basic rights, it should have embodied such a provision specifically in its own, the primary, legislation, and not left it to be dealt with by a subordinate legislative authority. Regulation 2A(a), therefore, was *ultra vires*, and it followed that the resolution of the general meeting, and the subsequent arbitrator's award, were unlawful, and could not be enforced.

For the above reasons, the appeals were dismissed.

Alex Samuel appeared for the Appellants; Meir Hefler for the Respondents; and Shulamit Wasserkrug, formerly Assistant State Attorney, and Davida Lachman-Messer, Director of the Department of Corporate Law in the Ministry of Justice, for the Attorney-General.

Judgment given on August 15, 1991.

MURDER CONFESSION REVIEWED

KUZALI v. STATE OF ISRAEL

In the Supreme Court, before the President Justice Meir Shamgar, in the matter of *Ahmed Kuzali and four others*, Applicants, versus *The State of Israel*, Respondent (Further Hearing 3081/91).

Murder—Criminal Law—Evidence—Confession—Criminal Procedure—Application to President of Supreme Court for Rehearing after Appeal Dismissed Evidence—Evidence Ordinance (New Version), 1971, section 12(a)—Courts Law (Consolidated Version), 1984, section 30(b).

The Applicants were convicted in the District Court of Haifa of the kidnapping and murder of Danny Katz. They were convicted, and their appeal to the Supreme Court was dismissed. They then applied to the President of the Supreme Court, under Section 30(b) of the Courts Law (Consolidated Version) of 1984, to order a further hearing of their appeal. An order under that section may be made if a ruling by the appeal court conflicts with a previous ruling, or if, "in view of the importance, difficulty or novelty of a ruling handed down in the matter", the President, or a judge or judges nominated by him, find room for a further hearing.

The District Court, the President said in his judgment, had relied on full confessions made by each of the Applicants in the course of the police investigation, and Applicants' counsel had now argued that the appeal court had erred in agreeing with that decision. It was necessary, therefore, to consider whether, *prima facie*, that argument had some merit and, if so, whether it provided grounds for a further hearing under Section 30(b) above. The President then pointed out that a distinction was drawn between the admissibility of confessions, and their weight after they had been received as evidence. Under Section 12(a) of the Evidence Ordinance (New Version) of 1971, a confession could only be admitted if the prosecution lead evidence as to the circumstances in which it had been made, and if it was proved to have been made freely and voluntarily. This the prosecution had to prove beyond a reasonable doubt.

Citing numerous precedents, including the case of *Muadi* (*The Jerusalem Post* of February 15, 1984), Justice Shamgar examined the principles governing the admissibility of confessions and the procedure of the court in applying the above section. Where the validity of a confession was challenged, the court conducted a "little trial" dealing specifically with that particular issue. Such a "little trial" had also taken place in the District Court in the present instance.

Although Applicants' counsel had attacked, in the main, the weight of the confessions, Justice Shamgar continued, he would nevertheless also examine the question of their admissibility. After pointing out that the prosecution had called as witnesses all the police officers, some 30 in number, who had been concerned in receiving the confessions, and that they had all been cross-examined by Applicants' counsel, he himself had analyzed in detail the evidence relating to the confessions of each Applicant.

The District Court, he said, was satisfied that the confessions had been given freely and voluntarily, and the evidence was sufficient to justify that conclusion. There was therefore no ground for interference with that finding by the appeal court, which had also itself examined in detail the evidence heard in the "little trial", and the grounds of the District Court for admitting the confessions.

Turning to the weight of the confessions, Justice Shamgar pointed out that the truth of the confessions was to be judged by the application of two tests — the intrinsic test, which weighed the confession in the light of common sense and experience of life, and the extrinsic test, which sought to support the confession by finding "something extra", some additional evidence lending credence to the confession.

This additional evidence, though not necessarily amounting to actual corroboration, had to be something substantial. The District Court had held that the confessions satisfied the "intrinsic" test, and the appeal court had justified that conclusion. He had found no ground, said Justice Shamgar, to interfere in that regard.

The District Court, Justice Shamgar said, had enumerated a number of factors, including videotapes of the reconstruction of the crimes by the Applicants themselves, and the decision of four of the Applicants not to give evidence in their defense (as distinct from their evidence in the "little trial"), which furnished the additional supporting evidence which the law required.

The appeal court had reviewed all the relevant evidence relating to the weight of the confessions, and after himself again examining all that evidence, Justice Shamgar held that no fault could be found with the appeal court's decision.

In summary, the President said that the Applicants' case, on the basis of the admissibility and weight of the confessions, was, in fact, an application for a new appeal, and not one for the rehearing of the appeal. It consisted in an attack on the findings of fact of the District Court, and that did not furnish a ground for a rehearing under Section 30(b) of the Courts Law.

Counsel had argued, said Justice Shamgar, that the appeal court had laid down a new, incorrect, principle, that where a confession had been admitted in evidence, the prosecution was not required to establish its truth, but the Defendant was required to adduce "strong evidence" to assail its credibility. This contention was based on a misunderstanding of the appeal court's decision. It was quite clear, said Justice Shamgar, that the prosecution was obliged to establish the truth of the confession by applying both the intrinsic and extrinsic tests mentioned, and the appeal court had not decided otherwise.

Finally, said the President, counsel had attacked the decision of the appeal court in refusing to order the further examination of the government pathologist, Dr. Bloch, on the basis of contradictions between the draft of his report on the autopsy performed, and his evidence in court. He agreed with the appeal court, said Justice Shamgar, that the contradictions in question were not sufficiently material to justify the pathologist's recall for further evidence.

For the above reasons, the application was dismissed.

Avigdor Feldman appeared for the Applicants, and Yiska Leibowitz, Senior Assistant State Attorney, appeared for the State.

Judgment given on August 25, 1991.

DETENTION BEFORE TRIAL

STATE OF ISRAEL v. GOLDIN AND BREZOVSKY

In the Supreme Court before Justice Aharon Barak in the matter of *The State of Israel*, Appellant, versus *Jackie Goldin and Golan Brezovsky*, Respondents (Miscellaneous Applications [C] 3717/91).

Criminal Procedure—Detention Before Trial—Gravity of Offence in Itself Sufficient—Penal Law, 1977, sections 372, 499(1), 381(a)(1), 26—Criminal Procedure Law (Consolidated Version), 1982, sections 21(A)(a)(1), 21A(b)(1).

The Respondents were charged in the Tel Aviv District Court with kidnapping for the purpose of extortion, conspiracy to kidnap and assault, in contravention of Sections 372, 499(1), 381(a)(1), and 26, of the Penal Law of 1977.

After the indictment was lodged, the State applied to the District Court to order the detention of the Respondents until the completion of the proceedings against them. The application was refused, the court directing that the Respondents be released on bail subject to certain conditions. The State then appealed to the Supreme Court.

The Respondents, said Justice Barak in his judgment, had admitted to kidnapping a three-year-old child from her mother. The plan had been conceived by Goldin with the object of procuring a ransom; and Brezovsky was to receive a fee for his participation. The latter did not know the true facts, having been told by Goldin that they were acting on the instructions of the child's father, who was having disputes with his wife.

Brezovsky entered the child's home, and pushed her mother aside with the aid of an electric shocker. The mother received burns and fell to the ground. Brezovsky then took the child, leaving a note demanding a ransom. Shortly afterwards, the Respondents were struck with remorse, and the child was restored to her family later the same day.

The District Court had pointed out that, *prima facie*, the Respondents had committed a crime of violence on a child with the aid of an electric shocker, and that there existed a basis for their detention, therefore, under Section 21(A)(a)(1) of the Criminal Procedure Law (Consolidated Version) of 1922. Under Section 21A(b)(1) of that Law, however, the District Court continued, a detention order was not to be made if the purpose of the detention could be achieved by releasing the suspect on bail, subject to proper conditions.

There was no danger, it said, of the Respondents repeating violent acts, or of their interfering with the course of justice; the purpose of their detention, therefore, would be to ensure the faith of the public in the effectiveness of the administration of criminal justice. This purpose, the court held, would also be served if the Respondents were released on bail.

The application for their detention was, therefore, refused, the judge ruling that the Respondents' detention would mean "exacting an installment in advance on account of the punishment they would eventually receive".

Justice Barak then analyzed Section 21A of the above Law. Discussing its legislative history, he pointed out that this section had been introduced into the Law in an amendment of 1988. There had been differences of opinion between the judges on whether the seriousness of a crime in itself — apart from of protecting the public from the suspect or ensuring that the processes of justice would not be interfered with — justified detention before trial.

The legislature had introduced Section 21A as a compromise. On the one hand, it had listed in sub-section (a)(2) certain offenses which, in themselves, justified the suspect's detention; namely, those involving drug trafficking, violence, the use of arms, abducting minors, exploiting the victim's inability to resist or his emotional or intellectual invalidity.

On the other hand, it had provided in sub-section (b)(1) that a detention order was not to be made if the purpose of the detention could be achieved by the suspect's release on bail, subject to suitable conditions. Whether an individual judge agreed or not, said Justice Barak, once the legislature had expressed its wishes, it was the court's duty to honor them.

Whether the purpose of the detention could be achieved otherwise than by detaining the suspect, Justice Barak continued, depended on the circumstances in which the crime was committed.

As the District Court had held, the purpose of the detention in the present case was to ensure the faith of the public in the effectiveness of the administration of criminal justice. In this context, the Supreme Court had already observed that in the struggle between the justice authorities and criminals it was important for the public to know that a suspect accused of a serious crime on the basis of prima facie evidence, should not be permitted to wander about freely awaiting his trial for what could be a very long period, as if nothing had happened.

Justice Barak then weighed the circumstances favorable to the Respondents, as against the gravity of the circumstances in which the crimes attributed to them had been committed. It was true that they had repented on the very day of the kidnaping, and had restored the child to her home.

On the other hand, not only were their crimes in themselves serious but the Respondents' conduct had also been serious. The object of procuring a ransom, the violence, the victim of the kidnaping being a young child — all these features outweighed the other considerations when the purpose of the detention in the present case was borne in mind.

Of course, the mitigating factors in the Respondents' favor would be taken into account when the question of their punishment was considered. In the present context, however, the issue of punishment did not arise, and there was no question of the detention being "an installment in advance" on account of the sentence to be passed.

In his opinion, Justice Barak concluded, the purpose to be served in the present case could only be achieved by the Respondents' detention, behind bars, until the completion of the proceedings against them. He had considered the possibility of placing them under "house arrest", but that would not satisfy the demands of the law in the present circumstances.

For the above reasons, the appeal was allowed, and an order made for the detention of the Respondents until the proceedings against them were completed.

Advocate Yiska Leibowitz, Senior Assistant State Attorney, appeared for the State, Advocate Shaul Bar-Oz for Goldin, and Advocate Razumov for Brezovsky. Judgment given on August 23, 1991.

ARBITRATION WITHOUT LAWYERS

KIDRON v. ISRAEL DIAMOND EXCHANGE

In the Supreme Court sitting as a Court of Civil Appeals before the President, Justice Meir Shamgar, Justice Ya'acov Maltz and Justice Theodore Orr, in the matter of *Advocate Bella Kidron (Kinderman)*, Appellant, versus *The Israel Diamond Exchange Ltd.*, Respondent (C.A. 468/89).

Arbitration—Legal Representation of Parties Precluded—Legality of—Chamber of Advocates Law, 1961, sections 20(1), 22.

Under the regulations of the Israel Diamond Exchange, a public company comprising some 2,000 members, commercial disputes between members are to be brought to arbitration before the directorate or members appointed by it for that purpose.

It was a recognized custom that litigants could be represented, if they so wished, by fellow members, whether or not such representatives were also lawyers. This right to representation was later embodied in a regulation of the exchange. Subsequently, however, a general meeting of the exchange amended the regulation so as to deny representation by a member who was also engaged in active practice as an advocate.

The Appellant, a member of the exchange and also an advocate, moved the District Court of Tel Aviv to declare the amended regulation invalid. His claim was dismissed, and he appealed to the Supreme Court.

The judgment of the Supreme Court was delivered by Justice Shamgar. The Appellant, he said, had relied on three grounds. He had argued that the amendment infringed two provisions of the Chamber of Advocates Law of 1961, that it was against public policy, and that it was against the best interests of the members of the exchange as a whole.

Counsel for the exchange had contended that the amendment was aimed at creating a position of parity between members in presenting their case before the arbitrators. Most of the disputes were of a professional nature, and had no connection with legal niceties. Allowing representation by practising advocates would complicate the proceedings, introduce inequality in some cases, and increase the cost of arbitrations. These factors, he argued, could lead eventually to the whole process of arbitration being destroyed.

Counsel had also pointed out that the Appellant had argued before the general meeting of the exchange that the amendment would damage his livelihood. The meeting, however, had passed a special resolution amending the regulation to its present form, on the basis of the reasons explained above, and not with any intention of damaging the Appellant's livelihood.

The Appellant had relied firstly, the president continued, on section 20(1) of the Chamber of Advocates Law, under which no person, other than an advocate, shall represent other persons, as a business or for a consideration, before courts, tribunals, arbitrators, or other bodies or persons exercising judicial or quasi-judicial powers. His contention was that a number of members of the exchange, who were not advocates, would concentrate on representing fellow members at arbitrations, and would turn this activity into a business, in contravention of the above section.

The simple answer to this contention, said Justice Shamgar, was that the Appellant had laid no factual basis whatsoever to suggest that the premise he foresaw would ever become a reality.

The Appellant, Justice Shamgar continued, had also relied on section 22 of the Chamber of Advocates Law, under which any person who has duly authorized a lawyer is entitled to be represented by him before all state or local authorities, and before bodies and other persons fulfilling public functions prescribed by law.

This argument too, Justice Shamgar held, had no merit, for the arbitrators in question, although acting as such under the Arbitration Law, were not "fulfilling public functions prescribed by law" within the meaning of section 22. Moreover, the right conferred by section 22 was the right of the client to be represented by the lawyer he had appointed, and not the right of the lawyer to demand that he, and only he, represent the client.

The Appellant had also argued, the president continued, that the new regulation was unlawful since it restricted his right to practise his profession, and was therefore against public policy. Citing Supreme Court precedents, Justice Shamgar agreed that provisions restraining a person's right of occupation were generally against public policy, and he was prepared to assume the possibility that a regulation of a company restraining a member's freedom of occupation could be set aside as unlawful.

In that context, however, both the Supreme Court and an English court had held that the regulation was unlawful only if the restriction it imposed arose within the relationship between the member and the company, and not outside that relationship. Both in the present case, and in the English precedent quoted in which the facts were somewhat similar, the member attacked the regulation not in his capacity as a member of the company, but as a lawyer.

Moreover, the grounds advanced by the exchange in support of the amended regulation were reasonable, and there was nothing to prevent the Appellant from acting as an advocate, and even exploiting his knowledge of diamonds and the diamond market, in areas other than arbitrations under the regulation.

The Appellant had argued lastly, Justice Shamgar continued, that the amendment complained of was unlawful as not being in the interests of the company. It was to be emphasized, he said, that the Appellant was thus obliged to establish that the interests of the company were adversely affected, as distinct from the interests of its members.

This the Appellant had not proved, and indeed the impression had been created that it was the interests of the Appellant as an advocate which had impelled him to attack the validity of the amended regulation. This motive was quite unconnected with the interests of the company.

Finally, Justice Shamgar pointed out that the regulations of the exchange provided for effective control procedures to ensure that only claims appropriate for arbitration were referred to arbitrators, and that the steps taken were fair and proper. Moreover, he cited English authority to show that the system of arbitration employed by the exchange was also practised in English commercial companies, for the same reasons for which it was adopted by the Diamond Exchange.

For the above reasons, the appeal was dismissed, and the Appellant ordered to pay the Respondent's costs in the sum of NIS 8,000.

The Appellant appeared in person, and Shmuel Eini appeared for the Diamond Exchange.

The judgment was given on August 25, 1991.

JUDGES VERSUS JUSTICE

HUSAAM HAJ YIHYEH v. STATE OF ISRAEL

In the Supreme Court sitting as a Court of Criminal Appeals before the Deputy-President, Justice Menahem Elon; Justice Gavriel Bach and Justice Theodore Orr, in the matter of *Husaam Haj Yihyeh*, Appellant, versus *The State of Israel*, Respondent (Cr. A. 2251/90).

Evidence—Admissibility of Written Statement of Witness out of Court—"Silent Witness"—Evidence Ordinance (New Version), 1971, sections 10A (a) and (b).

The Appellant was charged in the District Court of Tel Aviv, *inter alia*, with armed robbery. The robbery had been committed by three people, and the main evidence identifying the Appellant as one of them were statements made by one Mondar, another participant, to one of the latter's cellmates in prison named Hassan. Mondar was called by the prosecution at the Appellant's trial to confirm what he had told Hassan, but he refused to speak.

The prosecution then tendered as evidence a tape of the conversation referred to, which had been recorded without the knowledge of the participants. The court admitted the tape, and convicted the Appellant on the basis of what it contained. The Appellant then appealed to the Supreme Court on the ground that the tape had been wrongly admitted as evidence.

A written statement made by a witness out of court is admissible in evidence, subject to certain conditions, under section 10A(a) of the Evidence Ordinance (New Version) of 1971. Under sub-section 10A(b) of the ordinance, a written statement by a person who is not a witness may also be admitted if, inter alia, it is proved that "improper means have been used" to prevent him from giving testimony.

The first judgment of the Supreme Court was delivered by Justice Orr. The court had already held, he noted, that a taped record of what a person had said constituted a "written statement" by him within the meaning of section 10A above. The District Court, he continued, had admitted the tape under sub-section 10A(b) of the ordinance on the basis that "improper means" had been used to induce Mondar not to speak. The judge had relied, in this context, on his experience that "in most such cases, if not in all, the source of the silence is fear of testifying against a Defendant and implicating him in a crime".

In this finding, Justice Orr said, the District Court had erred. It was true that the Supreme Court, in recent years, had somewhat widened the basis on which "improper means" could be proved. Nevertheless, some evidence had to be brought to establish that element, and the judge's experience was not sufficient for this purpose.

It now became necessary to determine, therefore, whether the tape was admissible under sub-section (a) of section 10A of the ordinance, Justice Orr said. For this purpose, it was necessary to decide whether a witness who refused to speak was a "witness" within the meaning of that sub-section.

The court had considered this vexed question, in a panel of five judges, in the case of *Levi* (Cr. A. 254/88 — *The Jerusalem Post* of November 28 and December 5, 1990), and had decided by a majority of three to two, one of the dissentients being Justice Bach, that a silent witness was indeed a "witness" within the meaning of sub-section (a).

After a searching analysis of section 10(A), Justice Orr expressed his agreement with the majority decision in *Levi*'s case and held, therefore, that the tape was admissible evidence under sub-section 10A(a) above. He also agreed with the District Court that Mondar's statements in the tape, together with some supporting evidence that had been heard, were sufficient to justify the Appellant's conviction. He proposed, therefore, that the appeal be dismissed.

Both his colleagues disagreed with the majority decision in *Levi*'s case, and with his own opinion, in regard to the interpretation of section 10(A), Justice Orr continued. They proposed, therefore, to allow the present appeal despite a contrary ruling by the court in a panel of five judges.

This raised the question of whether it was proper for a panel of three Supreme Court judges to overrule a decision — albeit by a majority — of a panel of five of their colleagues. It was true that under section 20 of the Basic Law: Judicature, a ruling of the Supreme Court was binding on all lower courts, but not on the Supreme Court itself. Strictly speaking, therefore, the three judges could overrule the five, but the question still remained whether it was desirable to do so.

Justice Orr then pointed out that the court had held in several cases, including that of *Yehoshua* (H.C. 176/54, Selected Supreme Court Judgments [English], Vol. 2, p. 46), that only in the most exceptional circumstances should the court depart from one of its own precedents.

The late Justice Silberg had once commented that if the court did so frequently, it would no longer be a "court of justice", but a "court of judges".

In Justice Orr's view, his colleagues had not given this factor sufficient weight. He had suggested to them that they exercise their power under section 26(2) of the Courts Law (Consolidated Version) of 1984, and add two more judges to the present panel. They had not agreed, but he welcomed their acceptance of his alternative proposal that this panel direct a further hearing of the present appeal before another, enlarged, panel of judges.

Justice Bach agreed there was insufficient basis for the District Court's finding that improper means had been used to influence Mondar not to testify. He remained firm, however, in the opinion he had expressed in *Levi*'s case that a witness who refused to speak was not a "witness" within the meaning of Sub-section 10(A)(a) of the Evidence Ordinance. He understood that Justice Elon shared his view and the question arose, therefore, whether the court should now give a judgment which conflicted with the majority view in *Levi*'s case.

Citing Supreme Court precedents, including *Yehoshua*'s case, *supra*, and several legal texts, Justice Bach reviewed the principles affecting the question at issue. Judgments of the Supreme Court were binding on all other courts, and their consistency was vital to the stability of the law. The more the court departed from its own precedents, the more obscure the law would become, and lawyers and the public would be less equipped to know what the law was.

On the other hand, he maintained, rigid adherence to precedent stifled the development of the law, and restricted the professional and intellectual honesty of the individual judge who disagreed with the precedent quoted to him. Justice Bach then listed some of the considerations which, in his view, should guide the judge: To what extent did he believe that the precedent was incorrect? If it was clearly incorrect, it should not be followed. As the late Chief Justice Smoira had once said, "Between truth and stability, truth must prevail". On the other hand, if the judge believed that both points of view were possible, then, as Justice Barak had said, "Between truth and truth, stability must prevail".

To what extent would his following the precedent do injustice to one of the litigants before him, Justice Bach asked? What would be the effect of disregarding the precedent on the uncertainty in the law? To what extent did the problem at issue affect a basic legal right? If a basic right would be seriously infringed, the judge would perhaps be not only entitled, but also bound, to disregard the precedent.

And, finally, was the precedent one laid down by a routine panel of three judges, or was it a decision of a larger panel (in a rehearing, or because of the importance of the principle at issue?)

After full consideration, said Justice Bach, he had decided that his professional belief and approach in this case and his judicial conscience overrode his desire not to cause possible uncertainty in the meaning of the section in question: admitting hearsay evidence where the witness remained silent was to deprive the Defendant of the basic and vital right to test the evidence by cross-examination, exactly a result the legislature wished to avoid.

Justice Bach then commented that, had the majority ruling in Levi's case demanded the acquittal of a Defendant convicted in a District Court, and the minority ruled to convict, he might not have followed the minority opinion.

In the present case, however, following the majority opinion would mean convicting the Appellant of serious crimes, and sending him to prison for a lengthy period, in the knowledge and belief that his guilt had not been proved according to law. This no judge could do, unless the law compelled him to.

Finally, Justice Bach expressed the hope that the legislature would clarify the position of a silent witness, and so put an end to the present conflict of opinion on this point.

Justice Bach proposed that the appeal be allowed.

Justice Elon concurred, and dealt first with the interpretation of Section 10A of the Evidence Ordinance. He analyzed in depth the language of the section, reviewing its legislative history. Citing several precedents, and biblical and other Jewish law sources, he emphasized, in particular, the cardinal importance of a Defendant's right to cross-examine witnesses, which he could not do if the witness refused to speak.

Justice Elon concluded, without hesitation, that the majority decision in Levi's case was incorrect. The Deputy-President then referred specifically to the judge's duty of interpreting a statute, and the rule of law. A judge may not add to the language of a statute. The rule of law did not mean the rule of the judge. Citing Supreme Court precedents, including *Zarazevsky*'s case (H.C. 1635/90: *The Jerusalem Post* of March 6, 1991), he stressed that the amendment of a Law was the task of the legislature, which made the Law, and not of the courts.

Justice Elon then considered Section 20(b) of the Basic Law: Judicature; which provides specifically that the Supreme Court is not bound by its own precedents. Basing himself on its legislative history, including the debate in the Knesset, he held it was immaterial whether the precedent was one of a panel of three, or more, judges.

Citing rabbinical texts, he also pointed out that the binding nature of precedents was unknown to Jewish law, and also formed no part of Roman law, or the law of most Continental countries. Moreover, a change of attitude to this doctrine was discernible in recent times even in English law.

It was understood that the court was to exercise the utmost care in departing from its own precedents. At the same time, it was essential, in a developing society in which there were sharp conflicts of opinion on basic issues, that the intellectual freedom of the judge be preserved.

Referring again to *Zarazevsky's* case, *supra*, he pointed to differing attitudes of judges towards the growing intervention of the court, sitting as a High Court of Justice, in many sensitive areas. It was essential in a democratic regime that a judge's independence be recognized and his decisions be subject to examination and cautious criticism, in the light of the times and the subject in issue.

Reverting to the present appeal, Justice Elon again quoted that "between truth and stability, truth must prevail", a dictum borrowed from Jewish law. Was it at all conceivable that he would convict the Appellant (who, in his opinion, was entitled beyond any doubt to be acquitted for lack of evidence of his guilt) just to give the law stability?

For the above reasons, and by majority decision, the appeal was allowed and the conviction of the Appellant set aside, the court directing that the appeal be set down for rehearing before an enlarged panel of judges.

Osnat Bartur appeared for the Appellant, and Dr. Mishael Cheshin for the State.

Judgment given on September 4, 1991.

PRESERVING PURE LEGAL PRACTICE
ADVOCATE'S 'MORAL TURPITUDE'
IS ISSUE IN CURRENCY VIOLATION

TEL-AVIV CHAMBER OF ADVOCATES v. A.B.

In the Supreme Court, sitting as a Court of Appeal under Section 71 of the Chamber of Advocates Law of 1961, before Justices Aharon Barak, Eliezer Goldberg and Eliyahu Matza, in the matter of *The Tel Aviv Disciplinary Court of the Chamber*, Appellant, versus A.B., Respondent (C.A.A. 2579, 3093/90).

Criminal Law—Disciplinary Proceedings Against Advocate —Moral Turpitude"—Appeal to Supreme Court—Chamber of Advocates Law, 1961, section 75—Currency Control Law, 1978.

The Respondent, a licensed advocate, did not practise law but conducted a business involving large sums of foreign currency. He was convicted by a District Court on 10 counts under the Currency Control Law of 1978.

His offenses included possession of foreign currency without a permit in aggravating circumstances, and dealing in foreign currency without a permit in aggravating circumstances, including smuggling currency overseas.

He was sentenced to three years' imprisonment (suspended for three years), placed under probation for one year and fined NIS 50,000.

Pursuant to the Respondent's conviction, the Appellant moved the Tel Aviv District Disciplinary Court of the Chamber of Advocates to impose upon the Respondent an appropriate disciplinary punishment. The court sentenced him to suspension for a period of 100 months, this being a sentence, inter alia, provided for by Section 75 of the Chamber of Advocates Law where the advocate's offenses involved moral turpitude.

Both parties appealed to the Chamber's National Disciplinary Court, the Chamber arguing that the sentence was too light, and the Respondent contending that his offense involved no moral turpitude. The National Court rejected the Respondent's argument, but reduced the period of suspension to one of five years.

Both parties then appealed to the Supreme Court, the Respondent persisting in his contention that no moral turpitude was involved, and the Appellant requesting the court to order the Respondent's expulsion from the Chamber.

The judgment of the Supreme Court was delivered by Justice Barak. Section 75 of the Chamber of Advocates Law, he said, empowered a disciplinary court to sentence an offender to expulsion or suspension on the basis of his conviction alone, without itself conducting any inquiry, where his offenses involved moral turpitude. The cardinal point, therefore, was whether there was moral turpitude in the offenses of the Respondent.

Referring to Supreme Court precedents, including the case of *Udah* (H.C. 251/88, *The Jerusalem Post* of May 24, 1989, *supra* p. 84), Justice Barak then considered the meaning of "moral turpitude" in the present context. It designated the unethical element in the commission of the crime, or in the circumstances of its commission. Not every crime involved moral turpitude.

Since ethical conceptions changed, from time to time, and from one society to another, there was no point in trying to define what it embraced.

It was necessarily vague and for this reason it was purposely left undefined in the various statutes in which it appeared.

It was for the court to find its meaning in each case in the light of the ethical conceptions prevailing in the community at that time, and with the object of protecting those interests with which the particular statute was concerned.

Citing further Supreme Court authority, Justice Barak stressed that the object of disciplinary sanctions was not to impose upon an offender a punishment in addition to that imposed by the court, but to uphold the function of the Chamber of Advocates in preserving the standard and purity of legal practise.

Justice Barak then quoted examples of unethical conduct by advocates, in cases considered by the Supreme Court, and pointed to the possibility that the advocate's offense could be quite unconnected with legal practise and could, in itself, not be a serious crime.

Even offenses of absolute liability in which there was no element of criminal intent, could, in certain circumstances, involve moral turpitude if committed by an advocate. It was an advocate's duty to be faithful to the law of the land, and to maintain professional and ethical standards justifying the trust of his clients, the courts and the community.

Turning to the present case, Justice Barak cited the finding of the District Court (which convicted the Respondent) that he had dealt in foreign currency on a continuous, planned and sophisticated basis, and on a massive scale. This was not a single lapse, but a case of contempt for the law, and for the social and economic norms which it embodied.

It was true that the Currency Control Law was a regulatory statute, and that the Respondent might have secured a permit had he applied for one. This factor, however, did not detract from the seriousness of his offenses in the circumstances in which they were committed.

In his opinion, Justice Barak concluded, the crimes, committed by an advocate, involved moral turpitude, even if they were not associated with his profession as such.

Counsel for the Appellant, said Justice Barak, had cited precedents in support of its request that the Respondent be expelled from the Chamber of Advocates.

In all those cases, however, the advocate's offenses were more serious and were directly connected with his practise, or there had been previous breaches of professional discipline. On the other hand, the court had found no ground to mitigate the punishment imposed upon the Respondent.

For the above reasons, both appeals were dismissed.

Amos Weitzman appeared for the Chamber, and Meshulam Shafran for A.B.

Judgment given on August 28, 1991.

TAX RELIEF DENIED IF IT
BREACHES KNESSET STATUTE

ORANIT v. MINISTER OF FINANCE

In the Supreme Court, sitting as a High Court of Justice, before Justices Aharon Barak, Shoshana Netanyahu and Ya'acov Maltz, in the matter of *Oranit and Har Adar*, Petitioners, versus *The Minister of Finance and the Finance Committee of the Knesset*, Respondents. (H.C. 4472, 5399/90).

Income Tax—Regulations of Minister of Finance under Section 11 of Income Tax Ordinance (New Version), 1961—Regulations Confirmed by Knesset "Primary Legislation"—Regulation of State Enterprises (Imports and Rates) Law, 1991, section 12.

The settlement of Oranit in Western Samaria near Alfei Menashe and Sha'arei Tikva was established in 1984; and Har Adar, in the northern Judean mountains not far from Jerusalem and near New Givon and Mahaneh Givon, was established in 1986.

Both settlements tried for some years to obtain tax rebates under regulations issued by the minister of finance in terms of Section 11 of the Income Tax Ordinance (New Version), which empowers the minister, with the confirmation of the Knesset Finance Committee, to grant rebates on income earned in a new settlement or development area, and to authorize additional allowances for the assets of enterprises in such areas.

Since the repeated efforts of the settlement representatives were unsuccessful, they petitioned the Supreme Court for relief.

The judgment of the court was delivered by Justice Barak. He said the Petitioners' requests for tax relief had been consistently refused on various grounds, including their geographical situation and the income of their members. They had argued, however, that almost all the other Jewish settlements in Judea and Samaria, including those mentioned above, and others similar to them geographically, socially and economically, had received the rebates. They had therefore been the victims of unjust discrimination.

They relied, in this regard, on the judgment of the court in the case of *Kfar Veradim* (H.C. 678, 803/88: *The Jerusalem Post* of August 2, 1989, *supra* p. 95), in which the same question had arisen in connection with frontier settlements in the north.

The Finance Minister, Justice Barak recalled, had issued six sets of regulations under the above section. They had covered Eilat and settlements in the north and in the Arava; and by the end of 1990 they had included about 250 settlements, of which about 100 were in Judea and Samaria. The regulations, originally limited to three years, had been extended 16 times, the last extension having expired last December 31.

The Respondents' reply to the petition had been filed on December 27, 1990, four days before the validity of the regulations expired. They explained that the regulations would not be extended in their present form since it was intended to revise the criteria for granting the rebates, and also to ensure their proper application.

However, the Knesset thought otherwise. And on January 31, 1991, it passed the Regulation of State Enterprises (Imposts and Rates) Law, Section 12 of which provides that "regulations issued under Section 11 of the Income Tax Ordinance, the validity of which expired on December 31, 1990, shall continue to apply until June 30, 1991, and there shall be no deviation from, nor addition to, such regulations".

On July 25, 1991, the Knesset extended the application of Section 12 until December 31, 1992, the result being that that section is still in force.

The Petitioners had argued that, despite the statutory provision that "there shall be no deviation from, nor addition to, such regulations", Justice Barak continued, the Respondents were still empowered to add to the areas covered by the regulations so as to avoid unjust discrimination.

They had also contended that the above provision could be circumvented by amending the regulations retroactively, so as to make them applicable before Section 12 was enacted.

But, Justice Barak said, the Petitioners' arguments were quite unacceptable. It was idle to contend that extending or limiting the application of the regulations was not "deviating from" or "adding to" them. Moreover, he added, citing Supreme Court precedents, the court had already held that regulations whose validity had been extended by the Knesset became themselves primary legislation.

It was true that this ruling had been made in regard to emergency regulations; but it applied to all subsidiary legislation. The result was that the appellation "regulations" was no longer accurate in regard to the provisions now discussed. It was clear, accordingly, that the Respondents were not empowered to change a statute passed by the Knesset itself.

For the above reasons, the petition was denied, with no order as to costs. Gad Viskind and Yitzhak Enbar appeared for the Petitioners, and Uzi Fogelman, Senior Assistant State Attorney, appeared for the Respondents.

Judgment given on December 2, 1991.

REPUTED SPOUSE'S LEGACY RIGHTS

MESHULLAM v. RABBINICAL APPEALS COURT

In the Supreme Court sitting as a High Court of Justice before the President, Justice Meir Shamgar, the Deputy-President, Justice Menahem Elon, and Justice Shoshana Netanyahu, in the matter of *Shulamit Meshullam*, Petitioner, versus *The Supreme Rabbinical Court of Appeals*, *The District Rabbinical Court of Tel Aviv*, *and three others*, Respondents (H.C. 673/89).

Personal Status—Succession Rights of "Reputed Spouse"—Rabbinical Court Proceedings Set Aside by Supreme Court—Succession Law, 1965, sections 55, 151, 155(a).

Zion Yaffet died intestate and his children, the third, fourth, and fifth Respondents, applied to the District Rabbinical Court of Tel Aviv for a succession order, declaring that they were his sole heirs.

On the day of the hearing, Petitioner's counsel appeared and argued that his client was also an heir of the deceased by virtue of Section 55 of the Succession Law of 1965, which says "Where a man and woman, though not being married to one another, have lived together as husband and wife in a common household, then upon the death of one of them, neither being married to another person, and subject to any contrary direction, expressed or implied, in the will of the deceased, the deceased is deemed to have bequeathed to the survivor what the survivor would have inherited on intestacy if they had been married to one another".

Under Section 151 of the above Law, the relevant District Court has jurisdiction; however, under Section 155(a), a religious court which had jurisdiction in matters of the personal status of the deceased is also competent, *inter alia*, to make a succession order "if all the parties affected under this Law have consented thereto in writing.'

Petitioner's counsel then argued before the rabbinical court that since his client was an heir, and therefore "a party affected" under the Law, and since she would not consent to that court's jurisdiction, the whole proceeding should be referred to the District Court under Section 151 of the Law.

But the rabbinical court ruled that the fact that one or more persons, who were indisputable heirs of the deceased, had consented in writing to its jurisdiction, was sufficient, under Section 55 of the Law, to empower it to decide whether the Petitioner was an heir under that section.

If, indeed, she was an heir and refused to consent to its jurisdiction, the case would have to be dealt with by the District Court. If, however, she was not an heir, the rabbinical court could continue with the case, since all the heirs had consented.

The court then heard evidence and decided that the Petitioner did not fall within Section 55 of the Law.

Since it held, therefore, that all the heirs had consented to its jurisdiction, it upheld the children's rights to the estate and excluded the Petitioner.

The court's judgment was upheld by the Supreme Rabbinical Court of Appeals, and the Petitioner then applied to the Supreme Court to nullify the rabbinical court proceedings.

The first judgment of the Supreme Court was delivered by Justice Shamgar. He said that, as a general rule, a court or tribunal whose jurisdiction was challenged was required to decide itself, in the first instance, whether or not it was empowered to act.

The legislative scheme laid down in the Succession Law, however, and its legislative history, showed that this rule did not apply in the present context. Jurisdiction under the Succession Law was conferred upon the District Court and was only granted to a religious court, under Section 155(a), if all the heirs consented.

The plain intention was that a religious court could not deal at all with an application under the Law unless all the heirs agreed. The question whether a particular person was an heir was to be decided by the District

Court, and only if that person's status as an heir was established did the question of consent to the religious court's jurisdiction arise.

Counsel for the Respondents, the president added, had relied on a difference in wording between some sections of the above Law, which speak of all the "parties interested", as distinct from Section 155(a), which speaks of "parties affected". In his view, however, there was no significance in this distinction. He added that the whole conception of a "reputed spouse" enjoying rights of succession on intestacy offended against the Halacha.

Justice Shamgar proposed, therefore, that the court declare that the rabbinical courts were not empowered to decide on the Petitioner's status under Section 55 of the Succession Law, and that their proceedings, in the absence of the Petitioner's consent, were invalid.

Justice Netanyahu concurred.

Justice Elon dissented from his colleagues. Citing numerous Supreme Court precedents, he emphasized the general rule that the question of jurisdiction was to be decided, in the first place, by the court or tribunal before which that issue was raised.

After closely examining the Succession Law and the legislative background to its enactment, and referring, inter alia, to the difference in meaning between "interested persons" and "persons affected", in various sections of the Law, the deputy-president saw no ground for not applying the general rule to religious courts exercising jurisdiction under Section 155(a).

Justice Elon then turned to the ground advanced by the president that a rabbinical court would have difficulty in applying Section 55 since the whole conception of granting rights to a "reputed spouse" offended against its basic beliefs. Such fears, he said, were without foundation.

He said that it was now accepted as part of the law of the land even by those who disagreed with it, as was amply proved by the judgments of both rabbinical courts in the present instance. They had both analyzed the facts with the greatest care and it was only after the most detailed consideration of the evidence that they had rejected the Petitioner's claim.

By majority decision, the petition was allowed and an order made, as proposed by the President.

David Cohen appeared for the Petitioner, and Advocates Karet and Yigal Shapiro for the Respondent heirs.

Judgment given on November 11, 1991.

KNESSET AND THE HIGH COURT

PORAZ AND WEISS v. KNESSET SPEAKER

In the Supreme Court sitting as a High Court of Justice before the President, Justice Meir Shamgar, and Justices Aharon Barak and Eliezer Goldberg, in the matter of *MKs Avraham Poraz and Shevah Weiss*, Petitioners, versus *MK Dov Shilansky, Speaker of the Knesset, Uriel Lynn, Chairman of the Knesset Constitution, Law and Justice Committee and others*, Respondents (H.C. 5711/91).

Constitutional Law—Knesset Bound by Judgment of Supreme Court—Courts Intervention in Knesset Proceedings—Basic Law: The State Economy, 1965— Knesset Rules 124, 126.

On July 15, 1991, MK Lynn, in his above capacity, submitted a bill amending the Basic Law: the State Economy, 1965 to the Speaker, to be presented to the Knesset for its second and third readings. Since months passed without it being placed on the agenda, the Petitioners moved the court (in H.C. 4804/91) to order the Speaker to place the bill before the House. Lynn was cited in the petition as a second, formal, Respondent.

On December 11, 1991, the Court was requested to enter judgment enforcing an agreement between "the parties", signed by the Petitioners and by Advocate Arad, director of the High Court Division of the State Attorney's office on behalf of the State. Under it, the bill would be presented to the plenum on December 18, 1991. Judgment was then entered in terms of the agreement, and the bill was placed on the agenda as agreed.

On December 16, 1991, Lynn summoned the law committee to meet the following day. The meeting was attended by the chairman and two members and on the chairman's motion it was resolved to exercise the committee's powers under Rule 124 of the Knesset Rules and recall the bill to the committee for further consideration. (The above rule authorizes the committee to take this step even if the bill has already been placed before the plenum, provided the second reading has not yet begun.)

On December 17, Deputy Speaker MK Dan Tichon informed the House of what had transpired and the bill was not placed before the plenum on the 18th as ordered by the Court.

The Petitioners then moved the Court to declare the above steps unlawful and again to order the bill to be presented on the 18th for its second and third readings.

The judgment of the court was delivered by Justice Shamgar. The State Attorney, he said, did not question the validity of the agreement of December 12, nor of the judgment then given. She had argued, however, that the steps taken under Rule 124 above were also lawful and the Speaker, therefore, had had no alternative but to postpone the second reading.

The committee chairman (who had also appeared and submitted his arguments) had supported the above legal submissions, adding that the Speaker had not consulted him before the agreement was signed. He had, however, told the first Petitioner that he thought that the petition was a mistake and did not support the agreement, but indeed opposed it.

The Court had no doubt, the President continued, as to the committee chairman's good faith — but that was not enough. The question at issue was to what extent he was bound by the judgment of the Court, which had been given on a petition in which he was cited as a Respondent. As the authorities showed, a judgment given by consent had the characteristics of both a judgment and a contract and could be set aside on the same grounds on which a contract could be voided. Nevertheless, it was a judgment for all purposes; and a person bound by it could not disobey it onesidedly.

The court was of opinion, Justice Shamgar continued, that Uriel Lynn was bound by its judgment, as was the Speaker himself, to present the bill to the plenum, and was not entitled to take steps that would prevent this being done. He was a party to the previous proceedings in H.C. 4804/91; the meaning of the agreement then reached between the parties, subsequently embodied in a judgment, as well as his function in carrying out the agreement, were clear; and he was fully aware of the judgment and its provisions.

The fact that he was cited only as a "formal" Respondent in the previous proceedings made no difference; a "formal" party was not obliged to respond if he regarded himself as unaffected — but he was nevertheless bound by any judgment subsequently given. It was to be regretted that the first Petitioner did not inform the Court at the time that Lynn opposed the agreement; also, that the State Attorney did not ensure, before submitting to the Court an agreement between "the parties" that he agreed to its provisions.

Under Knesset Rule 126, the President continued, it was the function of the chairman of the Law Committee to present the bill to the plenum and answer any queries raised.

Justice Shamgar then pointed out that the Court did not readily intervene in parliamentary proceedings, even if it was approached by a Knesset member. Citing the precedents of *Sarid* and the *Citizen's Rights Movement* (H.C.6 52/81 and 1179/90, *The Jerusalem Post*, May 16, 1982 and March 28, 1990), he repeated that a balance had to be struck between enforcing the law and respecting the singularity of the legislature in deciding its own internal procedures.

In the present instance it was agreed by all concerned that the previous petition had been correctly brought before the Court and the present petition was only an extension of that proceeding.

In conclusion, Justice Shamgar said that it was the status of the Knesset that was at stake in the present case, and not that of the Court. It was inconceivable that an obligation undertaken by the Speaker before the Court, and embodied in a judgment, would not be honored or would be subject to tactical maneuvers.

The status of the legislature would be diminished if the mistaken impression were created that its obligation to honor a judgment of the Court was different from that of any other authority or individual in the State.

For the above reasons, the petition was allowed and the Respondents ordered to present the bill to the plenum for its second and third readings not later than December 25, 1991.

Ra'anan Har-Ze'ev and Edna Harel appeared for the Petitioners; Uriel Lynn appeared in person; and Dorit Beinish, the State Attorney and Uzi Fogelman and Menahem Mazoz, Senior Assistant State Attorneys, appeared for the Speaker and other Respondents.

Judgment given on December 22, 1991.